PELICAN BOOKS

Poverty: The Forgotten Englishmen

Ken Coates was born in 1930. A former
coal-miner, he now teaches sociology in the
Adult Education Department at Nottingham
University. He has written and co-edited
several books on socialism and industrial
democracy, notably *Industrial Democracy in
Great Britain*, *The New Unionism* and *The
Crisis of British Socialism*, and contributed to
*The Incompatibles: Trade Union Militancy
and the Consensus* (Penguin Special).

Richard Silburn was born in 1938 and was
educated at St Paul's School and Nottingham
University, where he now lectures in the
Department of Applied Social Science.
He is married, with three sons.

Poverty: The Forgotten Englishmen

Ken Coates and Richard Silburn

Penguin Books

Penguin Books Ltd, Harmondsworth,
Middlesex, England
Penguin Books Inc., 7110 Ambassador Road,
Baltimore, Maryland 21207, U.S.A.
Penguin Books Australia Ltd, Ringwood,
Victoria, Australia
Penguin Books Canada Ltd, 41 Steelcase Road West,
Markham, Ontario, Canada
Penguin Books (N.Z.) Ltd, 182–190 Wairau Road,
Auckland 10, New Zealand

First published as a Penguin Special 1970
Reprinted 1971
Reissued as a Pelican, with an introduction, 1973
Reprinted 1975
Copyright © Ken Coates and Richard Silburn, 1970, 1973

Made and printed in Great Britain by
Hazell Watson & Viney Ltd,
Aylesbury, Bucks
Set in Linotype Times

Contents

Foreword

We should like to place on record our thanks to the many people who helped us in the preparation of this book. Foremost among them we would like to thank the long-suffering people of St Ann's and the Edwards' Lane Estate in Nottingham, who not only endured long and inquisitive interviews, but who also suffered considerably from the blare of publicity, often less than objective, let alone kindly, when certain newspapers took up our inquiry and interpreted it in their own way.

Second only to them, our gratitude is due to the members of our tutorial class, sponsored by the Department of Adult Education of Nottingham University and the W.E.A., who laboured for endless hours in compiling, canvassing, and processing the questionnaires, and whose mature judgement has prevented us from making many more errors than we otherwise would have committed. It is very plain to us that the basic work of the inquiry was entirely accomplished by these dedicated and persevering students, so that all we have needed to do has been to make certain connexions with broader questions.

We should also like to thank the undergraduate students who so willingly helped us in the second and third stages of our investigation. If we had not had unstinting help from the heads of our Departments, Prof. H. C. Wiltshire and Prof. D. C. Marsh, we would have been quite unable to complete our work. They not only encouraged us in every possible way, but they bore with us through storms of local controversy in a manner which was staunchness itself. Our thanks also to Michael Barratt Brown and Dennis Marsden for their helpful criticism and advice, and to Robert Hutchison and Neil Middleton of Penguin Books for their patience and encouragement.

We are deeply grateful to Mrs Alison Brown and her colleagues, who worked tirelessly on the typing of successive manuscripts, and we are indebted to our colleagues and families, for their support and advice.

Naturally the conclusions from all this work are our own responsibilities as also are the mistakes.

Introduction to the Pelican Edition

Some water has gone under the bridges since this book was first published in 1970. There have been a number of changes in public policy, but although for every change there has been a considerable volume of debate on the issues involved, the basic theme which is developed in these pages remains all too vividly relevant, all too close to the experience of millions of our people.

The first part of this work concerns poverty and slum life in one city, and it is based on a study which was conducted, over several years, by groups of W.E.A. students in Nottingham. The main district which was investigated was the redevelopment area of St Ann's, which, as we have reported in the body of our text, was scheduled for early clearance at the time the inquiry commenced. Today, the bulldozers have made spectacular advances. Neatly patterned rows and crescents of open-plan Wimpey houses and maisonettes now cluster in brisk formations on one side of the valley, where until recently the long black slum terraces crawled along cobbled streets. On this side of the dip, bright low school complexes have sprouted out from the rubble, while at the bottom, the strangely futuristic chimneys of the district heating scheme point upwards to the noise of further demolitions, busily in progress further up the other hillside. The old panorama has gone.

In 1970 it was still possible to advise people to take a short walk from the city centre 'over a giant excavation, where, in what yesterday was a railway station, battalions of men are punching out the foundations of 1984 and, bang, you are in the middle of Dickens, or George Gissing. In one moment, the neon stops and the cobbles begin.'

Now the cobbles of Dickens and Gissing are almost gone, and the new order described by Orwell has become more vividly alive each day. One pre-cast concrete slab after another has been swung into position. The once stark contrast between the brittle glitter of the commercial centre and the sustained and ingrained dinginess of the old St Ann's (which before redevelopment visibly separated two adjacent worlds which were in sober truth worlds apart) is now blurred, fogged, indistinct. The giant excavation, the great divide of the late 1960s, has been more than amply filled in. Now the landscape seen from St Ann's and city centre alike is overshadowed by a grotesque new 27-storey palace of commerce, where car parks for hundreds of vehicles support an assortment of bus stations, supermarkets, trendy stores, eggburger serveries and multi-storied stacks of what is laughingly miscalled living accommodation. It is as if the welfare state had visibly materialized itself in an assortment of great plastic musak towers, symbolically embodying the principle of all-transcending mediocrity. Never before has it been possible for human beings to be boring on so huge a scale, to elevate philistinism and greed into monuments which can subdue a whole townscape.

But the progress of business has not been accompanied by any noticeable human advance among the poor. They are still poor, and even though many of them are now living in houses which are better than those which have been knocked down, their problems remain considerable. We have documented the processes by which people suffer from attempts to ameliorate their conditions in our forthcoming book, *The Partial View*, which is subtitled 'How Poverty May be Aggravated by "Reform".' In a nutshell, when we interviewed the rehoused members of our first sample population of St Ann's residents after a five-year interval, we found that family poverty had increased among them. The numbers of families in poverty had jumped from a third to a half, while the proportions of the total child populations involved had increased from 50 per cent to 60 per cent. Increased rents and travelling costs had reduced the amount of income householders could make available to meet expenses on food, clothing, and other basic necessities. The whole sample, even when living above the somewhat arbitrarily-determined 'poverty-line' described in this book, had been pushed down noticeably closer to it. As it happened, the people we spoke to in 1967 were among the first people to be allocated to different houses, before the newly-built ones were available, so that most of them were settled in older council houses, which had fallen vacant in the peripheral estates which encircle the town. However, for the people who are fortunate enough to be rehoused in their old neighbourhood, the effect on the family budget is even more drastic, since the new houses are let at rents far higher than those which apply in the pre-war estates. Of course, building costs and interest rates payable by local authorities are higher too, so that the fault for the deterioration of all except the housing standards of the people of the new St Ann's does not fall on the local authority, which must do the best it can within the framework allotted to it. Yet this was precisely the complaint we raised when this work was first published: such a framework was too narrow, and could only result in the adverse effects which we predicted, which have been all too evidently apparent in the event.

In this book we attempted to analyse and describe the complex of deprivations and hardships which afflict the lives, not just of this small cross-section of people in Nottingham, but of all those who live in decaying slum areas, in every one of our major towns and cities. We tried to relate this experience to the growing public discussion about housing and welfare policies, trade union strategies, and attempts at grass-roots community action. Much of the evidence was gathered during the period 1966–8, a period of particular economic stringency. Since then there has been one change of government, a complete change of politicians with ministerial responsibility and a dazzling series of shifts and reverses of policy. In an inconstant world the only obvious stability that remains is that economic uncertainty seems to continue indefinitely.

The political change, alas, did not surprise us. The manifest failure of the Wilson administration to attack the growing problems of poverty and deprivation which had been ever more fully documented from 1966 onwards, gave rise to an eleventh-hour debate in the weeks immediately preceding the 1970 General Election. The debate was a confused one: Mr Ennals for the Labour Government proposed the motion that, despite the contrary evidence, the plight of the poor had in fact improved during its term of office, while Mr Crossman, also presumably for the Labour Government, agreed that if low pay was a problem at all it was the fault of the trade union movement. Alas, the electors were to be converted to neither of these eccentric viewpoints. If the unions were sadly disillusioned, the poor were completely alienated. By and large they stayed at home on election day. But staying at home would only be a sensible strategy if everyone did it. The sad truth is that the new Government was anything but willing to follow suit, and busily went to work on a whole succession of novel measures (commonly described as 'abrasive'), many of which undermined still further the poor's already precarious standards of living.

As a result, during these past years, whichever politicians have held office, the condition of the poor has not improved. A few, the lucky ones, have held on to the precarious standard of living which they endured in the middle-sixties. But for many, ground between the millstones of inflation on the one side and the present Government's determined assaults against universal welfare provision on the other, poverty has become even more severe, deprivation even more manifest, hope even more elusive.

The Conservative Government which was elected in June 1970 faced, and continues to face, two dominant economic and social trends, which had both contributed greatly to the downfall of the Labour Government, and which have both been daily augmenting the numbers of people in poverty and increasing the hardships they have had to endure. These trends consisted of a uniquely painful combination of steadily rising real unemployment, and remorseless price-inflation. Since the middle-sixties the dole queues have steadily lengthened. For a while this process was dignified by new names, such as the genteel description 'redeployment', or the repulsively technocratic term 'shakeout'; but, as the numbers of victims involved nationally grew inexorably towards, and for a while even passed, the million mark, the fact of unemployment, even mass unemployment, could no longer be cosily explained away. For the first time since the war, unemployment on a large and permanent scale has become a reality, and the lives of millions of people have been affected by it. As is always the case, the impact of this unwelcome tendency has been most marked in the already struggling and depressed areas. As is also always the case, the shock has been felt most by the unskilled and economically vulnerable. But this time the 'shakeout' has shaken the upper branches as well as the lower boughs, and unemployment has caused many people to fall a very long way, from well up into the middle levels of management, administration and technical specialization. Economic insecurity has afflicted more people, and a wider cross-section of people, than most people who are younger than fifty can remember.

Severe price-inflation made itself felt even more insidiously than the steadily increasing unemployment rate. Even during the General Election campaign the leaders of the Labour Party hardly seemed to recognize the serious threat to their own administration that inflation represented. Since the election, this problem has assumed such a dimension that, were Mr Heath only able to re-establish the annual rate of price increases which helped to break Mr Wilson, he might be hailed as a national saviour. At the moment, alas, this picaresque vision seems as remote as does that of the Last Judgement.

Whatever happens in the community at large, rising unemployment and rising prices both bear down most savagely upon the poor. For the relatively unskilled worker and his family, loss of work precipitates an immediate financial and domestic crisis; while loss of work accompanied by little or no prospect of re-employment can only aggravate this crisis, producing a sense of bitter resentment, a loss of morale and self-esteem, and

13

a gnawing, corroding sense of uncertainty. As one redundant bricklayer from St Ann's told Stacey Waddy: 'It's almost devastating: you have to explain to the children, you have to keep up the appearance of being a father and provider, while at the same time you realize you are not. It has a demoralizing effect. The young girl says "Why haven't you gone to work?" So I answer that "Well, the job that I had was finished and I've been waiting to start the new one." They're born into a world where the father goes to work, and it doesn't matter whatever he does, whether he's a dustman or a stockbroker, to the child he's just a father and he goes to work. If he stops it's puzzling, especially when the other children's fathers go to work, and it's very difficult to explain.

'I'm fortunate really, because this is the first time that I've been unemployed, but it makes you think what it does to those who are almost permanently unemployed. I've heard them talking in the Labour Exchange, men who to my mind have no real chance of ever being employed – I know there are quite a few who don't want to be – but the rest, their situation is desperate.

'Today for instance, I've just come walking around, looking for anyone I know, to hear about work maybe. I've thought about applying for a job elsewhere. I've just been looking around for something. If I don't walk about I'd just sit in the house. I believe you should put your clothes on, take your tools, and go out to work.' A culture such as ours in large measure defines a man by the work that he does; it encourages him to achieve self-respect and social approval in that work, by the very fact that he works. In this situation, the denial of the opportunity to work robs a man not only of his livelihood, but also of his social status and his self-respect.

Everyone is adversely affected by the inexorable (and yet, from day to day, unpredictable) price-rises which have come to be a normal feature of the British economy. Basic and essential commodities, such as food, have been subject to runaway inflation, as growing and insistent public anxiety about precisely these price-increases amply reveals. But if all wage-earners suffer, the effect of such price-inflation upon the budgets of poor people can be little short of catastrophic. Commodity after commodity passes beyond their reach, so that the shelves of the corner-shop and the supermarket remain crammed with goods which have become more and more unattainable, while at the same time even the most trifling transaction becomes an agonizing choice of priorities, and the satisfaction obtained from every purchase is diminished by its implicit sacrifice and self-denial. Forbearance, in such cases, is not the sacrifice of indulgent luxuries in favour of necessities, it is the loss of one necessity in favour of another.

Any political party taking office in 1970, to the extent that it was pledged to tackle the growing problems of family poverty, would have faced an uphill task. The present Conservative Government inherited office with precisely this pledge. But if there has been every sign that the flesh has been weak, there have been all too few indications that the spirit was willing. Indeed, in many quite deliberately chosen ways, the present government has intensified the difficulties of the poor, and made the administration of their relief both more remote and more humiliating. To some extent this was because of the contradictory pledges upon which Mr Heath gained office.

In the 1970 General Election campaign the Heath team tried to make the need for urgent relief of family poverty a major campaigning point and, somewhat uncharacteristically, presented themselves as the champions of the poor. In particular both Mr MacLeod and Mr Heath personally stressed that an increase in the Family Allowance was the only appropriate short-term measure. At the same time their Manifesto committed the Government to reducing public expenditure and rates of taxation, and to 'concentrate welfare resources where the need for them was greatest'. Mr Barber, as Chancellor of the Exchequer, has certainly demonstrated his abiding enthusiasm for the reduction of public expenditure in a series of economy measures, many of which have borne most heavily upon the poor, the ill, and the young. Babies must no longer drink a daily pint of welfare milk; the ill must now pay twenty pence per prescription item; schoolchildren must pay more for their school-dinners and must, from the age of seven, entirely forgo their free school milk. Meanwhile the unemployed, injured and sick must no longer seek assistance for the first three days they are incapacitated or out of work. Yet, for all Mr Barber's keen efforts, public expenditure in general continues to increase, even while the universal welfare benefits are cut back further and further.

True, most of the social measures concerned have also claimed to safeguard the interests of the poor by maintaining means-tested exemptions for specific categories of people (this, presumably, in order to 'concentrate help where it is most needed'). In this way, each of these mean and vindictive measures enabled trifling economies to be made in the welfare budget, while each in succession also marked a further step away from universal welfare provision, in the direction of means-tested, selective measures.

The living standards of poor families thus came under a sustained attack from the Government from the very beginning of its administration. Simultaneously the living standards of a much larger section of the population have been challenged by the Government's Housing Finance Bill. This crude attempt to phase out government subsidies on council housing, by compelling local authorities to introduce substantial annual rent-increases until a new unsubsidized level (the so-called 'fair rent') has been reached on each tenancy, has made inescapable housing costs substantially more expensive for millions of council tenants. Here again, the Government has introduced a system of rebates to needy families, but, as always, this rebate is only available after a rigorous examination of means.

In these two important areas, social policy and housing policy, those who have floated just above the poorest have been particularly victimized, while the poorest themselves have only obtained relief upon completion of exhaustive tests. Moreover, all the evidence shows that the 'take-up' of such benefits seldom exceeds a fraction of the entitled population. On the other hand, the Government would claim that it has initiated a bold and positive social policy, the most important feature of which, as far as poor families are concerned, is the Family Income Supplement. This has been the only major innovation in social provision, and, predictably, it confirmed and extended still further the Administration's ideological commitment to means-tested, highly selectivist policies. Offered as a substitute for the promised increase in Family Allowance, the Family Income Supplement makes two important and, so far as they go, welcome innovations. It brings relief (as the Supplementary Benefits Commission may not) to those low-paid families whose breadwinner is at work, and it brings relief (as Family Allowances do not) to families with only one dependent child. In each case families who have hitherto been denied welfare assistance have, under some circumstances, become eligible for relief.

In brief, the Government has established prescribed income levels for families of differing composition (£20 per week for a single-child family, and an additional £2 each for subsequent children). Families whose total household income falls below the prescribed limit may, after an appropriate means test, receive as an Income Supplement up to half the difference between their actual income and the prescribed level, up to a maximum of £5 per week. The Government has estimated that about 140,000 families would be eligible to benefit from Family Income Supplement, but despite a considerable publicity campaign, the number actually receiving this supplement hovers around 90,000.

A number of practical criticisms have been directed at the F.I.S. For a start, it can be argued that the prescribed levels are set too low, so that, even with maximum take-up, only a small fraction of the poor would benefit at all. Given a take-up rate of about 60 per cent, the fraction benefiting is in fact smaller still. Secondly, this particular benefit, allied with increasing reliance on means-testing in order to restrict most government and local authority-administered benefits to 'those who really need them' on a harshly selective basis, has produced and (with each new selective measure) intensified what is known as 'the poverty trap'. This is the situation in which a worker who receives a low wage (and is consequently eligible for a number of benefits in both cash and kind including perhaps

17

F.I.S., rent and rate rebates, free prescriptions, free school meals, and so on) is awarded an increase in wages which, by raising him above the eligibility levels for these various benefits, results in his being worse off after the wage-increase than he was before. The small increase in wages is more than covered by the loss of benefit, and additional tax liability. The Lord, we are told, moves in a mysterious way; likewise He giveth and He taketh away. As far as the poor are concerned, He giveth and taketh away simultaneously; this is indeed a mystery, which surpasseth all understanding.

 The govt.

The 'poverty trap' has become an increasingly widespread and demoralizing fact, as the numbers and range of narrowly means-tested benefits has increased, and as the levels of public relief payment continue to overlap with the wage-levels of lower-paid workers.

For these reasons it is fair to say that the Social Security measures of the past few years have resulted in a situation of labyrinthine complexity, from the customer's point of view, which has not only been associated with humiliating and discriminatory eligibility procedures, but has also meant that the end result, for many people, has not been greater personal or family security, but a Catch-22 contradiction. There was a time when the administration of our Social Security system and associated welfare schemes was relatively comprehensible. There were scales of benefit which were payable, as of right, to those in need; it was by no means difficult to find out when and if one was entitled, and if one was, then there was a strong possibility that some payments would be made. There are still scales of benefit, indeed there are more of them; but many of them are classified as secret, as are the rules governing eligibility. One may still be entitled to benefit, not as an unqualified right, but after means tests, social inquiries, visits from inspectors, cross-examinations either at the dole office or at home, or both. Small wonder that many people find the whole wretched business too tiresomely sordid to be worth the effort. But most seriously, what is happening is that a welfare service, imbued once with a sense of social justice and compassion, is

18

being daily transformed into an obstacle-race, a complex of humiliating pit-falls to trip up, catch out, or simply put off the poor and the needy. And this dirty game is not being played by carefully selected sadists, but by overworked and under-trained clerks and minor officials who try, as conscientiously as they can, to administer the unadministerable and to under-stand the incomprehensible. They stand, divided in their loyalties, uncertain about their proper role, an unhappy buffer between their masters on the one hand and the most severely deprived citizens on the other. Many of them are themselves grossly underpaid.

But what of the future? Are the prospects brighter, or have the situations and circumstances described in this book become an integral, established and permanent fact of modern life?

At the time of writing it is hard to visualize a rapid improve-ment. On the contrary, with a pay-freeze in operation, but no parallel controls on food or house prices, with entry into the Common Market only weeks away, with V.A.T. impending, there seems little prospect of avoiding another massive dose of inflation. On the optimistic side there are some slight indica-tions of the long-sought-after 5 per cent economic growth rates, although there is no reason to believe that the poorest will share in any resultant bonanza. But because a solution seems unlikely it does not mean that one is impossible. In this book we have tried to indicate some of the ways in which a serious and sustained attack can be mounted upon poverty and depriva-tion in our society. But before this attack can even be dreamed of, the size and gravity of the problem must be recognized, and the will to confront it with determination must be gener-ated. The record of successive governments is a bitterly dis-appointing one, but among students and social workers, among trade unionists and constituency party members, among influen-tial and growing sections of the public at large, including the poor and deprived themselves, the problem is becoming more generally and more clearly understood, and the determination to eradicate it already forms a groundswell which democratically-elected governments can only ignore at their peril.

PART ONE

Poverty is Back
Among Us

A WORKER READS HISTORY

Who built the seven gates of Thebes?
The books are filled with the names of Kings.
Was it Kings who hauled the craggy blocks of stone?
And Babylon, so many times destroyed,
Who built the city up each time? In which of Lima's houses
That city glittering with gold, lived those who built it?
In the evening when the Chinese wall was finished
Where did the masons go? Imperial Rome
Is full of arcs of triumph. Who reared them up? Over whom
Did the Caesars triumph? Byzantium lives in song,
Were all her dwellings palaces? And even in Atlantis of the legend
The night the sea rushed in,
The drowning men still bellowed for their slaves.

Young Alexander conquered India
He alone?
Caesar beat the Gauls
Was there not even a cook in his army?
Philip of Spain wept as his fleet
Was sunk and destroyed. Were there no other tears?
Frederick the Great triumphed in the Seven Years War. Who
Triumphed with him?

Each page a victory,
At whose expense the victory ball?
Every ten years a great man,
Who paid the piper?

So many particulars
So many questions.

BERTOLT BRECHT

1 The Rediscovery of Poverty

I

During the fifties the myth that widespread material poverty had been finally and triumphantly overcome was so universally current, so widely accepted by politicians, social commentators and the general public alike, that for a decade and more, public controversy and political discussion were engrossed by the new (and fundamentally more encouraging) problems of what people are still pleased to call the 'Affluent Society'. The period since the end of the Second World War was interpreted as one of more or less uninterrupted and continuing economic growth, with the new wealth being distributed increasingly equitably throughout the population. The age-old malaise of poverty, far from being an endemic problem facing a mass of the population, was felt to be a slight social hangover: a problem affecting tiny groups of people who, through their incompetence or fecklessness, were failing to share in the new prosperity.

Increasingly the problems of affluence commanded public attention. This new mood was captured most aptly in Galbraith's book *The Affluent Society*: indeed, this very title was generally adopted as the vogue label to describe the society of the late fifties, and the problems which Galbraith underlined became the principal subjects of contemporary discussion. How should the tension between the demands of the individual consumer and the need for basic public amenities be reconciled; or must the new society always be typified by 'private affluence and public squalor'? What limits could or should be set to the acquisitiveness of the individual consumer? The argument about social policy and the Welfare State was increasingly switched from insistence upon the need for universal guarantees of social rights, to advocacy of the right of the individual to fend for himself, to contract out of involvement in State-sponsored welfare schemes.

Yet, only a decade later, we now know that throughout the fifties the numbers of people in poverty could already be counted in millions and were growing, not shrinking, that the distribution of national wealth was becoming less, not more, equitable; that the much-vaunted equalities of opportunity were to a great extent paper promises rarely carried into practice; even, that between 1950 and 1960 the diet of substantial sections of the population deteriorated to well below medically recommended levels. How was it that politicians of all parties, commentators of every persuasion, 'experts' in social inquiry, and professionals engaged in social work, should all have accepted so quickly and prematurely that poverty had become a memory of the past?

The first possible explanation is that until the early sixties only one major piece of research into poverty was undertaken, and this work seemed to demonstrate quite conclusively that poverty had indeed been overcome. Seebohm Rowntree, with his colleague G. R. Lavers, published, in 1951, the findings of the third and final survey of poverty in York.[1] These findings showed that in 1950 only $1\frac{1}{2}$ per cent of the survey population lived in poverty, compared with 18 per cent in the similar survey undertaken by Rowntree himself in 1936. No wonder that a *Times* leader rejoiced at this 'remarkable improvement – no less than the virtual abolition of the sheerest want'.

These conclusions were amply confirmed for most people by the less systematic but perhaps more compelling evidence of their own eyes. Was it not abundantly clear that there had been a striking and apparently permanent improvement in people's living standards? Was it not the case that for years the country had enjoyed full employment? Was it not true that wage levels were rising? Were not the shop windows stocked with a vast and ever-increasing range of new consumer goods at prices

1. *Poverty and the Welfare State*, Longmans, 1951.

which, with the aid of hire-purchase facilities, put them within the reach of most people's incomes? Was it not the case that the growing generation of children were taller, and heavier, and stronger than their parents, thanks to improvements both in diet and physical environment? Where were the hunger marches of the thirties? Even though the new-found affluence was most obvious in the Midlands and South-East, were there any areas of the country which were not substantially better off than they had been during the slump which had paralysed so many of them in the thirties? Indeed, for most people, it was this direct and vivid contrast between the thirties and fifties which was so striking. To those whose reflexes had been conditioned during the lean years of the Depression, the widespread prosperity of the fifties was quite undeniable.

How, then, had this quite remarkable transformation come about? According to Rowntree and Lavers there were two principal reasons. First, they cited the post-war policies of full employment and the associated rise in wage rates. They could show that, whereas in 1936 60 per cent of poverty was due to unemployment or low wages, in 1950 the figure was only 1 per cent. Secondly, the various welfare measures which were generally available in post-war Britain were supposed to have had a markedly redistributive effect, and to have considerably improved working-class living standards. Thus Rowntree and Lavers sought to evaluate the effect of such measures as food subsidies and family allowances in reducing poverty. Such poverty as remained was interpreted as a minor residual problem, concentrated mainly among the aged, and it seemed plain that it only required appropriate adjustments in the levels of welfare payments to overcome this lingering but final manifestation of hardship.

This plausible explanation in terms of post-war social and economic policies seemed to satisfy most commentators, including those of both the Left and the Right. Right-wing commentators tended to emphasize the primary importance of the wealth-producing mechanisms of the free market, in which the welfare services were to be seen as a short-lived expedient;

more radical writers dwelt on the beneficent effects of the Welfare State as a set of institutions which had civilized, if not quite transformed, the capitalist economic system. Thus, even so subtle a political analyst as C. A. R. Crosland, writing in 1956, accepted Rowntree's conclusions with little hesitation.[2] Although he correctly argued that Rowntree's assessments of the value of welfare benefits to individual households were crudely oversimplified, and although he acknowledged that there still remained some problems of hardship to be solved, he was hotly anxious to assert that the triumphant victory over poverty was a consequence of the economic and welfare policies of the post-war Labour Government.

Politicians, even Labour politicians, will probably always find ways to forgive themselves for failing to grasp that their efforts have not been entirely successful. More remarkable, perhaps, was the prolonged refusal of social workers throughout this decade, to acknowledge the continued existence of widespread and institutionalized poverty: a strikingly myopic reaction shared by numbers of others who were directly and professionally in close contact with social problems. To some extent, of course, they too were deceived by the obvious and widespread symbols of the new affluence, and were also, perhaps, somewhat over-impressed by the work of the welfare agencies in which they played such a major role. But a more fundamental reason for their inability to understand the significance of the social circumstances in which they were working lies in the systems of training which most social workers had undergone. The fifties were the heyday of what is now referred to as the 'psychiatric deluge' in social-work training programmes. During this period social casework was seen as a form of intensive social therapy, concentrating on revealing the 'latent' personality problems which underlie such 'manifest' symptoms as shortage of money. Heavily influenced by ideas borrowed from psychoanalysis, social-work theory emphasized the essential individuality of each client's problems; thus, by their training, social workers were encouraged to interpret all

2. *The Future of Socialism*, Jonathan Cape, 1956.

public ills as personal problems, and saw their role as helping each client adjust to the 'realities' of his environment. Thus discussion of poverty among social workers was concerned almost exclusively with the so-called 'problem family', whose members, through shiftlessness, low intelligence, or sheer incapability to budget, found themselves in poverty. The solution was discussed in terms of casework requirements.[3] Mercifully this regrettable era in the history of social work is past; increasingly social workers have come to understand that the problem of poverty is rooted, not in the inadequate personalities of its victims, but in the basic economic and class structure of our society. Increasingly social workers are to be found advancing or supporting suggestions for thoroughgoing structural reforms, just as a whole new range of social-work pressure groups such as the Child Poverty Action Group or Shelter have adopted a far more aggressive approach to the solution of social problems.

II

It was not until the beginning of the sixties that the small group of people who had consistently maintained that there was still a serious problem of material poverty began to make a serious impact on public opinion. As early as 1952, Peter Townsend, the most distinguished and persistent student of contemporary poverty, raised doubts about the validity of Rowntree and Lavers' conclusions. At the time Townsend was working for the independent research organization, Political and Economic Planning (P.E.P.), and in their bulletin *Planning* he challenged the validity of Rowntree's minutely calculated subsistence scales, from which he deduced his poverty line. Townsend argued that the list of items deemed to be a 'necessary expenditure' was too narrow, and urged a more

3. A guide to reading on this matter, and a sympathetic view of it, can be found in Philp and Timms, *The Problem of the Problem Family*. Family Service Units, London, 1957.

realistic appraisal of 'necessaries'. Two years later he returned to this theme in the *British Journal of Sociology*,[4] where he suggested that calculations of essential expenditure should not be based upon the prejudices of research workers or other experts who claim to know how other people's money should best be spent, but upon actual spending patterns of working-class groups. He recognizes here that spending habits are not 'rational' (in a strict economic sense), but take place in the context of a social system which applies certain pressure upon its members. Thus 'due regard must be paid to the conventions sanctioning membership of the community, to the influence of economic and social measures currently adopted by society as a whole ... and to the standards encouraged by advertisers, the press, the B.B.C., and the Church', to which list we would now, presumably, add the more potent and deliberate influence of I.T.V.

In 1958 Townsend attacked more directly the myth that poverty had been abolished. In an essay in the volume *Conviction* he drew attention to the existence of large groups of people, such as the old, the widowed, the disabled and sick, who were unable to play a full part in the productive life of the economy, and were consequently unable to take full advantage of improvements in living standards, to consume in the new levels which were becoming general. These vulnerable groups were not small in number and probably totalled about 7 million people.

In February 1960 a Fabian pamphlet by Audrey Harvey developed a powerful attack on the myths of the fifties. Based upon Mrs Harvey's considerable experience as a social worker in London's East End, 'Casualties of the Welfare State'[5] had two important themes. First, that many of the thousands of clients who sought help were suffering real economic hardship; even those with higher than average earnings did not normally have the institutional insurances against misfortune enjoyed by so many white-collar workers, so that sickness or

4. 'Measuring Poverty', *British Journal of Sociology*, 1954, pp. 130–37.
5. Fabian Tract No. 321.

some other interruption of earnings could quickly precipitate an economic crisis. Secondly, the network of welfare agencies and social service departments was so administratively complex, and so bureaucratically organized, that many of those people who were most in need were not getting the help they required.

This pamphlet initiated a prolonged discussion, which still continues, about the efficacy of the welfare services, which was a healthy corrective to the assumption that in, indeed because of, the Welfare State, all was for the best. Between 1962 and 1965 there were published a damning series of books and papers, each of which added further systematic evidence of the growing seriousness of the problem. The theory that the Welfare State had ensured a substantial redistribution of income to the benefit of the working class was shown to be very wide of the mark in Professor Titmuss's book *Income Distribution and Social Change* published in 1962.[6] In the same year Mrs Dorothy Wedderburn published two important essays. In the first, which she wrote with Mr J. Utting,[7] the hardship among retired old people was discussed in detail, while in the second, Mrs Wedderburn used a variety of official sources on income and expenditure to demonstrate that a large proportion of the population (about 12 per cent) was living at or close to the subsistence levels maintained by the National Assistance Board.[8] The following year, Tony Lynes published his occasional paper 'National Assistance and National Prosperity'.[9] This paper argued that at its establishment in 1948 the National Assistance Board had adopted a subsistence scale that 'could not be described as generous even by the standards of the thirties'; since then it had not been sufficiently revised to keep pace

6. Allen & Unwin, 1962.

7. Cole (Wedderburn) and Utting, 'The Economic Circumstances of Old People', Occasional Papers on Social Administration, No. 4, Bell, 1962.

8. Cole (Wedderburn), 'Poverty in Britain Today – The Evidence', *Sociological Review*, 1962, pp. 257–82.

9. Occasional Papers on Social Administration, No. 5, Bell.

either with changes in the cost of living, or with the growth in national prosperity.

In 1964 Royston Lambert's paper 'Nutrition in Britain 1950–60' [10] showed how during these years the diet of families with three or more children had deteriorated to well below the levels recommended by nutrition experts. Finally and most significantly, in December 1965 came 'The Poor and the Poorest' by Professor Brian Abel-Smith and Peter Townsend. [11] This document, based upon a careful analysis of the Ministry of Labour's Household Expenditure Surveys, compared household incomes in 1953 and 1960 with the scale of National Assistance operative at the time. The authors showed that, in 1953, 7·8 per cent of the population was living in poverty and the proportion was growing, so that, by 1960, 14·2 per cent of the population was affected. Thus it was claimed that in 1960 7½ million people were living in poverty. The publication of these findings so impressed an adult education class in Nottingham, that it reconvened six months later as the St Ann's Study Group to plan the local poverty research project that forms the basic subject of Part II of this volume.

10. Occasional Papers on Social Administration, No. 6.
11. ibid., No. 17.

2 But what is Poverty?

Much of the discussion about contemporary poverty has been frustrated because of confusion over or ambiguity in the meaning of the word. This was recently exemplified almost perfectly by George Schwartz in his column in the business section of the *Sunday Times*.[1] 'What significance and value,' he asked, 'attach to the definition and measurement of poverty in the Western world and other advanced communities? Before long it will mean non-possession of a coloured television set.' In justification of this judgement, Mr Schwartz went on to add:

> Is this a disgustingly frivolous statement? I retort that to proclaim that millions of families in the U.K. are on the poverty line and being driven remorselessly below it, and that over thirty million people in the United States are living in conditions of poverty is not only disgusting and frivolous but also blasphemous. If poverty is to be measured on those standards, I would agree, that 80 per cent and more of the world is below the level of subsistence . . .

Of course, Mr Schwartz thinks it self-evidently ridiculous to assume that four fifths of the population of the world are in want. Undoubtedly many people will agree with him.

We encountered a similar, if more humanely conceived, argument in the correspondence column of the *Nottingham Evening Post* after we had published the preliminary results of some of our local research into poverty. One correspondent made the point that in comparison with the millions of people in underdeveloped regions of the world where life expectations can be below thirty years, and where physical hunger and even

1. *Sunday Times*, 18 August 1968.

33

starvation are all too common, even the poorest person in this country is well off. Beyond any doubt, this is a valid argument. The co-existence of rich nations plagued with widespread diseases of overconsumption and poor communities existing at the barest imaginable level of livelihood, cannot be morally defended. But to assume that this implies that there is some easily discovered, absolute and apparently universal, line below which there is poverty and above which there is not, is fundamentally to misunderstand the problem. That this misunderstanding is widespread should, however, cause no surprise: most of the research into poverty in Britain during the past eighty years has been based upon just such a misconception. This is well illustrated by Rowntree's three classic surveys in York.[2] It does not minimize the importance of these surveys in the very slightest, to emphasize their rigidity in one fundamental respect: in each case Rowntree calculated a fixed minimum weekly sum of money which, in his opinion, was 'necessary to enable families ... to secure the necessaries of a healthy life', and he emphasized that 'the standards adopted ... are on the side of stringency rather than of extravagance', being 'the lowest standards which responsible experts can justify'. In accordance with this principle, and with the help of the British Medical Association, a diet sheet was compiled which combined (supposedly) adequate nutrition-value with minimum cost. This sum of money was then allowed for spending on food; presumably the housewife was supposed to buy exactly the same quantities of exactly the same commodities every week, or else risk either over-spending or lowering the nutritional value of her purchases. The 1950 dietary used by Rowntree is shown in Table I, and we can see the quantities of food, at 1950 prices, deemed necessary for a man, wife, and three children under fourteen. Six pounds of swedes, and no tins, not even of baked beans, may have seemed a little austere to the average working-class family, even in 1950. To these

2. *Poverty: A Study of Town Life*, Macmillan, 1901; *Poverty and Progress*, Longmans, 1941; *Poverty and the Welfare State* (with G. R. Lavers), Longmans, 1951.

food costs Rowntree added £1 7s. 9d. for clothing, 6s. for household sundries, 7s. 7d. for fuel and light and 11s. 6d. for personal sundries, giving a total weekly subsistence-level income for a man, wife, and three children (excluding rent) of £5 0s. 2d.

Table 1. Dietary for man, wife, and three children (based on B.M.A. Report on nutritional needs, published 1950)

Breast of mutton – 2½ lb. at 8d. per lb. (imported)	1.	8.
Minced beef – 2 lb. at 1s. 4d. per lb.	2.	8.
Shin of beef – 1½ lb. at 1s. 6d. per lb.	2.	3.
Liver – 1 lb. at 1s. 6d. per lb.	1.	6.
Beef sausages – 1 lb. at 1s. 3d. per lb.	1.	3.
Bacon 1¼ lb. at 1s. 11d. per lb. (cheapest cut)	2.	4¾.
Cheese – 10 oz. at 1s. 2d. per lb.		8¾.
Fresh full cream milk – 14 pints at 5d. per pint	5.	10.
Herrings – 1½ lb. at 8d. per lb.	1.	0.
Kippers – 1 lb. at 1s. per lb.	1.	0.
Sugar – 3 lb. 2 oz. at 5d. per lb.	1.	3½.
Potatoes – 14 lb. at 9 lb. for 1s.	1.	6½.
23½ lb. Bread – 13½ loaves at 5½d. each	6.	2¼.
Oatmeal – 2 lb. at 6d. per lb.	1.	0.
Margarine – 2½ lb. at 10d. per lb.	2.	1.
Cooking fat – 10 oz. at 1s. per lb.		7½.
Flour – 1¼ lb. at 9½d. per 3 lb. bag		4.
Jam – 1 lb. at 1s. 2d. per lb.	1.	2.
Treacle – 1 lb. at 10d. (in tins)		10.
Cocoa – ¼ lb. at 8½d. per ¼ lb.		8½.
Rice – 10 oz. at 9d. per lb.		5½.
Sago – ¼ lb. at 9d. per lb.		2¼.
Barley – 2 oz. at 9d. per lb.		1.
Peas – ½ lb. at 10½d. per lb.		5¼.
Lentils – ¾ lb. at 10½d. per lb.		8.
Stoned dates – ½ lb. at 10½d. per lb.		5¼.
Swedes – 6 lb. at 2½d. per lb.	1.	3.
Onions – 4½ lb. at 5d. per lb.	1.	10½.
Apples – 4 lb. at 5d. per lb.	1.	8.
Egg – 1 at 3½d.		3½.
Extra vegetables and fruit	1.	6.
Tea – ½ lb. at 3s. 4d. per lb.	1.	8.
Extras, including salt, seasoning, etc.		9.
	47.	4.

This inflexible, but easily understood, conception of a fixed poverty line has been tellingly criticized by Peter Townsend. He complains that the adequacy of such a subsistence standard depends on its being spent efficiently, that is to say as the compilers of the standard have thought best. Against this, though, 'it may be that people do not know what goods are "necessary" and where they can be obtained cheaply. Or it may be that spending habits are determined by the conventions of the lowest stratum of society, and by economic and social measures ... currently adopted by the community as a whole. All this is quite apart from individual habits and inclinations.' But more than this: what is to be considered 'necessary' and what is not? 'If clothing, money for travel to work and newspapers are considered to be "necessaries" in the conventional sense, why not tea, handkerchiefs, laundry, contraceptives, cosmetics, hairdressing and shaving, and life-insurance payments?'[3] Here Townsend is demonstrating that what is deemed 'necessary', once sheer physical survival is assured, is a matter of convention, not of principle; and conventions are socially formed. Now this is by no means a new idea; on the contrary, quite explicit statements on the relative nature of poverty can be found even in the work of the classical economists.

Thus, in *The Wealth of Nations*, Adam Smith says, 'By necessaries I understand, not only the commodities which are indispensably necessary for the support of life, but whatever the custom of the country renders it indecent for creditable people, even of the lowest order, to be without.' Karl Marx writes in *Capital* that the worker's 'natural wants, such as food, clothing, fuel and housing vary according to the climatic and other physical conditions of his country. On the other hand the number and extent of his so-called necessary wants ... are themselves the product of historical development and depend, therefore, to a great extent on the degree of civilization of a country.' The principle of the relativity of poverty was developed by Marx in that section of *Capital* which has so often been quoted as setting forth 'the law of increasing misery'. Far

3. 'Measuring Poverty', *British Journal of Sociology*, 1954, p. 131.

from seeing the growth of capital as a simple tendency to the material deprivation of the workpeople, Marx enunciated a much more subtle proposition: 'in proportion as capital accumulates, the lot of the labourer, *be his payment high or low* [our italics], must grow worse.'[4] In support of this notion he quotes Gladstone's budget speech of 16 April 1863, where Gladstone, describing a period of economic growth, reports an 'intoxicating augmentation of wealth and power', which, while 'entirely confined to classes of property ... must be of indirect benefit to the labouring population ... while the rich have been growing richer, the poor have been growing less poor. At any rate, whether the extremes of poverty are less, I do not presume to say.' To this 'lame anticlimax' Marx replies that 'if the working class has remained "poor", only "less poor" in proportion as it produces for the wealthy class "an intoxicating augmentation of wealth and power", then it has remained relatively just as poor. If the extremes of poverty have not lessened, they have increased, because the extremes of wealth have.' Turning to the social definition of needs, we find that Marx writes in his much earlier work, *Wage-Labour and Capital*:

A noticeable increase in wages presupposes a rapid growth of productive capital. The rapid growth of productive capital brings about an equally rapid growth of wealth, luxury, social needs, social enjoyments. Thus, in comparison with the state of development of society in general although the enjoyments of the worker have risen, the social satisfaction that they give has fallen in comparison with the increased enjoyments of the capitalists which are inaccessible to the worker. *Our needs and enjoyments spring from society; we measure them, therefore, by society and not by the objects of their satisfaction. Because they are of a social nature, they are of a relative nature* [our italics] . . .[5]

Seen in this way, poverty is not so much a simple lack of wealth as a more basic lack of power. While it is true that

4. Ed. Torr, Allen & Unwin, p. 661.
5. *Karl Marx Selected Works*, Vol. 1, Lawrence & Wishart, 1946, pp. 268–9.

socially expanded needs can displace the 'natural' priorities of consumption, so that social pressures may persuade a man to go hungry rather than naked, or undernourished rather than lag too visibly far behind the Joneses, so that it becomes possible to find children exhibiting many of the signs of malnutrition and yet familiar with every televised exploit of Batman or Tarzan, it is also true that the moral consequences of poverty in an advanced society are far more dire than its physical results. Loss of power is the most serious of all the losses entailed in poverty, because it is the most permanent and self-reinforcing. 'Needs' themselves can be increasingly manipulated in the most cynical and conscienceless way, where men lose control over their own joint activities. In this, Gladstone was right to point up the 'intoxicating augmentation of wealth and power' which accompanied the economic growth he was describing. As Marx had written over two decades earlier: 'If ... the income of the worker increases with the rapid growth of capital, the social gulf that separates the workers from the capitalists increases at the same time, the power of capital over labour, the dependence of labour on capital, increases at the same time.'[6] Such a loss of power affects all employees as capital becomes more concentrated and continuously extends its dominance. But if some are able to defend themselves with varying degrees of success, there are others for whom the task becomes increasingly onerous, increasingly difficult, even increasingly vain.

The weak, who go to the wall, are not only in want, but are also manifestly ill-placed to complain effectively about their condition. To the burden of individual deprivation, they too often have to add the additional imposts of social neglect, and of consequent exclusion from even such normal opportunities for self-defence as might exist for people only slightly more favoured than they themselves. Material lack becomes loss of morale: and this in turn may well serve to inhibit collective action in any form, and still further atomize and intimidate the poor community.

6. *Karl Marx Selected Works*, Vol. 1, Lawrence & Wishart, 1946, p. 279.

At the other pole of society, as Professor Meade has pointed out:

A man with much property has great bargaining strength and a great sense of security, independence and freedom; and he enjoys these things not only *vis-à-vis* his property-less fellow citizens but also *vis-à-vis* the public authorities. An unequal distribution of property means an unequal distribution of power, even if it is prevented from causing too unequal a distribution of income.[7]

These long-established pleas for an understanding of the relative nature of poverty have had numerous modern echoes. One notable voice to have taken up the cry has been that of Professor J. K. Galbraith, who, in Delphic mood, claims that

people are poverty-stricken when their income, even if it is adequate for survival, falls markedly below that of the community. Then they cannot have what the larger community regards as the minimum necessary for decency; and they cannot wholly escape, therefore, the judgement of the larger community that they are indecent. They are degraded, for, in the literal sense, they live outside the grades or categories which the community regards as acceptable.[8]

Or, again, Marshall Clinard says:

Poverty is both an absolute and a relative term. In an absolute sense, it means a lack of resources for specific needs; in a relative sense it refers to the extent of these resources in comparison to what other individuals in the society have ... a poor urban family today may have technological possessions and education superior even to those of the upper socioeconomic classes in the eighteenth century. In other words poverty must be defined in terms of the aspirations and expectations of a culture and its capacity to produce these goods ...

Finally, Michael Harrington, in his important book *The Other America*, argues that 'To have one bowl of rice in a society where all other people have half a bowl may well be a sign of

7. J. E. Meade, *Efficiency, Equality and the Ownership of Property*, Allen & Unwin, 1964.

8. J. K. Galbraith, *The Affluent Society*, Hamish Hamilton, 1958, p. 252; Penguin Books, 1962.

achievement and intelligence ... to have five bowls of rice in a society where the majority have a decent, balanced diet is a tragedy', but he goes on, beyond the notion of relativity in terms of conventional social expectations, to assert that 'poverty should be defined absolutely, in terms of what man and society could be. As long as America is less than its potential, the nation as a whole is impoverished by that fact. As long as there is the other America, we are, all of us, poorer because of it.'[9] In other words, the only tenable absolute standard is an optimum one, based upon the maximum possible social achievement. Placed in this context, the stringently calculated subsistence-level poverty line is seen to be an aberration on the part of those whose yearning for precision and parsimony exceeds not only their common humanity, but also their desire for sociological sophistication.

Following Harrington, we *could* agree on an absolute standard, which would involve an optimum based on a universal community. While men identify themselves with Britain, or the United States, or France, or Nigeria, their standards will be those of their own immediate surroundings. If men ever come (and who can deny that they are trying?) to see themselves as human beings, part of one human fellowship, then one of the first realities of their vision will be the appreciation of the fact that Mr Schwartz' caustic and cynical equation is all too close to the literal truth.[10]

9. *The Other America: Poverty in the United States*, Macmillan, 1962; Penguin Books, 1963.

10. Mr Schwartz' objections to modern poverty research go beyond dismissing any identity between the deprived people of English slums and the Egyptian fellahin. 'Do you realize,' he asks, 'that many of the definitions of poverty and other social phenomena derive from what should be strictly objective statistical classification? Line up 100 people in order of height,' he enjoins us. 'When they are sorted out properly, mark off the 25 on the right. That's a quarter of the group and you are entitled to say that one quarter of the group is below the height of say 5 ft 5 ins. What you are not entitled to do is to proclaim dogmatically that one quarter of the group is physically stunted, and then go on to assert that this is the result of capitalist exploitation over the years.' To hammer home his point, Mr Schwartz appeals to us: 'Let me set

II

Acknowledging that, in the absence of world-wide community, poverty is a relative notion, we find ourselves confronted by an entirely practical problem: for the purposes of both social policy and social research, some defining line has to be drawn to distinguish the relatively poor from the more affluent. The calculation of a precise subsistence minimum below which physical survival is endangered is now generally accepted as a hazardous and shortsighted operation, but what alternative measure can be adopted? An examination of American poverty studies indicates that there are several possible alter-

---

and mark a general knowledge quiz for our M.P.s and I undertake to show by the classification of my marks that 25 per cent of them are afflicted by intellectual impoverishment.'

If we *did* take the I.Q.s of M.P.s, and found that they ranged between a small group at 160 and a slightly larger group at 85, with the vast majority in the middle (their traditional posture), this of course would be quite usual. Perhaps the normal curve of distribution might entitle Mr Schwartz to be fussy about calling any given 25 per cent grouping names, or describing their position pejoratively. If we take and classify men by their heights, we anticipate such a normal curve, with a few in the extremes, and many in the middle. In such circumstances, finding most people between 5 ft and 6 ft 6 ins., we might be likely to say that the two men who were less than 4 ft 6 ins. were physically stunted, and both they and Mr Schwartz might be inclined to agree with us.

But when we look at the statistical distribution of wealth, we don't get a normal curve. To use Mr Schwartz' rather naughty analogies, we find some few people three miles high, most of us about a yard high, and too many, a very sizeable group, about eighteen inches high. The eighteen inch people are expected to live among the yard-high ones, and pass themselves off as 'normal'. The three-milers can buy all kinds of inter-mediaries, six-footers who think like Mr Schwartz, to argue that eighteen inches is a perfectly nice height and three miles a terribly burdensome and uncomfortable one, involving infinite self-sacrifice and asceticism. To those of us who have an inkling how tall three miles is, though, eighteen inches seems short. Further, many of us have an uncomfortable suspicion that Mr Schwartz would not be totally miserable if, in the interest of economic growth, eighteen inches were agreed to be a perfectly proper standard of height for all commoners, and all yard-tall men accordingly shrunk.

natives.[11] Most studies choose an arbitrary annual income, very often 3,000 dollars for a family of four: but also recommended as a criterion has been the level below which no income tax is levied, or a sum of 1,500 dollars for the first person, plus 500 dollars for each additional member of the family: while others arbitrarily select some fraction such as the bottom fifth, quarter or third of the income distribution. To base a poverty line on the actual distribution of income within society seems a sensible procedure; it avoids the paternalism of a calculated subsistence scale, it is sensitive to growth in the national economy, and it demonstrates that at root the discussion about poverty is concerned as much with economic equality as with economic survival. There are however serious, perhaps insuperable, practical obstacles to using a measure based on distributed income in this country. These obstacles have been closely examined in Professor Titmuss's book *Income Distribution and Social Change*.[12] He shows how difficult it is to get accurate information on income distribution. This difficulty is partly due to the complexities of our system of taxation, direct and indirect, with its intricate mysteries of concessions and allowances, and partly due to the added difficulty of assessing the relative worth and costs of fringe benefits such as expense accounts, private pension and other welfare schemes, not to mention conceptual difficulties when an attempt is made to define income-units in relation to the overall possession of wealth.

Consequently, British research has developed another approach to defining poverty, using the scale of benefits paid by the National Assistance Board (now called the Supplementary Benefits Commission) as its standard. This device was used by Mrs Dorothy Wedderburn in 1962[13] when she estimated that

11. See Mollie Orshansky, 'Counting the Poor: Another Look at the Poverty Programme', in *Poverty in America*, ed. Louis A. Ferman, Joyce L. Kornbluk and Alan Haber, University of Michigan, 1965.

12. Allen & Unwin, 1962.

13. 'Poverty in Britain Today – The Evidence', *Sociological Review*, 1962.

12 per cent of all households were living below, or no more
than 25 per cent above, National Assistance Board scale rates.
Abel-Smith and Townsend used essentially the same technique,
but they showed the percentage of households and of the population living at different levels up to 40 per cent above the
basic N.A.B. scales.

The argument used to justify this means of identifying the
poor is a simple one. The task of the National Assistance
Board was 'to assist persons in Great Britain who are without
resources to meet their requirements, or whose resources ...
must be supplemented in order to meet their requirements'.
The rate of payments made by the Board and its successor
has varied in accordance with appropriate scales, which take
account of the individual circumstances and responsibilities of
each applicant. Precisely how these scales are arrived at is
something of a mystery, and there is ample scope for discussing their adequacy. The scales do however 'have the advantage
of being in a sense the "official" operational definition of the
minimum level of living at any particular time'. They represent
the level below which the State will not normally allow a
household to fall, and so represent a convenient and appropriate yardstick for poverty. Certainly no serious critic would
argue that the scale rates are too high; indeed, as Tony Lynes
pointed out in 1962,[14] the N.A.B. scales established in 1948
were 'roughly in line with the Beveridge recommendations.
Since the Beveridge subsistence level was below Rowntree's
1936 poverty line, it is clear that the 1948 assistance scale
could not be described as generous even by the standards of
the thirties.' Furthermore, while between 1948–60 the real value
of the scales was increased by about a quarter, real disposable
income per head increased by twice that rate. Thus, far from
being over-generous, the N.A.B. scales were demonstrably over-
stringent. In recent years they have been very much more
generously increased, but even so it would certainly be unreasonable to accept a lower level as an appropriate poverty line.

14. 'National Assistance and National Prosperity', Occasional Papers
on Social Administration, No. 5.

The justification for drawing the line at 40 per cent above the basic scale-rates is that the N.A.B. always had it in its power to make certain extra discretionary payments, and was charged to overlook certain amounts of capital or savings. In practice, many recipients of National Assistance do receive payments as much as 40 per cent above the basic scale rates, or are living in households whose level of living is 40 per cent above the minimum. In any event, the conclusions of 'The Poor and the Poorest' were based on this assumption, as were the findings of the Nottingham research which was inspired by 'The Poor and the Poorest'. There is no need to be dogmatic about this particular poverty line: as we shall see, poverty is so much more than a crude shortage of resources that to bicker about a marginal few shillings would be vulgarly obscurantist. We would rather see 40 per cent above scale rates as one indication, not necessarily the most important or significant, of relative hardship.

III

The establishment of a 'poverty line' that is sensitive to the relativity of wealth and acknowledges that as circumstances change so do human needs, distinguishes in a most important respect the research of the decade from the classic poverty studies of before the war. Consequently, it is striking that, this point of definition apart, there is a very considerable measure of agreement as to the principal causes of poverty. The relative importance of these causes has changed from time to time as circumstances have altered, and different pieces of research reveal marginal differences from one situation to another, but the headings listed by Rowntree as the immediate causes of poverty in his first study of York in 1901, are almost identical with Abel-Smith and Townsend's 1965 classification, thus:

(1) Death of chief wage-earner (the problem of the fatherless family).

(2) Incapacity of chief wage-earner through accident, illness, or old age (Townsend divides this group into two, separating

the aged from those whose earnings are intermittent because
of sickness or disability).

(3) Chief wage-earner out of work.

(4) Chronic irregularity of work; here Rowntree seemed to
refer to the chronic work-shy, a group who are nowadays
known to be so small in number as to be for the purposes of
this discussion, insignificant.

(5) Size of family.

(6) Lowness of wage. Townsend produces one category to
include all those whose income is below the accepted level,
either because of family size, or because of lowness of wage, or,
of course, because of both factors.

Rowntree went farther than merely listing causes; in a strikingly insightful passage he describes what he calls the 'cycle
of poverty':

The life of a labourer is marked by five alternating periods of
want and comparative plenty. During early childhood, unless his
father is a skilled worker, he probably will be in poverty; this will
last until he, or some of his brothers and sisters, begin to earn
money and thus augment their father's wage sufficiently to raise
the family above the poverty line. Then follows the period during
which he is earning money and living under the parents' roof;
for some portion of this period he will be earning more money than
is required for lodging, food, and clothes. This is his chance to
save money ... this period of prosperity may continue after mar-
riage until he has two or three children, when poverty will again
overtake him. This period of poverty will last perhaps for ten years,
i.e. until the first child is fourteen and begins to earn wages; but
if there are more than three children it may last longer. While the
children are earning, and before they leave the home to marry, the
man enjoys another period of prosperity – possibly however only to
sink back again into poverty when his children have married
and left him, and he himself is too old to work.

This description is much more than an elaborate spelling-out of
the truism that at some points in one's life one's income is particularly stretched; it certainly shows how any individual
may drift into poverty and out again several times in his life,
but even more it suggests that although the absolute number

of people in poverty may not differ greatly between any given set of dates, the particular people who make up that number may have changed substantially; as one family rises out of its poverty, so its place is taken by some other family whose responsibilities have increased or circumstances changed so that it in turn falls below the line. Thus, of course, the numbers in poverty at any given time are only a fraction of the numbers who are in poverty at some time in their lives.

A comparison of Rowntree's three surveys of 1899, 1936, and 1950 (see Table 2) shows how the relative importance of

Table 2. A comparison of Rowntree's three studies in York

Cause of Poverty	Percentage of those in poverty		
	1899	1936	1950
	%	%	%
Unemployment of chief wage-earner	2·31	28·6	Nil
Inadequate wages of earners in regular employment	51·96	42·3	1·0
old age ⎫	5·11	14·7	68·1
Sickness ⎭		4·1	21·3
Death of chief wage-earner	15·63	7·8	6·4
Miscellaneous (including large family)	24·99	2·5	3·2

the poverty-causing factors changed during the course of fifty years. As the table shows, by far the most important factors in the first survey were low wages or large families, and in many cases a combination of both. In 1936 unemployment was very much more important; this was, of course, the effect of the economic depression which caused so much hardship in all the industrial areas. Illness and old age were also much more prominent in the thirties than earlier; it must be remembered here that we are discussing relative proportions. It is not necessarily the case that between 1901 and 1936 the numbers of sick or old people increased nearly four times. On the contrary, Rowntree claimed to show a gratifying reduction in the total numbers in poverty; what these figures show is the change in relative distribution of the various poverty-causing factors among this smaller number. When the 1950 figures are examined, the change is even more clear. Bearing in mind that Rowntree estimated that the total number in poverty was now very small indeed, we can see that low wages or unemployment, far from being the principal causes of poverty, were by now almost completely insignificant, a fact which was universally acclaimed as a result of post-war economic and social policies. Old age and sickness, growing in importance in the thirties, had by 1950 become by far the most significant factors and both, in modern circumstances, require action through developments in social-welfare policy rather than economic policy as such. Provided unemployment remained low, and wage rates remained higher than Rowntree's subsistence levels, then poverty would remain a very small-scale, residual social problem.

However, once we abandon a stringently calculated subsistence level as the yardstick for adequate wages, and substitute the appropriate scales of public relief which will take direct account of individual and household circumstances, and once we have some limited awareness of the minimum standard of life that social convention (rather than physical survival) demands, then we must expect low wages and/or large families to become a much more significant factor. In Table 3 where we

Table 3. A comparison of Rowntree's 1950 study and Abel-Smith/Townsend 1960

% Rowntree 1950	Cause of Poverty	% Abel-Smith/Townsend 1960
4*	Inadequate wages and/or large families	40
68	Old age	33
6	Fatherless families	10
21	Sickness	10
Nil	Unemployment	7

* This figure includes all of Rowntree's miscellaneous group, of which only a part were large families: hence this figure is somewhat of an exaggeration.

compare the different categories of Rowntree's 1950 survey with the Abel-Smith/Townsend estimates for 1960 (which adopted the Assistance Board scales) the contrast is clear. In 1960 40 per cent of the poor households were in poverty because their wages were inadequate to meet their requirements as defined by National Assistance Board standards, almost the same proportion that Rowntree found in 1936. Old age accounted for one third of poor households in 1960, a proportion that might be expected to increase as the proportion of old people in our population increases. Fatherless families, or families where one member (not necessarily the wage-earner) is disabled or has been ill for some while, are the other main groups of impoverished households.

But the really striking feature of 'The Poor and the Poorest' was not its description of the characteristic poor groups, but the estimates of the absolute size of the problem. In 1960, it is claimed, there were:

(a) 3 million people in families in which the head is in full-time work, but has either a relatively low wage or several children or both.

(b) $2\frac{1}{2}$ million of pensionable age.

(c) 750,000 people in families composed of a mother and dependent children but no father.

(d) 750,000 people in families with one parent disabled or sick.

(e) 500,000 people in families with the father unemployed.

This total of $7\frac{1}{2}$ million, or 14 per cent of the total population, was nearly twice as large a proportion in poverty as in 1953, and there is reason to believe that the proportion has increased even more since 1960.

Particularly disturbing was the revelation of the extent of poverty among children. According to 'The Poor and the Poorest', 31 per cent of those in poverty were children under fifteen – altogether more than 2 million children. The accuracy of this finding has since been strikingly confirmed by the Ministry of Social Security itself; in 1967 the Ministry published its own survey of families with two or more children. *The Circumstances of Families* [15] showed that there were 345,000 such families living at or below Supplementary Benefit level. If an estimate is added of one-child families then, by Supplementary Benefit standards (making no additional allowance of 40 per cent), 'approaching half a million families, containing up to one and a quarter million children' were in poverty, of whom half a million were actually below the Supplementary Benefit level.

Since 'The Poor and the Poorest', Professor Townsend and his associates have embarked upon a series of research projects concerned with specific groups of poor people. We now have, or soon will have, detailed studies of such vulnerable groups as the sick, the fatherless families, the unemployed and so on. In the meantime, however, there have been some notable additions to our knowledge and understanding of deprivations other than cash poverty. In 1965 the *Milner Holland Report* on housing in Greater London [16] published a detailed account of the stark housing conditions endured by the residents of London's 'twilight areas'. Although referring only to Greater London the revelations of Milner Holland could have been duplicated in the decaying neighbourhoods of all our major industrial cities. Just as the *Milner Holland Report* documented housing deprivation, so the 1967 *Plowden Report* on children and their schools [17] emphasized the extent and nature of the educational deprivation of slum children.

Each one of these studies was of course primarily concerned with its specialist interest, be it poverty, poor housing, or inadequate schools and each study made its valuable contribution to the growing debate on poverty and deprivation. People in the real world, however, cannot live such specialized lives, and it seems only too apparent that the family which lives its life in a Milner Holland slum may well do so in Abel-Smith/

15. H.M.S.O., June 1967.
16. Cmnd 2605.
17. *Children and their Primary Schools*: A Report of the Central Advisory Council for Education, H.M.S.O., 1967.

Townsend poverty, while its children are sent to a Plowden school. If this is so, then there is a need for one more study focused on one impoverished community, which would try to show how all these different types of deprivation mesh one into another, to create for those who must endure them a total social situation shot through and through by one level of want after another. What sort of a life is there for a person who grows up, works his life away, or is pensioned off in a society where gross hardship is commonplace and some serious deprivation is universal? How do the different kinds of shortcoming, documented so vividly in 'The Poor and the Poorest' and the *Milner Holland* and *Plowden Reports*, relate to one another, feed off one another, sustain and help to perpetuate one another?

Much of the material in the second part of this book was gathered in one community in Nottingham. The district of St Ann's is a typical city-centre twilight area, which could well have provided the basic material for any of the investigations we have mentioned. In most of our large cities can be found similar districts; no doubt many of them are even more deprived and forlorn than is St Ann's. Certainly no two such districts are identical, but in so far as any place can be called typical, St Ann's is a typical late Victorian, working-class, city-centre neighbourhood in acute decline. It is in such an area that can be found the worst housing, the most run-down public services and, as we shall see, an alarming proportion of people who are poor and needy.

PART TWO

How the Poor Live: The Case of St Ann's

Nothing, therefore, is really in question, or ever has been, but the differences between class incomes. Already there is economic equality between captains, and economic equality between cabin boys. What is at issue still is whether there shall be economic equality between captains and cabin boys. What would Jesus have said? Presumably he would have said that if your only object is to produce a captain and a cabin boy for the purpose of transferring you from Liverpool to New York, or to manoeuvre a fleet and carry powder from the magazine to the gun, then you need give no more than a shilling to the cabin boy for every pound you give to the more expensively trained captain. But if in addition to this you desire to allow the two human souls which are inseparable from the captain and the cabin boy and which alone differentiate them from the donkey-engine, to develop all their possibilities, then you may find the cabin boy costing rather more than the captain, because the cabin boy's work does not do so much for the soul as captain's work. Consequently you will have to give him at least as much as the captain unless you definitely wish him to be a lower creature, in which case the sooner you are hanged as an abortionist the better.

GEORGE BERNARD SHAW

Preface to *Androcles and the Lion*

3 Poor People in Nottingham

I

Nottingham has for many years enjoyed the reputation of being a wealthy city. Local industry is very varied, ranging from coal-mining, manufacture of hosiery, lace, and tobacco, to such twentieth-century growth industries as Ericsson's telephones and Boots pharmaceuticals. There have always been job opportunities for women and girls, particularly in the hosiery factories, so that two-income families are no new phenomenon in Nottingham. Thus, while Nottingham has a housing problem, a traffic problem, and has, indeed, its share of problems common to all big cities, it has never been described as a poor city.

Between October 1965 and June 1966 Nottingham University's Department of Adult Education sponsored an evening class under the title 'Anatomy of Britain'. The dozen or so students who enrolled for the session studied and discussed the basic characteristics of the British social structure under the supervision of one of the present authors, Ken Coates. For this group, the publication of 'The Poor and the Poorest' was an occasion of particular importance, and it was read and eagerly discussed. These discussions were somewhat frustrated in that Abel-Smith and Townsend had based their analysis on a national survey of expenditure made by the Ministry of Labour, and it was difficult to interpret the significance of the figures for a city like Nottingham. Nonetheless, the idea that some 7,500,000 people should be living in poverty was shocking and, to some class members, incredible. At this point the class, anxious to continue their study for a further year, began to

55

speculate whether or not it would be possible to spend this
year in an investigation of conditions in Nottingham, in order
to discover if the local picture corresponded with the overall
position as presented by Abel-Smith/Townsend. A second
tutor, Richard Silburn, was recruited and in a short course in
the summer of 1966 plans were laid for the coming year's work.

Having decided in principle to carry out a social survey, it
was quickly realized that with the time and resources at the
class's disposal, an inquiry covering the whole of Nottingham
would be hopelessly superficial. The class had, therefore, to
choose a specific area for its concentrated inquiry. In fact, this
choice was made without difficulty, for within five minutes'
walk of the class's meeting place lay the district of St Ann's,
a run-down but centrally situated area scheduled for comprehensive redevelopment. St Ann's was not only convenient, but
it seemed, at first sight, to be an appropriate locale for poverty
research.

Once we had selected St Ann's as the area for our investigations, we were still faced with the need to mask out an appropriate sub-area which would accurately reflect conditions
throughout the district. Although, after the publication of our
preliminary findings, it was possible to mobilize enough volun-
teers to complete a survey of the whole redevelopment area,
the fact that it contains a population of some 30,000 was sufficient to persuade us that we must, initially, narrow our scope
in order to gain anything like a precise focus on conditions in
the area. A handful of people in an adult class, meeting weekly,
could not have conducted a thorough inquiry covering the whole
of so crowded a territory. So we shrunk our attention to a part
of the district containing 2,000 houses and 6,000 people, embodying, as far as we could ascertain, all the main characteristics of the wider area. This included some of the most dejected
and decrepit streets, with some of the worst housing conditions,
just as it also incorporated one or two of the roads in which
are clustered the most solidly-built and well-equipped houses
to be found anywhere in the district. Cut in two by the ward
boundary which separates St Ann's from Market wards, the

survey area presented us with one immediate problem, that official statistics based on ward-units were difficult to relate to our own work. In the event, the disadvantage was to prove all too slight, for the very good reason that the local authority treats such ward-based statistics as it may possess as official secrets, and presents almost all its data on health, educational, and welfare problems only as general, city-wide figures, which obviously conceal more than they reveal about the real rhythms of life in different specific areas. We rapidly came to feel that it would be easier to coax officialdom to give us the recipe for a hydrogen bomb than to persuade them to tell us anything we wanted to know about the conditions in the schools they control, or to get anything more from them than the most pious generalizations.

When the study group assembled in October, twenty people registered. A number of these recruits had a professional interest in the area, and some had access to facts, records, and statistics not generally available. More importantly they already knew the district well and had profound, albeit specialized, insights into its structure. The class included three probation officers, a schoolteacher who was married to an immigrant and who lived on the border of the area, an accountant in the corporation's housing department, and another, privately employed accountant, together with an architect, two journalists, three secretaries, and a number of housewives. It was thus a group of people of very varied experience and outlook which began its inquiries in October 1966.

As the group familiarized itself with the part of St Ann's which was to be investigated, it quickly became obvious that the discussion about poverty was not merely about levels of income. The first and dominant impression of St Ann's is of the poor housing; then one notices the inadequacy of the public amenities and facilities. One rapidly becomes aware that deprivation takes many forms; poverty has many dimensions, each one of which must be studied separately, but which in reality constitute an interrelated network of deprivations. It was through seeing this complexity, and observing how far it contributed to the character of social life in St Ann's, that the study group began to develop its own particular perspective, its own particular understanding of the poverty, not just of individuals, but of a community.

At the end of our first year's work, we had completed 176 interviews in our area, a result which gave us a response rate of 70 per cent from all the approaches we made. Since we were using a long and complicated questionnaire, we were satisfied that this was a representative sample. The findings of this stage of the inquiry were published in some detail in a brochure issued by the Department of Adult Education at Nottingham University.[1] They caused a considerable stir in the local press, which had at least one useful side-effect in that it encouraged a large number of undergraduate students at the University to volunteer for work in our next two projects which were both completed in the first half of 1968.

The first of these consisted of an investigation of poverty and its effects on people living on a council housing estate on the outskirts of the city. This sought to try to evaluate the effect of bad housing conditions on the poor, by examining the differences in community life and social aspirations in a district in which there were a large number of people close to the poverty line, but which enjoyed tolerable housing amenities. The estate consisted of 650 houses built in the middle nineteen-thirties, separated from its surroundings by a railway cutting on one side and two major roads on others. Known locally as 'The Island' because of its relative isolation, it is a fairly typical pre-war council estate, built to accommodate people who had been moved in slum-clearance schemes. We had reason to expect that there were a large number of old people and low-paid workers housed there, so, with a questionnaire which was modified very slightly from our original to allow for the differences in conditions, we conducted 77 interviews on two consecutive Sunday mornings, which gave us a sample of approximately 12 per cent. Undergraduates were

1. 'Poverty, Deprivation and Morale', 1967.

carefully briefed to act as interviewers, and were supervised in groups by experienced members of the adult class.[2]

Meanwhile, in early June, the second-year students of the University Department of Applied Social Science were preparing for the practical research experience demanded by the department. It was agreed to employ these students in St Ann's to build up a more comprehensive dossier on conditions in the development area; by the end of June over 200 additional interviews had been completed and the preliminary analysis of the data had begun. It is upon the data gathered in these three projects that much of the discussion which follows is founded.

II

Firstly, how many people in this one community are poor by modern standards, and what proportion of the community do they comprise? Secondly, do these people fall into any particular categories which might make one set of remedies more appropriate than another? The largest group of poor households we discovered in our Nottingham inquiries was that of the retirement pensioners; in all, in St Ann's we interviewed sixty-three such households. In some cases, we met elderly married couples, but more frequently we met widows living alone. Indeed, because most of the aged were living alone, the actual number of people in these households was relatively small, and only 15 per cent of our total poor population fall into this category. Although many of these elderly people were among the very poorest we encountered, particularly if they were dependent upon the basic old age pension and did not apply for the supplementary pension to which most would have been entitled, any further generalization about their circumstances is extraordinarily difficult. Their styles of life depend as much on their past resources, both physical and moral, as on their present condition, and the specific problems they face are consequently very different. This may be illustrated by citing two

2. 'The Morale of the Poor', Nottingham University, Dept of Adult Education, 1968.

examples. We interviewed one old lady of eighty-one or eighty-two; she has never married and lives alone. She is physically very frail, and her eyesight is failing; because of this, she lives and sleeps in her downstairs living-room in order to avoid having to struggle upstairs. Since the death of a sister who had lived near by, she has no relatives at all, and most of her friends have died. Although the neighbours help her with the shopping, she feels very lonely. Her isolation worries her. She has an abiding fear that she might hurt herself in a fall, and be unable to attract help. Her needs are very simple, and she 'manages to get by' on her pension, but she dreads the winter-time because the cost of coal is so high. She seldom gets out, and spends much of her time daydreaming and 'remembering her good times'. In contrast, another pensioner we talked to, a seventy-eight-year-old widow: she has excellent health and is an active and cheerful soul. She has lived on the same street since she married more than fifty years ago, and knows everyone. Two of her sons live with their families nearby, and she looks after a great-grandson on two days a week. On her street, she attends many home births as an unofficial midwife, and also helps to lay out the dead, and sits with the dying. She is full of purpose and enthusiasm. She describes herself as being 'not wealthy at all, but I just about get by. Of course, my boys are very good.'

Quite clearly those two old ladies are in very different situations, and although both are (technically) poor, poverty does not hit them in the same way. For our first old lady, lack of money is by no means the most pressing problem. Of far greater moment is the sense of loneliness and isolation that develops as friends and contemporaries die, and the growing fear of being left alone, unwanted among strangers. As one becomes ill, or begins to feel frail, this fear can become a real obsession.

Certainly the relief of old people's poverty would help them: they frequently face agonizing decisions about the coal bills in the autumn. To be able to keep warm without having to make inroads into one's budget for food and clothing would be, for very many people, a liberation. Fundamentally, however, the plight of the aged requires more than cash relief: it not only calls for a complex of welfare services, but even more for a community sensitive to the various and changing needs of the old.

The second largest category of poor households we interviewed included by far the largest number of persons (accounting for 50 per cent of the poorer population). This consisted of those families with breadwinners at work whose incomes did not entitle them to receive public relief. As Townsend has explained, there are two elements here, which alone or in combination cause poverty. The first is found where the breadwinner's wage is very small, too small perhaps to support even the smallest family. The second is seen when the numbers of dependants in the family stretch the income further than it can go. Of course, both elements combine in the case of a large family trying to live on a very small income. We interviewed people who fell into each of these groups.

It is a commonplace that dependent children impose some strain on almost every family budget; at the same time, much of the discussion about family poverty has seemed to assume that only the very largest families are normally seriously affected. Quite obviously, the more dependent children there are in a family, the more likely it is that the family will be in poverty. However, the fact is that this risk becomes significant at a very much earlier stage in a family's growth than many people seem to realize. The argument is not only about the families of eight, nine, or ten children, but in a depressingly large number of cases, it is about the families with only two or three children. Thus, in St Ann's, nearly one in five of the one-child families, over a third of the two-child families, and approaching half the three-child families, were in poverty. This poverty became more aggravated as the family grew larger, so that all the families with seven or eight children were in poverty, as were four of the five families with six children. On the other hand it can be stressed that of the 214 families with children who were interviewed, only 24 had five or more children, and of these 24, 8 were not in poverty. In brief, the important discussion about family poverty is *not* primarily about 'problem families' of feckless breeders; consequently remedies in terms of birth-control, sterilization or other even zanier and less humane eugenic recommendations are not of great relevance. This will probably not impede those who noisily canvass them. There is, it seems, a fairly large body of well-wishers of the poor which begrudges them not only the legendary pleasures of Bingo and television, but also even the rudimentary distractions which they have been offered by the Almighty. In our study, 60 per cent of the poor families had three children or less. Doubtless there will be some philanthropists who will argue that those who cannot afford it should not have a family of even these modest dimensions; such critics might refer, before holding forth, to the arguments used by Seebohm Rowntree in the thirties, which stressed that the physical survival of the race demanded a large number of three-child families. This utilitarian consideration might impress them, even if they find it distasteful to ponder further the paradox of an apparently rich society in which substantial proportions of the population can only maintain a family of average size by enduring soul-breaking hardship.

These facts about family poverty should encourage the rest of us to examine more closely the question of working-class wage levels. What is quite evident is that, even in a city as relatively prosperous as Nottingham, there are large groups of workers whose basic wages are extremely low: many of these men depend upon crucifyingly long hours of regular overtime to secure themselves a decent income. The size and character of the problems of the low-paid worker will be examined more fully later; at this point it suffices to say quite baldly that the most important single cause of poverty is not indolence, nor fecundity, nor sickness, nor even unemployment, nor villainy of any kind but is, quite simply, low wages.

Obviously, it is the category of low-paid workers, or workers with large families and inadequate wages, which is most prone to feel the effects of what Rowntree described as the 'cycle of poverty',[3] in which families find themselves, at different points in their lives, above or below the poverty line. But we were compelled to notice another important contributive element to this cycle, when we began to scrutinize the data we collected about wage levels in Nottingham.

Almost two fifths of the people employed in Nottingham are women and girls, as compared with a proportion of slightly over one third, nationally. Nottingham is a centre of light engineering, in which far larger proportions of women workers are normally employed than in heavy industry. It has a thriving pharmaceutical industry, where thousands of girls find jobs. Although mechanization has changed the constitution of the labour force in the tobacco industry, a high proportion of the workers at Players are women, and indeed a few years ago, half the people working there were women and girls. Traditionally, of course, Nottingham was a centre of the lace trade, which employed many thousands of women. As the fashion for lace faded out, so the hosiery industry, and new factories for the making-up of garments, expanded, absorbing the girls who were displaced from lace-making. Ericsson's telephones, now part of the Plessey group, employs more than 5,000 workers, a quarter of whom are women. The transport, distributive, banking and educational services, together with public utilities, employ two fifths of the workers in the Nottingham area, and half these are women. There is thus a constant and unremitting shortage of female labour.[4]

The effect of the numerous job opportunities for women and girls is, of course, to augment family earnings wherever women are able to hold jobs at the same time as their menfolk. This fact accounts, in great measure, for much of the apparent 'prosperity' of Nottingham. But it also implies something else. Wherever women workers are employed in large numbers, their presence has a tendency to depress the levels of earnings of the men working alongside them. Where a family

3. See above, p. 33.
4. See F. A. Wells, 'Industrial Structure' in *Nottingham and its Region*, British Association, 1966.

has two breadwinners instead of one, it will, of course, normally be better off, even if both earn individually somewhat less than a single breadwinner might command elsewhere. But if it becomes the norm to rely on two sets of earnings, there is an additional dimension to add to Rowntree's cycle. Quite simply, during all the time that women are rearing small children, their inability to work will, whenever their husbands are low paid, thrust the young family either below, or perilously close to, the poverty line. That they will rise above it again after the children are old enough to 'look after themselves' (at ages which will vary greatly according to the degree of stress under which the family finds itself, as well as the cultural influences under which it lives) does not mitigate the fact that the degree of insecurity in such conditions is greater than that in areas where men's wages are cushioned from the pressure of female competition. Of course, the answer to this problem is, quite simply, equal pay for equal work. This will overcome the adverse pressures on men's earning power at the same time that it brings a greater element of justice into the working conditions of women. But until this simple gain has been registered, 'prosperity' will continue to be replaced by periods of great stringency, whenever and wherever young married women from such areas become mothers.

The third general category of poor people consists of families without a male breadwinner. In our sample we encountered twenty-one fatherless families. The greatest unhappiness and hopelessness can be found in this group. Premature widowhood, or, more frequently, desertion, leave a mother alone to support dependent children. For these mothers, there is not only the emotional anguish over losing their husbands (and let it also be said that in some cases such a loss may bring a certain emotional relief), but all the brute practical difficulties of earning enough money to keep the family. This is more complicated than merely finding a job; it is often far more difficult to find someone to look after the children while their mother is out at work. If she has relatives near by then maybe the family can rally round and suitable arrangements can be made.

But for the mother who is quite alone, the situation is much more overwhelming, and usually she is obliged to rely upon help from the Ministry of Social Security. Here again, we must beware of generalizations, for while it is true that many of these families are considerably distressed and even severely demoralized, we did encounter some very much more positive cases. One in particular sticks in mind, of a woman who, although apparently quite alone and friendless, rejoiced in her anonymity; she had, she told us, moved into St Ann's precisely because she knew no one there and, despite her difficulties, she obviously relished her freedom from what had been a particularly unhappy and complicated family situation. The most disturbing fact about this category of poor families is the large number of children in them; of the 94 individuals we found in this situation, 70 were children. It can only be supposed that they are suffering not only the pain of a broken home, but also all the other deprivations that poverty imposes.

We found very few households in which poverty was caused by sickness, the fourth general category with which we were concerned. The numbers of people involved amounted to only 5 per cent of the poor population. Sickness becomes a more serious threat as one grows older, and can be expected to affect most wage-earners towards the end of their working lives. We only encountered two or three households where poor health was affecting a young man with family responsibilities; but although they are mercifully few in number, the plight of these families is particularly grievous. The hardest-hit are not necessarily those where the health problem is chronic; for these the family, although dependent upon sickness or disability benefits, has at least a limited security of income. Much more seriously affected are those men whose illnesses are intermittent, whose regular working lives are constantly interrupted by short periods of sickness. With each bout they will suffer a period of two or three days during which they are not earning, nor yet eligible for sickness benefit. The family income may, in such cases, constantly oscillate between extremes. Families in this situation will find it exceptionally difficult to predict, from month to month, what their circumstances may be. What are, for most people, perfectly normal expenditures, such as a television rental or a hire-purchase repayment, can become, for these families, nightmarish transactions, which impose their exhausting strain on every member of the household. It remains true that the persistent sickness of any member of the family can cause great hardship; the invalid wife and mother is a distressingly familiar example. Not only may special, perhaps expensive, diets be necessary, but it may be necessary to meet the cost of a home-help or other domestic assistant; sometimes the father himself may have to take time off work to care for his wife or look after the children. Unless there are other members of the family near by, or exceptionally helpful friends or neighbours, school holidays can be an insistently nagging worry, at least until the older children are able to look after the younger ones.

The fifth broad grouping of poor people consists of those on the dole. In St Ann's, 13 per cent of the poor population lived in households in which the breadwinner was unemployed. This group has been increasing in recent years as, first, economic recession, and later, Government economic policy determined that the rate of unemployment should be allowed to reach a much higher level than was acceptable in the fifties. These policies, which have been styled (as it now seems, all too gently) as 'redeployment', originally assumed that in most cases the period of unemployment suffered by those 'shaken out' would be a very short one, little more than a brief passage between jobs. For some breadwinners this may be the case. With others it is certainly not and we came across examples of men who were finding it extremely difficult to find work. This was a forbiddingly common experience among the older men, and among men who lacked heavily-demanded technical skills. For these people unemployment is a bleak and dispiriting reality, which casts its shadow into the factories themselves as an all-too-present fear.

Thus, in St Ann's, out of a total of 413 households in which we obtained interviews, 156 were found to be in poverty; of the interviewed population of 1,395 people, 547 were living in impoverished households. From these figures it is immediately apparent that our estimates of the extent of poverty in St Ann's are very much greater than Abel-Smith and Townsend's for the whole country. Where they found 17·9 per cent of households at or below the poverty line, we found over 37 per cent: where they found 14·2 per cent of the population to be poor, we found nearly 40 per cent.

These figures seem staggeringly high, and might easily inspire a first reaction of disbelief. With a little thought, however, it must be clear that poverty is not distributed evenly across the country or within our cities. Every town has its whole areas of comfortable, centrally heated houses with wide gardens, its streets seeded with E-type Jaguars, in which it is difficult to meet anyone who does not possess an income three times the average in St Ann's. In short many cities have a 'stockbroker belt', in which an ordinary income would represent insupportable penury for its inhabitants. One would obviously not expect to find, in such places, numbers of people living at standards close to the National Assistance Board levels. Similarly, in most cities, there are areas of relatively cheap housing, usually rented; in these live the families of semi-skilled and unskilled workers, people who have never enjoyed great wealth, but who live from one weekly pay-packet to the next with, at best, only a slender margin of savings. The shortest interruption of earnings, through sickness or redundancy, means, for these people, sudden and considerable hardship. Slight fluctuations in the economy, a reduction in overtime of two or three hours a week, mean, inexorably, for them, a substantial lowering of living standards. It is precisely in these districts that one would expect to find the poor, because here is a population that is economically vulnerable, less able than others to protect itself against the shifts of fate which can precipitate a family into poverty. In addition to this, we might expect poor people to move into such areas of a city from elsewhere, attracted by the relatively low rents. No one, we think, would suggest that in a city like Nottingham, 40 per cent of the people live in poverty; but it is perfectly reasonable to suppose that in the poorest areas of any major city, there might be found just such a concentration of poor people.

But if so large a proportion of a community are living so close to the standards permitted by public relief, then it becomes necessary to study closely not only the poor people themselves, but also the community of which they form such a substantial part. Abel-Smith and Townsend, in presenting their evidence in 'The Poor and the Poorest', identified, as we have seen, and partly imitated, five sets of circumstances or family situations which were most likely to thrust people into poverty. Since then, much of the recent research effort has been to examine the particular difficulties of each group in detail. Thus we now know a great deal about the lives and problems of the old, of the unemployed, of the fatherless families and so on. This is, of course, valuable and important work; any serious student of modern society will require this sort of detailed knowledge, and no intelligent discussion of remedies is possible without it. In one respect, however, these studies can be misleading; when the field of inquiry is narrowed to cover a specific group, it is always possible to see more of the trees than the wood and it can be dangerous to consider any sub-group in isolation from the wider society in which it has its place. This means much more than paying due attention to such exotic matters as the class system, or kinship patterns; it means that we must constantly remember that the poor do not necessarily see themselves as a group at all and are not necessarily aware that their own immediate and personal difficulties are elements of a public problem. They live ordinary lives in a normal social environment; they are expected to live in the same manner as their neighbours, and they will expect this themselves; they share in all the attitudes, assumptions and expectations of the community in which they live, and of course they contribute as much as their neighbours to the formation of these attitudes and assumptions. Lacking sufficient money to mesh comfortably into the fabric of this community's standards, the poor must be seen not simply as isolated individuals, abstracted from society, but as human beings formed in the very society from which they are to a greater or lesser extent excluded.

This perspective on poverty helps us to locate each case of individual or family hardship in its wider social context. Once appreciated from this wider viewpoint many of the most frequently encountered assumptions about the nature of poverty, and the personality flaws of the poor people, are themselves exposed as the vulgar myths they really are. One such myth needs to be emphatically and directly confronted at once. In its crude form it is very widespread, and in many apparently subtler statements it is implicit, so that no coherent or sensible discussion about poverty is possible until it has been dealt with. It is the conviction that if people are poor, it is, in some way, their own fault.

Since our interest in family poverty first started to attract local attention, we have received dozens of letters, not all from callous people, telling us that we were mistaken. 'Go to the Bingo halls,' we have been told. 'Look at the pubs: they're always full!' someone recently wrote to the local newspaper. 'They spend the Family Allowances on drink and betting,' said a caucus of staid ladies at a Townswomen's Guild meeting which invited one of us to give a talk.

The belief that the poor have only themselves to blame for their condition is, of course, a time-honoured one. In his first survey of poverty in York, Rowntree divided poverty into two types. Some people were poor because their total income was insufficient to allow them to obtain what he adjudged to be the minimum necessities for physical efficiency. These people, he said, were in *primary* poverty. Others had an income which would have been sufficient, were it not that some portion of it was pre-empted by other expenditure, either useful or wasteful. These, he considered, were in *secondary* poverty.

The critics whom we quoted above all seem to assume that primary poverty, a sheer shortage of money, cannot exist, but that secondary poverty, especially that proportion of secondary poverty which is caused by foolish and wasteful expenditure, can. To this charge there is of course one immediate answer. All the calculations which we made were designed to reveal the adequacy or otherwise of the family income. If this income is found to be inadequate, then no matter how wisely and shrewdly it may be spent, the poorer families cannot escape from their poverty.

Our estimates are, in this sense, confined to cases of primary poverty. To this extent they are, of course, underestimates of the total amount of poverty, precisely because cases of secondary poverty are never included. It may well be that there are families with adequate incomes, whose dissipated or eccentric conduct leaves them short of all manner of 'necessaries'. They are not included in our estimates. It is obvious that if a family's income is already hovering around the standards of public relief, and it then decides to spend its money unwisely, the standards of comfortable life, which would be unattainable in any case, only become that much more remote. But we have made no allowances for such spending. This fact, properly understood, does not attenuate matters: on the contrary, it intensifies the scope of the problem. To the extent that it may take place, the riotous deployment of resources in Bingo halls and pubs will not in any way diminish the problem of poverty: it can only increase it, by ensuring that families which could, conceivably, live at an acceptable standard, are, in fact, precipitated into secondary poverty. In that sense, the existence of distractions like gambling aggravates the problem. It certainly does not cause it, let alone excuse indifference to it.

A casual observer might be excused for supposing, at first blush, that over-indulgence in drinking or excessive betting were widespread in a district like St Ann's. On most streets there seems to be a public house, and one of the largest community buildings in the area, a converted dance hall, invites you, with a flourish of neon, to win a fortune at Bingo. In the first area of St Ann's which we examined closely, there were twenty-one pubs and eight betting shops as well as the Bingo hall. This area was however bisected in two directions by the principal thoroughfares across St Ann's, so that the number served by some of these enterprises was considerably larger than the 6,000 people who lived in the immediate vicinity. The Bingo hall, for example, is not only in a busy main road, but two buses stop directly outside it and it is adjacent to a main bus terminal, so that it certainly has a clientele which is very widely spread, and by no means confined to the local residents.

Is obsessive gambling widespread? Much less so than some people are inclined to think. Mrs Pont, who lives in the middle of the area, told our interviewer: 'Well, I think, taking this street, there's only about one person that goes to Bingo. She can go because she's got no children and she goes out to business, and her husband does, so she can afford to go. But I think she's about the only one that I know of. She quite openly says that she goes to Bingo, because it's somewhere for her to go. She goes for the company and entertainment as well. But I don't think they are a good thing, not for the poorer people to go to. Mind you, I'm not against anyone having a bet. The Lincoln, or something like that. My Dad always used to have a go on the Lincoln.'

This seems to be about it: most people will have an occasional flutter on one or another of the major horse races. A very much smaller number gamble regularly, on a daily or weekly basis, and then the sums of money involved are usually small ones. Most people have no Puritan disapproval of betting, but at the same time, they are not persistent and foolhardy gamblers. Of the people we met, about one in eight said that they had been to a betting shop in the past three months, and the same fraction had been to a Bingo hall. The most widely used amenities were free: the city parks and libraries. The most patronized commercial entertainment was the cinema: three out of ten people had been to the pictures in the preceding weeks.

To those who wish to view slum life as a cut-price bacchanalia, the pubs tell an equally dull story. Each street, it is true, is likely to have a local at the corner; but most of these inns are very small, with just one or two rooms. The public bar will open every evening, but as often as not the best room is only used at the week-end. Most of these pubs are quiet places, with a great deal less drama and crisis than 'Coronation Street's' Rovers Return. Far from being fleshpots, dens of vice and indulgence, the drink most commonly served to most customers, men and women alike, is a half-pint of mild ale. The local is certainly a cheerful social centre, and a welcome one at that; at the week-end it will be jammed with people, someone will rattle away on the upright piano in the best room and there will be boisterous singing. But the bottles of spirits take a lot of emptying, and the publican's car is a modest one.

All the amenities we have mentioned are used from time to time by some of the poorer people. Sometimes the unemployed father will attempt to back a winner; several times old age pensioners talked of the company at the local, and said they welcomed a seat near the fire during the winter months. An old person can make a tenpenny glass of mild last a long time, while he stays near the warmth. Tenpence will not buy much coal to heat the house, so it may be a provident investment. But the poor do not contribute greatly to the publicans' and bookmakers' trade. Such amenities are not only used much less frequently, but, even then, more modestly, by the overwhelming majority of the poorer families, than by the rest of the populace.

But this does not end the argument. Ostentatious and wasteful expenditure need not, apparently, be confined to such ephemeral pleasures as beer and Bingo. The houses of the poor, our critics assured us, bulge with the most expensive of luxurious consumer durables. Refrigerators, record-players, cocktail cabinets, radio sets, even colour television sets. Certainly a hallmark of 'affluence' is the gadgetry which has accompanied it, and, of course, some of that gadgetry has made its way into St Ann's. Four fifths of the people living there own television sets, and two fifths have washing machines or vacuum cleaners. Among the poorest people, verging on the poverty line, the ownership of television sets is less general (69 per cent), while the ownership of washing machines is almost halved, and of vacuum cleaners even more drastically reduced. But these figures do not really speak very clearly, because they neither spell out the difficulties which such purchases involve, nor the quality of the articles purchased.

Of course, the cycle of poverty allows families to acquire various properties when they are above the poverty line, which are not, normally, all shed once hard times recur. Nonetheless, hard times do take their effect, as can be observed by watching the two busy pawnshops which do a constant and bustling trade, or the hundred and one second-hand dealers who have proliferated in the little sidestreets. We found one of these with a very revealing inscription in its window: 'Pawn-tickets bought for cash' it read. Debt is no stranger to St Ann's. In our first survey area, when we investigated County Court Judgements for debt, we found that in the nine months prior to our inquiry there had been fifty-seven judgements for amounts of £30 or more against people in our part of St Ann's, out of a total for the whole city of 1,244. That is to say, 4½ per cent of these debts were in our area, which comprised only 2 per cent of the city population. If there is double the amount of actual default, is it fair to assume that there is also considerably more than average difficulty in maintaining payments, among the people we talked to?

Yet consumer durables are not necessarily bought on hire-purchase. They wear out, and when they do, they are either thrown away or traded in. What happens to decrepit television sets when their better-off owners have decided to replace them? Part of the answer can be found at Sneinton Market, on the borders of the St Ann's area. Twice a week, on Monday mornings and Saturdays, the junk market convenes outside a swimming bath, and alongside the wholesale fruit and vegetable warehouses. It is a hectic place. You can hardly browse around the stalls, because, unless it is pouring with rain, you will be pushed and battered between the stalls until your feet find a place to grip and you are able to stand your ground amid the crowds. Robust ladies cry out their wares, which may be reject pots from the works, or faulty shoes, or rolls of cheap lino: it is not *all* old stuff, at Sneinton. But a solid mass of

73

stalls are piled with worn goods. You can buy a three-piece suite, with all the woodworm guaranteed dead, or an old clock 'which only needs a bit of tinkering' to keep perfect time, or a battered refrigerator for three pounds; you can take your pick of radio sets and used gramophone records, or you can find 'a good strong bed with a clean mattress' if the fancy takes you.

If you were handy at mending things, you could probably equip, after a fashion, a whole house, by shopping at the market. It would cost you less than a tenth of the prices you would expect to pay in the big shops, although whether the equipment so bought would live a tenth of the normal time is an open question. However, when it comes to a straight count of how many spin dryers there are in St Ann's, there is no way of knowing whether the items included in the result came straight from the factory, or whether they had been spinning away for nearly twenty years in suburbia before being barrowed home from the stalls at Sneinton.

Of course, many people buy new television sets, or rent them. This doesn't necessarily mean that they make no calls on the second-hand market. Either at Sneinton, or in the dingy little stores which announce 'houses cleared', you can often save heavily if you value your pennies more than your pride, or sometimes more than your comfort. A new pair of shoes? For two bob you can find a nice pair of second-hand ones, with only very small holes, which nearly fit. You can get the kiddies' breeches at the same shop. If the old man needs a suit, a rummage through the barrows can find him a lovely one for thirty bob, if you know where to look, and if he doesn't mind a bit of slack at the back. To an outsider, the meanness, the sad shabbiness of poverty, comes alive in these little shops, with their tired fat ladies scratching a living from the clothes of the recently dead.

Poverty among children cannot simply be measured by counting the pairs of plastic sandals they wear to school. To know for sure who is deprived and who isn't, you have to know whose nice, clean shoes are pinching. A lot of kiddies have got very nice, very clean, little shoes which came, via the little second-hand stores, from other feet with different contours. This fact is well-recognized not only by the merchants of the junk-trade. Legions of stout philanthropists who want to raise money for a hundred causes from preventing cruelty to animals to promoting the gospels overseas, know very well exactly which are the best spots for jumble sales. They are never in suburbia.

Reachmedown. The word helps to form a whole personality. In St Ann's, private affluence lives at one remove from itself, a mocking half-echo of the standards established over the hill. The poor pale scavengers who root through piles of cast-off underwear in order to scrape up a livelihood perform some sort of service. They help to maintain the decencies where they would otherwise collapse, they assist in cutting the corners on the meanest little budgets, they relieve what might otherwise be open and crying distress. But what is the power of a wearer of old clothes? How often does he see himself as a free man? Naked, he is an equal with any: clad, his dependence is reinforced every time he fastens his shoes. You can count, you can parse, you can reason with impeccable rigour about the condition of the poor, and still you will remain miles from understanding it, until your own feet can feel the ache that accompanies the proud display of little John's 'new shoes' from the reachmedown shop.

It is these emotional and moral consequences of being poor that are hardest to grasp for those who have never experienced such deprivations themselves, but they are the very heart and substance of poverty. They rob a man of his pride and his dignity; ultimately they dehumanize him. This is why it is worth while to describe, in some detail, what life is like in an impoverished community.

4 Housing in St Ann's

I

The thing about St Ann's is that you can step right into it from the very centre of the City of Nottingham. One minute you are standing in the shadow of the huge new office towers, counting the 'to let' signs in their windows, or cat-walking through screened wooden tunnels which rattle and jig to the tune of concrete-mixers, or rubber-necking along under the artificial concrete cliffs of Maid Marion Way ('the ugliest street in Europe' one well-known town-planner has styled it) which already, half-finished, show that Britons, too, have mastered the architecture of claustrophobia; the next moment you have passed across over a giant excavation, where, in what yesterday was a railway station, battalions of men are punching out the foundations of 1984, and, bang, you are in the middle of Dickens, or George Gissing. In one moment, the neon stops and the cobbles begin.

St Ann's is a slum. It is a slum which crawls on, wearily, over more than three hundred of Nottingham's dirtiest acres and more than eighty of its greediest years. The money which has been sucked out of the people of St Ann's has accomplished remarkable improvements in the suburbs of Nottingham and even further afield. At least one of the landlords of the first sector scheduled for clearance had an address in Cannes. But St Ann's itself has just gone on and on, and down and down.

In 1909, the Board of Trade explained the social geography of Nottingham: 'The surface of the plateau on which the city stands is thrown into elevations of varying height, and this hilly character contributes in some degree to [the] division between the poorer and richer neighbourhoods.'[1] Whatever has changed in the commercial centre of the city, this remains true. Climb up to the top of any of the tall buildings there, and you will be able to peer down through the smoke into the wide valley of St Ann's. At the top of the hill on its northern side you can see the beginning of Mapperley Park. Trees begin to sprout out as the rows of cramped terraces give place to large houses encircled by shrubberies or rose gardens. Off the valley's southern slopes, after switchbacking downhill and down the social scale, you begin to climb again to Sneinton, with its ruined windmill, new skyscrapers, black old church ('but it has a beautiful reredos ...' says the Vicar) which crawls up sullenly over the skyline.

In the middle of the valley itself runs the St Ann's Well Road, the hectic main thoroughfare, which is also the shopping centre for the district. Bristling up on both sides are rows of tributary streets, jammed with busy workshops, factories, and file on file of narrow terraces. Until the middle of the nineteenth century this part of Nottingham was known as the Clay Field and was common land: enclosed by an Act of 1845, and made available for development as building land, the new district of St Ann's was built, more or less as we see it today, by the 1880s. 'Most of the dwellinghouses ... were of the same type and size, small houses intended for the lower-paid working classes. The street pattern is somewhat depressingly drawn in straight lines ... and was no doubt designed to accommodate as many houses as possible, about 40 to the acre.'[2]

Most of these houses themselves are of a standard type, as the 1909 Board of Trade Inquiry reported:

Five-roomed houses form the predominant type of working-class dwelling in Nottingham ... The five-roomed house is usually plain-fronted and built straight from the pavement line. It contains

1. Board of Trade, *The Cost of Living of the Working Classes*: Report of an inquiry by the Board of Trade into Working Class Rents, Housing and Retail Prices, together with the Standard Rates of Wages, H.M.S.O., 1909.

2. From a memorandum submitted to the study-group by Mr G. Oldfield on the history of the St Ann's district.

a parlour, about 12 feet by 11 feet by 9 feet, and a kitchen on the ground floor, two bedrooms on the first floor, and above these a fifth room, which is sometimes an attic lit by a skylight ... the street-door usually opens directly into the parlour. Behind the parlour is the kitchen and beyond that commonly a small scullery. There is as a rule a small back-yard and a back entrance ... The water-closet and sometimes the coal-cellar are in the yard.[3]

This neutral description does not set the houses in their context. It is a dull one. The front doors open straight off the pavement, and lead straight into the parlour. Access to the back of the houses is usually through a narrow arched entry leading to the backyards which are made of black brick. Sometimes these backyards are open, communal. Rather more frequently, each house has fenced off its own portion, although as often as not access to one person's back door may be gained only by walking through the neighbours' yards. At the end of the yards are lined the lavatories, in brick-built, sometimes tottering, sheds. The backyard serves as a playground for the children, and a meeting place for the adults. Many of the streets are cobbled, treacherous in the rain. A few are still gas-lit. Today these streets are often dirty and litter-strewn. Of course, they are swept as regularly as any other streets in the city, but St Ann's Ward has a population density of 62·6 people per acre, compared with a density of 17 per acre in Nottingham City as a whole.[4] This fact alone ensures that there is an appropriately greater density of waste-paper and other litter too, carpeting the streets. If you walk through the alleys and backstreets of St Ann's, all too often you can find the gutters ankle-deep in debris, and the pavements and roadways covered in a thin layer of rubbish.

At first sight this, then, is St Ann's: a large deteriorated district, geographically distinct, with a certain sense of identity; perhaps, it might be expected, even of community. It is an area threatened with comprehensive demolition and reconstruction which is bound to change its whole character. It is an area of manifest environmental and social deprivation in which

3. Board of Trade Report, p. 352.
4. According to the 1961 Census.

general amenities are at the most rudimentary level; where the scarce trees stand as stunted hostages to rotting bricks and grey stones; where until recently there have been no play facilities for the children except the yards and streets, and where, during our investigation, a little boy was killed while playing on a derelict site. It is an area where the schools are old and decrepit; with dingy buildings and bleak factories and warehouses, functionally austere chapels, a host of second-hand shops stacked out with shabby, cast-off goods; overhung throughout the winter by a damp pall of smoke. Greater familiarity with the district prompts other judgements, more difficult to sustain by physical evidence: to those of us who have come to know it and to feel involved in its life, St Ann's is an area dominated by a certain hopelessness, in which the sense that things are inexorably running down weighs constantly on every decision, and inhibits many positive responses to make or mend. And yet its people have, somehow, shaped out of this unpromising environment a way of living full of wit and humanity.

There are in St Ann's about 10,000 houses, crushed into a space of some 340 acres. It has been suggested that 'when they were first built they represented a considerable improvement compared with the conditions in other parts of the town'.[5] Even so, to speak gently, most of these houses do not fit even the most lax of modern housing standards. In consequence, after some considerable public controversy, the entire district is now scheduled for redevelopment in the next fifteen years. The houses do not leave much room to breathe: at 40 houses per acre, the density of housing in the area contrasts with a figure of something like 12 houses to the acre on more recent council housing estates. St Ann's is therefore a tightly cramped neighbourhood; smallish houses are spilled together in terraces or blocks very close to one another.

Very few houses are larger than those described as typical by the old Board of Trade Report: the standard five rooms provide two living-rooms downstairs, two bedrooms upstairs, and an attic in the roof. A small number of properties are even

5. G. Oldfield, op. cit., p. 3.

smaller, lacking the attic garret. In principle, these houses might be thought suitable for a family of average size; in practice, however, this rubric is complicated because the deteriorated condition of some of the property has made some of the rooms virtually or totally unusable. The attic rooms are usually the first to go: they are normally exceptionally difficult to heat, and are often, therefore, extremely damp, even when the roof is sound. In some cases, rain pours in, to be trapped in a whole battery of pails and cans; in others, the ceilings have fallen, the plaster is leaving the walls, the woodwork is powdered away. In one house you could see daylight in the attic, not through the roof (where it is a fairly common sight) but through the wall itself: the plaster had fallen away, leaving a chink between the bricks through which a very healthy sunbeam frisked. Closer examination showed that this attic's outer wall was only one brick thick. Exactly a quarter of the houses we examined had one or more rooms which were considered by their inhabitants to be unusable; and we did not find that such complaints were unduly pernickety. Rather the contrary: people were wont to accept conditions which we would have judged intolerable, as if they were perfectly normal. When they did complain, it was for cause.

In one case, for example, the floorboards in an upstairs bedroom were so rotten that on two occasions a leg of the bed had broken through the floor, and burst through the plaster of the ceiling below. Weak floors have other disadvantages. When the rot really takes hold it can imperil life and limb. One lady we interviewed told us that when she was making the bed upstairs, 'my foot went right through the floor, and there I sat, hollering for help, with my leg waving about through the living-room ceiling'. Mercifully, many of the downstairs floors cannot rot away, because they are laid directly on the earth beneath. These floors get wet and sometimes mouldy. If the floors are less than sturdy, the walls themselves are none too strong. Constantly we came across complaints concerning doors and windows, where the surrounding brickwork is often at its weakest. For instance, another house we visited had, in its main living-room, a wooden window-frame which had so deteriorated that it was in constant danger of falling away from the masonry; it was tenuously held in place with string. The window itself could not be opened with any confidence; but fortunately, the cracks between the frame and wall ensured a constant supply of fresh air. In all these cases, the rooms concerned had to be used because of the acute shortage of space their abandonment would have produced.

The major cause of such poor conditions is natural decay through age: the houses were none too carefully finished when they were built and they have long reached the end of their useful life. In many cases the very brickwork itself is powdered with age; it crumbles beneath the fingers when touched. The pointing between the bricks has often flaked away, leaving a delicate tracery of corrosion through which the wind and rain find ways to continue their work of destruction. The slates on the rooftops are frequently cracked or broken, and many of them are missing. Rusted guttering and fractured drainpipes sag and lean around some houses, pitching water down the sides of their outer walls, to mark out its own mouldy patterns in the reeking patches which appear indoors. Rot, in any one of its forms, and sometimes in several together, visits the woodwork. Often, neither doors nor windows will open properly, or shut again once opened. The dismal catalogue of complaints is endless:

'All the bricks under our back window are rotten. The damp comes through all the time. The back-room floor has sunk in in parts, and damp comes up there, too. You can put your hand through the wall in places.'

'The damp comes through so much that all the plaster has come away. We can't decorate. The windows won't open, and the back door is falling off.'

'The cellar is half-full of water every time it rains.'

'We are scared what will happen if our kitchen door falls off again. One of these days the kitchen itself will fall down.'

'Our house has sunk two inches at the back, and none of the doors will shut.'

'The pantry wall falls down every year.'

Again and again we were told 'our kitchen's just not fit to cook food in'; 'we can't go down the cellar, because the steps are rotten'; 'we've got an open lavatory' (meaning that the lavatory roof has a sizeable hole in it, since a mere leak would be taken for granted); 'the lavatory's falling down'; 'the chimney has collapsed': the list could be extended almost indefinitely.

In this welter of disintegration, animals other than men come to find their homes. Dogs are invited in by the residents: St Ann's is packed out with dog-lovers, and its canine population is even more mixed than its human one, and quite as friendly. But other animals are not invited. Cockroaches, mice and rats all find comfortable resting grounds. The corporation is willing enough to acknowledge the first two species of invader: the responsibility for attacking them falls mainly upon the residents. But it strenuously contests that rats exist in St Ann's. One corporation official has become quite legendary for his description of some particularly aggressive beasts, whose presence he had been summoned to register: 'Oh, they're just large mice' he is reported as telling the complainant. Such 'large mice' abound. They help to explain why people like keeping dogs. 'In Hedderley Street, St Ann's, I met another young mother,' wrote David Roxan in the *News of the World*. 'Mrs Heather Hayes married at 16, had her first baby before she was 17 and now, at 25, she has six children. They live in a substandard council house, along with two dogs kept not so much as pets as to kill the rats that roam nearby.'[6]

The rats come up from the sewers, which are in no better condition than the houses. Some of the feeder sewers were built of bricks, and laid down at the beginning of the St Ann's development. The same decline of solidity which has set in among the houses has also, apparently, been under way beneath the ground. As the old bricks rot away, the sewers collapse, not only frightening the rats, but blocking the pipes and, in wet seasons, causing floods. Some people complained, not only that their cellars had been filled with evil-smelling effluent, but that on especially bad days their backyards had been overrun by sewage. Since these yards are frequently the only play-

6. 19 November 1967.

ground for small children, it is clear that it is not only un-pleasant and undignified, but also hazardous to health, to have them periodically overrun by ordure.

All these symptoms of collapse could be documented separately. But for St Ann's residents, they all exist in concert, and they merge to present a total life-style, in which the separate burdens are sometimes quite difficult to unravel. There are serious grounds for arguing that such conditions as these have been dramatically worsening in recent years. Intensified neglect has considerably accelerated the decline of many houses which were already in a poor state. It is obvious that normal standards of maintenance and repair have by no means always been upheld, so that the property has deteriorated more rapidly than might otherwise have been the case. Drifting neglect has intensified to avalanche proportions in recent years, as the talk of ultimate demolition and redevelopment has discouraged both landlords and tenants from undertaking many of the most necessary repairs, or improvements.

It was impossible for our survey team, usually working after dark and without any expert guidance or help, to make any detailed or 'objective' assessment of the general state of repair; although we could see some of the worst problems very easily, we were not qualified surveyors. Therefore, we were forced to rely upon a sounding of our respondents' own feelings, by asking the direct question 'Is this house in good repair?' The answers were, as might be expected, quite unambiguous. Out of our whole sample of 413 householders, 220 replied, without qualification, that their houses were in 'bad repair'. But we found that there was an important difference between the replies which we got from owner-occupiers, as a group, and the answers given by tenants. While the vast majority of the owner-occupiers felt that their properties *were* in good repair, over six out of ten tenants thought that their rented houses were *not*. Of the handful of owner-occupiers who were dissatisfied with the repair of their houses, half had been living in them for less than a year; in these cases it seems pretty likely that sooner or later they will start work on the necessary programme of repairs and improvement, to restore the property. Tenants, however, have no such hopeful prospects; most of them must reconcile themselves to remaining in substandard housing until the corporation's housing programme reaches down to rescue them. Obviously there are important distinctions to be made between the kind of difficulties faced by people who have bought their own houses, and those who are rent-paying tenants. One might reasonably expect people who fall into these two groups to have attitudes which differ from one another in a number of ways. For example, it is plausible to suppose that an owner-occupier will feel more involved in the condition of the property in which he lives, and will accept a greater responsibility for its maintenance and repair, than will a tenant. Under most contracts of tenancy, responsibility for structural and external repairs lies with the landlord; clearly the standards of maintenance in rented houses depend upon how seriously the landlord takes, or can be made to take, his responsibility. Again, it is less likely that a tenant would invest substantial sums of his own money, even assuming he *had* substantial sums to invest, in the provision of such household amenities as bathrooms (once more assuming that there was space for an addition or conversion to be made), than would an owner-occupier. It is also probable that would-be owner-occupiers would choose to buy houses which already had such amenities, if they had any choice in the matter. In short, on the whole, one might expect owner-occupiers to live in properties which enjoy more household amenities, and are in better repair, than those occupied by tenants.

However, amidst all the dilapidation, and in spite of the disincentive to repairs which is provided by the redevelopment plans, repairs *are* constantly being made, and not only by owner-occupiers. We were curious about their extent. We tried to find out how many tenants had ever complained to their landlords, and what proportion of these complaints had ever been acted upon. The first thing we found out was that, whether people said their house was 'in good repair' or not, they still found the need to make some sort of complaint to their landlords. Nearly three quarters of all the tenants we interviewed had complained during the twelve months before our survey took place; and two out of every three of those who were 'satisfied' with the state of their houses had nevertheless registered a complaint of some sort. Of those who were dissatisfied, five out of six had complained.

The landlords had done something: two thirds of the tenants reported that they had had repairs of one kind or another carried out by their landlords during the previous year. When we examined *what* was done, its character varied considerably: a great many repairs were fairly modest, such as making good the guttering, or fixing a window-pane; but a few were more substantial, such as making good an unsafe chimney-stack, or rebuilding a wall. In spite of the fact that these efforts have been made, it is clear that the need is infinitely greater than the response. If it were not so, many more of our respondents would have put themselves in the 'satisfied' category. The fact is that in many cases repairs are virtually impossible; where, for instance, the brickwork is quite rotten, there is no way of keeping out the damp, no matter how frequent and painstaking the re-plastering. If the need for renewal is overwhelming, the task has become hopeless.

Whatever one's conclusions about the physical repair of the property in St Ann's, there is little scope for optimism. There can be even less hesitation or doubt about the distribution of basic household amenities. On this question we have precise and objective information, which is summarized below.[7]

Table 4.   Housing Amenities

		%		%
Lavatory	Inside	9·0	Outside	91·0
Bathroom	Yes	15	No	85
Hot-water system	Yes	45·5	No	54·5

The overwhelming majority of the respondents have an out-

7. These figures are from our final, comprehensive survey. They differ very slightly from those for the first survey area. cf. 'Poverty, Deprivation and Morale'.

side lavatory, and no bathroom. The lavatories are most frequently found at the end of the yard, sometimes in an individual brick shed, and sometimes in a terraced file of several adjacent units. Apart from being less than appealing aesthetically, and apart from their excruciating discomfort during the wintry weather, these outside lavatories can present very real difficulties, particularly to people who are old and frail, who may find the journey down the yard and back both time-consuming and physically exhausting, if not, in high frosts, actually dangerous.

Recently, people with outside lavatories have been subject to another hazard. As areas have been marked off for clearance, so individual houses which have fallen empty have been boarded up. Macabre twilight streets have emerged, sometimes housing two or three old people who are literally surrounded by abandoned ruins. One such old lady told us that she had gone to the lavatory one morning, only to find that it had disappeared! Thieves had apparently discovered a market for lavatory pedestals, and had swooped on a whole row of apparently deserted houses, clearing all marketable fittings from their outdoor sheds. In their devotion to the task in hand, they had apparently failed to observe that some of the equipment with which they were making away was still in use.

Extreme cases like this apart, the inconvenience of an outdoor lavatory can perhaps be imagined only with difficulty by those fortunate enough not to be compelled to rely on one. It takes some effort for people who are comfortably housed to appreciate such conditions, and this effort is obviously seldom made. If even a little more thought had been given to this kind of problem by successive Governments and local administrators, it would, long ago, have been tackled with real force and ingenuity. Perhaps there is a case for arguing that Ministers of Housing should be compelled, upon their induction to office, to live in such a fashion for a couple of months or so. Consequent upon each public revelry in which they then engaged, they would come to learn the health-giving values of fresh air, or, for that matter, of cold fog, as they scuttled up and down the yard in the middle of the night, or joined their neighbours in the dawn chorus before reassuming the burdens of responsibility in the mornings.

The lack of a bathroom imposes a different and more severe burden. In most houses in St Ann's, the only source of water is the kitchen tap. Consequently the kitchen sink has to be used not merely for washing up kitchen utensils, but also for preparing food, washing and shaving, and laundry. This is an insanitary and inconvenient arrangement, made even more difficult for more than half the housewives in the area, who do not have a hot-water supply. They have to boil a kettle every time they need warm water, and that is an expensive business, as well as an inconvenient one. At bathtime out comes the zinc tub, in front of the fire. The effort required to fill this, working from saucepans on a gas stove, needs to be imitated if it is to be fully understood.

It is not very pleasant to live in a house which is rotting away. Old and decrepit dwellings are uncomfortable, even if you have to live in them on your own, but they are much worse when they are overcrowded. Most of the redevelopment area of St Ann's lies in the St Ann's and Market wards of the city, and the Census information on the density of occupation in these wards is very instructive. It reveals that while the density of the population living in overcrowded conditions (i.e. at more than $1\frac{1}{2}$ persons per room) is not only higher than anywhere else in the city, but is about twice as large as the average for the city, yet, at the same time, the average number of people per room is the same in both wards as it is in the city as a whole. This apparent paradox is a reflexion of two features of St Ann's – first, there are a large number of old people living alone, and secondly there is also a considerably larger than average child population, some of whom come from biggish families living in little houses. (About a quarter of the people in St Ann's are under fifteen years old.) The old people frequently occupy whole houses, although these houses may have more rooms than they can conveniently use. This under-occupancy serves to reduce the statistic of density per room. There is no standard measure for under-occupancy, and any measure one devises is bound to be arbitrary. We adopted two devices: the first was a subjective assessment by the respondents, who were asked if they had any rooms that they did not require. In this way we could calculate the numbers of households who said they had a surplus of rooms, and also the total numbers of unused rooms. Secondly, we devised and applied an arbitrary scale of adequacy, thus:

1 person in not more than 3 rooms
2 persons in not more than 4 ,,
3 ,, ,, ,, ,, ,, 5 ,,
4 ,, ,, ,, ,, ,, 6 ,,
5 ,, ,, ,, ,, ,, 6 ,,
6 ,, ,, ,, ,, ,, 7 ,,
7 ,, ,, ,, ,, ,, 8 ,,
8 ,, ,, ,, ,, ,, 8 ,,

This is clearly a very crude scale: it is based upon an assessment of the probable pattern of relationships in households of varying sizes and it is not by any means sensitive to all the possible variations that could be suggested. The application of these two standards yields slightly contrasting figures. The subjective assessment showed that 175 households said they had rooms that they did not need – the total number of surplus rooms being 272. Applying the arbitrary scale, 176 households have surplus space, amounting however to only 193 spare rooms.

Whichever of these standards one prefers, it is quite clear that there is an inefficient use of housing resources on a fairly significant scale. There is not much doubt that this problem arises because of the lack of variety of housing types available, in an area dominated by the five-room house. A married couple without children, or whose children have left home, do nor normally require the use of three bedrooms and so must under-occupy their property. On the other hand, the large family who may require a fourth bedroom can only satisfy this need by encroaching on the already limited living-room space downstairs. There are 58 households in our sample with six or more members, who might find the typical St Ann's house cramped; on the other hand, there are 163 one- or two-person households who will find a five-roomed house more than big enough. Perhaps (although it is doubtful) when the houses were built they might have been ideally suited to average contemporary requirements. Important changes in the age and family structures of the population have occurred, however, and nowadays the inflexible standards of eighty years ago cause more than a few problems.

Nestling alongside this under-occupation there are also pockets of substantial overcrowding, where large families are living in houses far too small for their needs. The spasmodic incidence of serious overcrowding (more than $1\frac{1}{2}$ persons per room) is very clearly shown both in the Census and in our survey figures. Indeed, our first survey area, divided as it is between the two wards, almost exactly splits the difference between the two sets of ward statistics for overcrowding. In detail, the first survey figure of 11·4 per cent of the population living $1\frac{1}{2}$ to a room (or more) involves 70 people living in ten households. A particularly disturbing feature of this story is that the figure includes 46 children, which is 19·6 per cent of the child population of the first survey area. In other words whereas about one tenth of the total population live in overcrowded conditions, one fifth of the children are at this disadvantage. As will be seen, this is a recurrent feature in the profile of the social problems of areas like St Ann's. Wherever one can detect and quantify a social problem area, there is always a disproportionately large number of children involved. The gravity of this finding is self-evident: whatever personal or social harm is caused by physical or material deprivations, such damage is being disproportionately inflicted upon the young, the vulnerable and impressionable.

Overcrowding is not simply inconvenient, and involves more than discomfort. There are obvious and serious questions of public health involved; the risk of infection is multiplied considerably, the capacity to isolate the ill is reduced, and the standards of hygiene demanded of those affected are abnormally rigorous. For example, it is extremely undesirable that people should habitually sleep in the room in which food is prepared or served; this, however, may be unavoidable. The general health problem posed in areas where the only source of water is the tap in the kitchen sink, where all cleaning (whether of food, pots or persons) must take place, is aggravated in ratio to the numbers of persons dependent upon that tap. At its very worst, overcrowding occurs in multi-occupied tenement houses, where one room is allocated per family, and where several families might share the lavatory, the bathroom, if there is one, the water supply, and even the cooking installations. The health risks in this situation must be extraordinary. Our survey area contained only isolated examples of this sort of occupancy, although in adjacent areas of Nottingham, which have not been scheduled for clearance, this is a very much more typical condition.

Because of the especially difficult problems of accommodation facing the coloured immigrants, many of whom are forced to live in such multi-occupied tenements, we strongly suspected that the abnormally high incidence of mortality among West Indian babies might be at least partly attributable to the unhygienic housing circumstances. The infant mortality statistics as presented in the 1965 Report of the Medical Officer of Health were as follows:

National Rate	19·0	deaths per thousand
Nottingham Rate	27·38	,, ,, ,,
'West Indian' Rate	52·02	,, ,. ,,

We sought the help of the Medical Officer of Health, in the hope that some light could be thrown on the possible influence of housing factors on this appalling statistic. In fact, the Nottingham 'West Indian' rate is very close to that prevalent in the West Indies themselves. But we feel sure that it ought to be very much lower if only because of the existence in this country of the National Health Service. Reasons other than bad housing can be offered as a speculative explanation for this fact. However, nothing has been done by the Nottingham health department to take the problem out of the realm of speculation: Nottingham's health statistics are collected in such a way that it is a practical impossibility to obtain information which would throw any light whatsoever on the question. Under the circumstances, it must remain an open question: and a sore one, at that.[8]

The public health hazards of overcrowding are not the only ones: the social difficulties it brings in its wake can be prodigious. For children, it can mean savage limitations: not only do they have to learn to play outside on all possible occasions, but study and the development of private pursuits are quite impossible. Even the material comforts of the consumer society are not easy to reconcile with such housing conditions: assuming a family is able to afford them, it may well find that many of the labour-saving or recreational machines which are taken for granted in suburbia are very cumbersome in so narrow an environment. A question which must be asked of all modern houses is obvious enough: is it possible to find room in them for such things as washing machines, refrigerators, television sets, radiograms and so on? In St Ann's, and many districts like it, there are thousands of houses which were designed when the sewing-machine was the only domestic machine in common use, and when elbow-grease was the standard technique to be applied to most household chores. Such houses are totally unsuitable for twentieth-century living habits. Nor will today's standards remain constant. The television set, which is now almost universal, carries a daily message to everyone who lives in St Ann's or anywhere like it, that their homes are inadequate in a hundred ways as instruments for modern living.

It is generally true to say that it is the character and quality of its housing which is the first determinant of a neighbour-

8. Since this was written, a new Medical Officer of Health has been appointed, so that it is possible that policies might change: we are happy to report that recently the overall figure has shown a marked improvement. Naturally, it remains very important that such statistics should be presented in sufficient detail to enable intelligent judgements to be made.

hood's 'personality'. Certainly, in St Ann's, the condition of the houses bears immediately on the lives of the people. Englishmen widely believe in a thing they are pleased to call a 'private life'. You can live something like it in a commuter suburb, where if you have a blazing row with your wife, neighbours will only get to know about it if she tells them. Private lives require a sturdy minimum of investment in bricks and mortar: there are, for sure, numerous disadvantages in such private lives, but these are disadvantages which many people in St Ann's might well like to taste. In some of the streets of St Ann's nothing is personal unless it is whispered. The shape and structure of the houses project even the most individual activities into the social domain. If you go to the lavatory, you meet your neighbours in the yard. If you want to make love you may well feel it discreet to listen for your neighbour's snores before you start the bed-springs rattling. Even when the houses were brand new, they were suitable only for people who lived very similar lives, and whose conduct varied very little from a fairly restrictive norm. Eccentricities of behaviour are immediately noticeable in such places. Badly insulated, they transmit noise, smells, heat, cold, and personal secrets with complete impartiality. This is true of well-maintained houses in St Ann's as well as decrepit ones, but openness to the wind and rain do not mitigate the difficulties of life under such conditions.

All these deprivations add up. Their sum is backbreaking toil and hardship. And these pains are suffered in houses that are too small, too densely concentrated together; houses that are in various stages of dilapidation and decay; houses that lack the basic amenities taken for granted by most people. You get dirty in St Ann's quite easily, but it is hard to get clean. It is often damp. It is often cold. It is never easy to make it dry and warm. Any one of these drawbacks would, on its own, constitute at least a serious irritation, but a combination of all of them, compounded in so many cases by material poverty, becomes well-nigh intolerable. The heaviest burden falls upon the housewives, whose task it is to raise their families in these circumstances. The one thing that makes decent family life possible in these unpromising environments is stark drudgery; the role of the wife and mother involves an endless round of unremitting, indeed, heart-breaking, but thankless, labour. Such toil could easily be made unnecessary if a little social effort and investment could be applied. The household linen hanging on the clothes-line stretched across the backyard is certainly clean and white when it is first put on the line to dry. The children's clothes are clean before they go to play in the street. The municipal wash-house, with its heavy ranks of steel basins, its fantastic sculpture of steaming pipes, and its forbidding scales of drying racks, is, seen from St Ann's, a vital addition to the local amenities. Seen from outside, it is a symbol of the house-wives' enslavement. But this dichotomy is, itself, a great deal of the trouble in St Ann's. Things can appear to have a different significance if you view them from a different vantage-point.

Human beings are almost infinitely adaptable, and provided that they are ill-treated consistently, they are apt to regard ill-treatment as 'natural'. If the lavatory leaks a little, and always has leaked a little, one comes to regard the leak as 'normal'. If the roof blows off such a lavatory, of course one will expect to be annoyed. But all the myriad petty discomforts can too easily be borne with remarkably little complaint. Damp, cold, rot, decrepitude are as 'natural' in St Ann's as is the smoky atmosphere: for all most people know, they have been sent by Providence and must be endured. Indeed, since Providence has never sent anything else, what other response would be possible? Only *exceptional* damp, *unusual* cold, *excessive* rot, and decrepitude to the point of collapse are felt to be legitimate subjects of discussion. If you hang your washing out in the yard to dry, normally it will be attacked by numerous little black smuts: you will not normally complain. But when a particularly sulphurous bath of smuts burns holes in all your clothes while they are on the line, then you will complain. In the same way people mute their criticisms of what others would regard as intolerable housing amenities. This, and not a fear of exaggeration, is the hazard we have to be aware of when interpreting the remarks of the people of St Ann's about these housing conditions.

While this complex of overcrowding and decay colours the lives of all who live in St Ann's, it has a special significance for those who are in poverty as well. Everyone finds necessary household maintenance and repairs an unwelcome financial burden, but for the poorer such expenses may be quite nightmarish. Indeed, here one can detect a good example of how rich one has to be to be poor: precisely because a poor family cannot afford expensive but once-and-for-all repairs (assuming such repairs to be feasible), household maintenance must either be neglected, or undertaken in a cheap but piecemeal fashion, where any improvement is partial and temporary in its effect. In the long run of course, not only is this inefficient, but it costs more than the single, substantial investment. To neglect maintenance however is only to shift the burden from one part of the household budget to another. An ill-fitting window-frame which lets in draughts and damp will, during the passage of a season, considerably inflate the heating bill. To fight dirt costs more if you have only a gas stove on which to heat water. The cost of hot water is reduced in relation to the capital expenditure which can be undertaken, so that an efficient boiler system is more costly to install than a simple immersion heater, but cheaper to run. To lack even the rudiments of a hot-water system is to pay more per pint of hot water than anyone else has to pay. To fight damp when it is constantly present means laying out vast sums of money on coal or coke, which become more expensive because small quantities have to be purchased for want of ready money to meet large bills. To air clothes when there is no airing cupboard is not only a chore, but an expensive one, while to fail to air all the unworn clothes is frequently to write them off to mildew. This was vividly illustrated in one household we visited where the bedroom was so damp that clothes stored in the cupboard had to be removed daily and spread on a clothes-horse in front of the fire to dry out. The man who lived there showed us why this was necessary; he produced a pair of trousers mouldered beyond recall, obviously now only suitable for the dirtiest of tasks. These trousers had fallen from their hanger, and had lain unnoticed in the wardrobe bottom for a damp week. To buy food for a day at a time because there is no pantry in which to store it is to meet higher bills at corner stores than would be involved in larger purchases from supermarkets. It would be valuable, if people had the spare cash, to line damp rooms with some form of insulating material before wallpapering them: for want of that small capital outlay, they may spend more on frequent re-decoration than they otherwise might have saved; but since the outlay in papering a room three times a year is piecemeal, it is possible, while root-and-branch solutions to the problem are not. The less you have, the more you need to spend. Low wages are conjoined, in this picture, with atrociously bad houses in which money is eaten away far more voraciously than would ever be thought conceivable in suburbia.

The expense of necessary heating and drying is not only considerable, but is ultimately hopeless – it is not a tax which in any way augments a person's living standards, but, like protection money, merely staves off for a little longer an absolute loss. Yet the poorest and neediest must spend substantial proportions of their scant resources in these negative, and, it should surely be added, demoralizing, ways.

To be poor is to pay more, and to pay more often. And there is no slum problem which is not at the same time a poverty problem. The conventional image, still current in some quarters, of the rehoused poor 'putting coal in the bath' is very sour in St Ann's, because for all too many people it might be nice to have the option of putting the coal they can't afford in the baths they haven't got.

II

For some years now the City of Nottingham corporation have declared their intention to redevelop St Ann's; and to this end they have prepared a plan for the total demolition and recon-struction of the entire neighbourhood. The whole area has been divided into eleven phases (some of which have since been sub-divided), and the public health authorities are already well advanced with their examination of all the properties prior to application for a compulsory purchase order. Already, however, there has been some considerable controversy about the process of selection, and the whole principle of phasing has been questioned by the newly formed St Ann's Tenants' and Residents' Association, which emerged, under the tutelage of the young writer, Ray Gosling, during the last weeks of our investigation. S.A.T.R.A., as it has become styled, contends that wholesale demolition is an inappropriate remedy for the problems of the area:

Today the great industrial centres contain large inner areas simultaneously a-fester: generally incapable of meeting the minimum housing standards of today. It is impossible to modify, adapt or repair the whole of the existing fabric in these rings of decay that encircle our town centres. But within any given Redevelopment Area this condition is not total: always there is the odd good street, the several scattered fine houses – and always there are people of spirit. ... We intend to show ... that it is economically possible and humanly desirable to take the very bad out now, patch for the present the not so bad, improve the reasonable, preserve the good.[9]

In accordance with this view, two apparently contradictory petitions from residents of St Ann's were presented to the corporation within one week. One came from inhabitants of phase one, who wanted their street to be reprieved from demolition, while the other came from an area which has not yet been represented, asking to be brought forward in the corporation's schedule. The suggestion that 'selective renewal' is both economically and humanly preferable to comprehensive redevelopment was very largely inspired by a well-publicized and provocative Government Report.

In 1966 the Ministry of Housing published the results of a survey of an area of Rochdale, called Deeplish,[10] which has a

9. Ray Gosling, 'St Ann's', Nottingham Civic Society, 1967, p. 2.

10. *The Deeplish Study – Improvement Possibilities in a District of Rochdale*, H.M.S.O., 1966. See also *Our Older Homes – A Call for Action*, H.M.S.O., 1966.

number of superficial similarities to St Ann's. The Ministry's researchers had made a very thorough investigation into the attitudes of the local people to the houses they lived in, and to their neighbourhood. They also surveyed the condition of the local property. Their inquiry resulted in a series of recommendations about the possibility of 'selective renewal' of Deeplish housing. The researchers meant the systematic improvement of the amenities of the individual houses, and also of the surrounding neighbourhood. At first sight this may appear to be an attractive alternative option to that of wholesale demolition, which must usually involve the uprooting of the inhabitants of condemned properties.

Inspired in part by the results of *The Deeplish Study*, coherent and detailed plans for this kind of selective renewal of St Ann's have been advanced by three architects, whose researches were pursued parallel with our own. Such plans hinge on the systematic provision of improvement grants, which would normally permit the construction of a bathroom, of a cold food store, and of an inside lavatory, while also allowing for the installation of hot and cold running water. However, it is customary for such Government grants to be provided only for houses with a life-expectation of at least fifteen years. True, some authorities have reduced this period to as short a time as seven years, but so far the Nottingham Corporation has proved reluctant to do this. A possible reason for this could be that if the houses which came late in the demolition queue were substantially improved in the meantime, the cost of redevelopment would be increased by the increased value of the property to be demolished. There is, of course, a great deal to be said for the improvement of houses like these, even if they are to disappear in seven to ten years' time. Seven or more years without hot water is a school-life in dirt, or in a frantic and constant losing battle against dirt. The architects, Davis, Strickland, and Wilkinson, have shown that it would be possible to mount an operation to provide the four basic amenities at very small cost, provided only that it was conducted on a sufficiently large scale to allow standardization of materials. The feasibility of this proposal has already been well established by the National Coal Board's scheme for the modernization of colliery houses. But even if the municipality were to agree to the spending of Government money in this cause, it is clear that there are extreme difficulties which would have to be met in order to go to work on the appropriate scale. Not only the apathetic landlord, but also the tenant who has no conception of his elementary rights, must figure in the social equation which is a vital part of all such calculations as these. Improvement grants would be a help in St Ann's: but, if the scheme were to touch more than a fringe of the needs of the area, lively individual and collective effort would be imperative, both in disseminating news of the possible amelioration, and in pressuring recalcitrant landlords to take up the offer.

But whatever might be said about the desirability of stop-gap, short-term, improvements, they have a distinctly limited applicability in St Ann's. The justification for a strategy of wholesale patching-up of old properties in order to lend them another few years of life involves two separate but equally important judgements. The first is a purely technical one: are the properties capable of such renewal, is the basic structure and fabric in such a condition that a limited expenditure on improvements would make a real difference, or are they already so deteriorated that no reasonable amount of money could effect any substantial improvement? On this technical matter we are not competent to make judgements but three students of architecture, whose detailed investigation of St Ann's we have already mentioned, demonstrated clearly that the houses in St Ann's varied considerably in quality. If the worst houses were to be demolished first, then such demolition would take place here and there all over the redevelopment area. In this sense the corporation's phased plan of total demolition will necessarily involve the destruction of some relatively sound properties months or years before some of the worst houses are destroyed. The keyword here is 'relatively'; to our inexpert eyes there is very little property in St Ann's which reaches even a minimally acceptable standard. True, in comparison with the very worst, some might seem tolerable, but in contemplating the long-term future of a district it does not seem very desirable to use the very worst standards as a yardstick. As some indication of the average level of housing standards, we can take the results of the Medical Officer of Health's examination of the first five phases scheduled for redevelopment. It is fair to assume that, in general, a Medical Officer will err on the side of caution when assessing the fitness of a house for habitation. Nevertheless, of the first 4,000 houses examined, 74 per cent have been declared absolutely unfit for habitation. True, there remain the other 26 per cent, which could, presumably, be improved. But the improvement of every fourth property would by no means preserve the character or quality of St Ann's in the way Deeplish has been preserved. There may well be areas of Nottingham suitable for selective renewal, but we are not convinced that St Ann's is one of them.

On this first, and technical, question then, the evidence seems powerful, although there is clearly still room for discussion. On the second and, some would think, the most important question, however, there is less room for doubt: when asked for their opinions about their homes, their neighbourhood and what they want in the future, the residents of St Ann's show a clear consensus, and one moreover which is in sharp contrast to the declared feelings of the men and women of Deeplish. In the latter nearly three fifths of the people interviewed before the programme of renewal was carried out said they were 'very well satisfied' with their houses, while the same proportion were 'very well satisfied' with the neighbourhood, and over two fifths were 'very well satisfied' with both house and neighbourhood. On the other hand, only about one in ten of the housewives was 'rather dissatisfied' with either the houses or the neighbourhood, and fewer than one in twenty was dissatisfied with both house and neighbourhood.[11] In St Ann's a quarter were 'very dissatisfied' with the neighbourhood, while nearly half were 'dissatisfied' to a greater or lesser extent. Only 10 per cent were 'very satisfied'. The implication of this contrast seems

11. *The Deeplish Study*, p. 23.

clear; in terms of contentment with the neighbourhood, St Ann's and Deeplish are totally dissimilar.

In our second survey in St Ann's we attempted to locate such dissatisfactions more specifically. Nearly two thirds were glad that the area was scheduled for redevelopment while nearly a half said that they would like to leave the area altogether. When asked what they disliked so much, the poor housing was mentioned most frequently, but the dirt, the damp, the noise, and the steady deterioration were constantly cited. Our own findings on this score are fairly closely paralleled in a survey carried out by the corporation in the first phase scheduled for redevelopment. The corporation sought data on the incomes of the people in the area, and also on their desire to remain in or near the area, or otherwise. In response to their queries about where people would prefer to live, the council's investigation found that 37·5 per cent of the residents would not mind moving right away from the area, while 20 per cent wished to remain 'fairly near', and 42·5 per cent preferred to remain 'near'. On the positive side, the closeness to the city centre and the good shopping facilities were features that many of our respondents said they would miss: in fairness it should be added that three people said they would miss their particular houses.

All in all, this does not, in our judgement, even approximate to the situation reported in Deeplish. This, of course, may not be a decisive answer to the case for selective renewal. All that we are saying is that Deeplish and St Ann's are by no means comparable areas, so that what may be appropriate for one is by no means necessarily appropriate for the other. Indeed a policy of selective renewal, as a substitutive for redevelopment, while it would no doubt be preferable to nothing, would seem to ride roughshod over the declared wishes of a majority of the residents of the St Ann's redevelopment area.

But if we remain unconvinced about the feasibility of selective renewal as a satisfactory policy in this particular case, this does not by any means imply that we can regard the alternative strategy of wholesale demolition as a panacea. Certainly, given an appropriate sense of priorities, this country has both the necessary wealth and techniques to be able to renovate her industrial townships in a relatively short time, creating habitable dwellings wholesale, on the ruins of the present slums. But in the absence of an overall view of the real sociology and economics of slum life, and in the absence of a serious allocation of resources to meet the whole range of needs which have been stifled or distorted in the slum environment, then even the boldest efforts at reconstruction can frequently produce effects which are very far from those intended.

The gap between the intentions of planners and their achieved results is not simply a problem to be solved by the involvement of sociologists in the planning process, or even, as more radical advocates will rightly insist, by increasing 'participation' by the community in the formation of plans. It goes without saying that these devices are a precondition for any adequate redevelopment policies. Such policies must be concerned to find means of throwing out the slum bathwater without at the same time rejecting the baby, i.e. whatever elements of community structure may be felt by the people concerned to be worthy of preservation and development. Certainly our experience, up to now, of housing estates, be they private or municipal, reveals all too clearly the difficulty (perhaps, even the impossibility) of creating communities by design. There is a clear need for many more imaginative experiments with varied types of housing schemes. Selective renewal, where it is appropriate, is, of course, one such scheme, which is self-consciously concerned with the maintenance of existing community sentiments.

But apart from the aesthetic and 'sentimental' objections to root-and-branch redevelopment, it also poses a very grave economic difficulty. Both land values and building costs have increased steadily in recent years, so that the unit-cost of rebuilding has grown, almost daily, more expensive. The more costly a house, the greater, under present conditions, the rent that must be charged to the tenants. In the case of St Ann's, the new flats and houses, when they are built, will almost certainly be let at three or four times the rents that are being paid in the condemned properties. No doubt the new properties will be, from the point of view of physical standards, an extraordinary improvement on the existing stock and so will be, in market terms, genuinely 'worth' a higher rent. Many people in St Ann's are only too anxious to pay this, if it is to be the price of some possibility of civilized living. But, as we have seen, there is a very substantial minority of householders who, with all the will in the world, will be unable to afford the new rents, or whose determination to pay them will necessitate the most drastic economies in an already overstretched budget. While some people will tighten their belts, others will be unable to do so. Many of those who are rehoused will surely, within a fairly short time, be compelled to decide to find cheaper accommodation. In search of it, they will shop around in the remaining areas of the city where cheaper, albeit grossly substandard, accommodation is still to be found. In so doing, they will not only increase the demand for, and the price of, low-priced houses, but to the extent that they are successful they may well become, in spite of themselves, 'newcomers', inadvertently contributing to the social disruption of yet another neighbourhood. For the poorest people redevelopment may offer very little real improvement. For them, new tenements, more depressed slums, will emerge. The shrinkage of the area given over to slums will mean an intensification of the density of slum overcrowding. Far from being 'elevated' the poor will be precipitated into an even more abject ghetto. The bulldozers will have brought in their wake, not new hope, but fortified despair. This is an old story. In his description of conditions in Manchester in 1844, Frederick Engels drew a horrifying portrait of 'Little Ireland', a slum clustering in the Medlock Valley, which was an outstanding disgrace even for the Manchester of those days.[12] Little Ireland was cleared to make way for a railway station and some celebration of this hygienic advance took place at the time. In 1872 Engels had occasion to return to his

12. 'The Condition of the British Working Class in 1844' in *Marx-Engels on Britain*, Lawrence & Wishart, 1953, p. 94.

old theme about Little Ireland: floods devastated the adjacent area to the old slums and drew attention to the existence of the most dreadful squalor in a new setting.

It was then revealed that Little Ireland had not been abolished at all, but had simply been shifted from the south side of Oxford Road to the north side, and that it still continues to flourish ... this is a striking example of how the bourgeoisie solves the housing problem in practice. The breeding places of disease, the infamous holes and cellars ... are not abolished; they are merely shifted elsewhere. The same economic necessity which produced them in the first place, produces them in the next place also.[13]

This may seem an unduly gloomy point of view, but it is one which grows more, rather than less, apt, as the costs of urban renewal increase substantially and more rapidly than do wage rates – particularly the wage rates of the lower-paid workers. The only possible solution would be to treat housing as a welfare service rather than a marketable commodity, and to approach the housing problem with the urgency that a national crisis merits. This would obviously involve direct exchequer financing of housing, and would certainly mean removing from rents the liability to defray large interest charges, assuming it did not immediately mean the abolition of rents altogether. Administratively there is no doubt that these problems are complex. Their complexity arises not primarily from the nature of the human needs which remain to be met, nor from the difficulties presented by building techniques, but from the web of competing interests and authorities which have to be assuaged before one brick can be placed upon another. Until the direct pressures of the market are totally excluded from the sphere of housing policy, what is fundamentally a very simple social decision will remain almost impossibly difficult. Meanwhile, in districts like St Ann's the poverty problem cannot be solved without tackling the housing question, but similarly the housing question cannot adequately be dealt with without a

13. Frederick Engels, *The Housing Question*, Lawrence & Wishart, pp. 78ff.

strategy to cope with poverty. Rather than an administratively separate group of policies, each proceeding with its own logic and priorities, what is required is a unified drive based upon an understanding of the interrelationship of social problems, one which recognizes the necessity for a comprehensive and simultaneous attack on all of them at once. To streamline the administrations and integrate their efforts would not, of course, be to *solve* the problem: but it would be to *confront* it and, quite possibly, to help make plainer what is presently concealed from the welter of agencies and from the majority of the population: that we are members of one society, and that, if the humble are to be exalted, the mighty must be cast down from their seats.

5 Neighbourhood and Slum Life

Even a limited understanding of the character and condition of the housing in an area like St Ann's should make it plain that, in such a district, houses are by no means simply 'little boxes made of ticky-tacky' separating people who live similar lives. Of course, the physical appearance of the rows of terraced dwellings is more closely uniform, more forbiddingly alike, than that of the suburban commuter estates satirized by Pete Seeger. But such houses do not merely *separate* the people who live in them: they also bring people together, even when they may well not wish to be together. The backyards are not only a kind of semi-public forum and a playground: they are also, sometimes, a battleground. Contact between people is obviously more pronounced in a densely packed slum than would be normal on the straight avenues of the big estates, or even than it is reputed to be, by sociologists, in cul-de-sacs.

'Togetherness' is supposed to be nice, and, indeed, one can easily see how a slum community might seem an enviably friendly place to the lonely commuter. D. H. Lawrence has evoked some of the forms of community contact in a similar environment: a convenient image of its closeness is called up by his description of the semaphore between neighbours in a colliery row, as they rattled with the poker on the fireback in order to call for assistance or to propose a chat. A lot of romantic ideas have emerged from this kind of picture of a slum community. Shades of George Orwell's decent poor, of Richard Hoggart's richly insular Hunslett, notions of fond and active community come, perhaps inevitably, to mind when one sees the long uniform rows of terraced houses, the warm and colourful crowded corner shops, the dozens of little pubs, packed, and the streets and yards themselves, bursting with life. Ray Gosling has conjured up such a picture, in which he enjoins us to 'think of Coronation Street. ... We say, if only Al Capone's Chicago hadn't shot so many: if only St Ann's had good houses. If only ...'

We had not been in St Ann's very long, however, before we came to realize that these romantic ideals of plebeian community fit it rather ill. Of course, they reflect one part of the truth in almost any deprived district: life among people who have to work or live closely together is seldom completely red in tooth and claw. The St Ann's of this world, though, for all their apparent consistency and sameness, are very complex places indeed. For a start, such restricted housing conditions heighten, to an extraordinary degree, the constant and unavoidable conflict between the desire for community and social contact on the one hand, and for some elements of privacy on the other. This is not by any means a new problem. Sir Leonard Woolley[1] records an excavation at an Egyptian necropolis, in which he uncovered some rows of funereal artisans' houses, blocked together back-to-back with entrances giving on to parallel common lanes. One inhabitant of a corner site had, however, bricked up his original doorway, opposite or adjacent to those of all his neighbours; and he had knocked a new hole in the other wall, facing away from the throng. Obviously, even in those days, it was possible to find one's neighbours just a little tiresome. In St Ann's, sharing an outdoor lavatory, as did nine of our respondents, may conduce to heightened social contact, but not always in an entirely happy way. Nor is there at hand as ready a solution to the problem as was found by the anti-social Egyptian.

First impressions of overcrowded districts can stimulate many easy but misleading generalizations about 'community'. But if there is a rational core, for instance, to racial resentments (apart from the remnants of the old imperial xenophobia which was sedulously fostered in every child, to say nothing of

1. *Digging up the Past*, Penguin Books, 1937, p. 36.

every conscript soldier, until more recently than we may care to admit) then it might profitably be sought in the housing standards of places like St Ann's. These districts invite the poor immigrants because they are both relatively open and relatively cheap, but they are the most difficult territories imaginable for the co-existence, never mind the intermingling, of cultures, simply because privacy can only be discovered in their buildings when everyone goes on tiptoe.

Noise can very easily pass down the terrace from house to house. This means that if life is to be tolerable, it must conform to a common rhythm. If people's habits do not approximate to a very rigid common norm, their physical conditions will produce savage tensions. A fondness for late-night revelry in one house can easily reduce the next-door neighbours to nervous exhaustion. Sometimes the dividing walls between houses are only one brick thick, and every untoward disturbance, every tiff, even every reconciliation, is broadcast to the ears of the adjacent residents. People can learn tolerance in such surroundings, and become warmly involved in one another's problems. They can also learn jealous resentment, a cumulative and gnawing annoyance, a dumb but potent hostility.

It is easy to see why people are drawn to eulogize the sense of community which is supposed to exist in slums. Anyone who walks down St Ann's Well Road, or along Alfred Street which bisects it, during shopping hours or on a fine evening, must at once be aware of a mood, an atmosphere, something mysterious, even vibrant, occasionally violent. You are aware of it as you pass the brightly lit but opaque windows of the pub. The interior may be functional, may even be austere: but the loud hubbub of chatter, the many different voices and inflexions mingling with the distinctive Nottingham accent, evoke a world of spirited confusion. You sense the cosmopolitanism of St Ann's when you pass the crowded Italian corner-shop, open until late at night, with its baskets of aubergines and green peppers on display outside, and inside a passing glimpse of pasta in every shape and size, bottles of cheap Chianti, and nubile women, who might easily have come, last year, from Naples. On the corner of the Central Market is the Central European delicatessen, run by and supplying the large Polish community. The Bombay Emporium now stocks sweet potatoes and yams and is called the Commonwealth Stores. From Tsang's Fish and Chip Bar you can take home a carton of chop suey. Those in the know talk darkly about the elusive 'Shebeens', where liquor and West Indian curry are served until dawn.

Certainly an important part of the unique character of St Ann's is due to the extraordinary variety of residents, the Poles and Ukrainians from war-time days, the Italians shortly after, more recently the Asians and West Indians. To these expatriates must be added the British immigrants, the Scots and Irish, the Geordies and the Liverpudlians, all drawn to the Midlands in pursuit of work. Some will stay a few days or weeks and then move on south, while some remain for months or years. But they all live with, in and among the people born and bred in St Ann's, a key part of Nottingham's industrial working class, many of whom have the assurance of three generations of life in the heart of the city. It was this variety and confusion, this mêlée of people both deeply rooted and newly arrived, that prompted Ray Gosling to write: 'St Ann's is a remarkable district. People of all manners, creeds, colour and fancy live there – against all odds, so far so lucky, in harmony and with humour.'[2] But where so many different people must share a relatively confined space, tensions and cleavages will always arise. St Ann's is a neighbourhood with many newcomers, and newcomers are not always welcome. Our earliest and most preliminary inquiries revealed something of the extent and character of these tensions.

We talked to two women who ran a fairly large off-licence and general store. They told us that they both thought the area had deteriorated, and they mentioned new families coming in all the time. These, they said, included 'particularly people who have proved bad tenants on the council estates: they just

2. Ray Gosling, 'St Ann's', Nottingham Civic Society, 1967. See also *Architecture East Midlands* No. 13, April/May 1967.

move them into corporation property in this area.' They mentioned other newcomers: two West Indians had been stealing cigarettes from a showcase while they were getting other items for them. Normally they had very few coloured people in, because there was another shop, further down the road, owned by a West Indian family. 'Most of them shop there.' But the few black people who did come in were 'always very nice and very friendly'. Besides the Italians who had settled, though, the main body of newcomers was English: there were a lot of young couples who came to the area because they could pay low rents while they were saving for somewhere of their own. Both these ladies said, without being asked, that the people were very friendly and would always help each other. 'If someone isn't around for a day or two, then we try to find out why.'

Again, we spoke with a seventy-six-year-old ex-dustman who had lived in the area 'for a very long time'. He was very insistent that the area had 'changed a lot'. Two coloured families had moved into the street, which he mentioned without comment. But complaints followed thick and fast about the behaviour of the other new people on the street. 'There are forty children now playing on this street. The row is unbelievable. They take no notice at all when you tell them to make less noise. The teenagers make nothing but trouble. They even put fireworks through the letterbox.' This complaint was to become distressingly frequent. If the children are often, in any neighbourhood, the messengers who knit it together, and whose playgroups make many introductions for their parents, it is also true that in such conditions as these, unwittingly, the children can be the initiators of a thousand feuds.

A housewife in her mid-thirties told us that she had been in the area for nine years, having previously lived on a large post-war council estate. She was quite convinced that the area was changing for the worse as new people came in: 'Our children have got far worse since they came here. Now they're always answering back. It's going down all the time here.' New arrivals, however, were concentrated in some parts of the area: 'They're all right at this end of the street, but they're no good at the bottom. Mind you, I was brought up decent, not like them round here.' Again, it was the upbringing and behaviour of the newcomers' children that really scandalized this lady. A woman of sixty who had lived in St Ann's for thirty years was equally certain that 'the district has changed considerably, especially since the coloured people have moved in'. She did not dislike them, but, she said, 'they're not like us'. But, yet again, the main complaint she had was not against West Indian or Pakistani immigrants: it was once more about the *English* newcomers to the area, and especially the young ones: 'The children,' she said, 'are a menace – there is little for them to do except damage. They are always making bonfires on this demolition site, or breaking into places like those rented garages opposite, which they keep busting up.' She knew nothing about any club facilities for teenagers.

Another woman in her late forties, whose family had been in the district for seventy years, thought, 'The area has changed a lot in the past two years – the council keep moving problem families in as the old people die, or when folk move out. People who can't afford the new house rents move in here. I myself like the area, because I have always lived here, but I don't like these new people. They use foul language. You should just hear them, sometimes. It's really rough.'

Then there was a shopkeeper who had been there for thirty of his fifty years. He thought that fewer people were living in the district, and that there were fewer large families. He also said: 'The newcomers are of a poorer type than the old residents. The older people are very friendly. You know, it's better here than on the estates, because on the estates so many of the women have to go to work to pay the extra rent and the fares.'

Yet in some streets there were other views. One man, an owner-occupier who had lived in St Ann's for thirty years, said that as far as he could see, the houses were well built and remarked, 'It's a friendly sort of place. Everybody knows each other. Most of the people here are middle-aged, and have been here a long time.' This man mentioned, quite without

110

excitement or remark, that he did have two Italian neighbours. It was quite apparent that they, at any rate, had not dislocated the pattern of local behaviour. One reason for this harmony was very simple: he pointed out at once that there was only one child in the immediate block. In the same street, another old lady who was interviewed agreed with him that it was 'nice and quiet'.

After this, we found one of the newcomers, a woman in her thirties, who had moved in eighteen months ago. She had known the area when she was young, and felt that it had 'gone down a lot since then'. Although she liked being near the shops, after living on a suburban council estate, from which she had come by exchange of houses, she said that the thing she really disliked was 'having to be so careful who you're friends with, and who your children can play with'.

So much for the assumption that areas of old, long-established housing necessarily generate a serene sense of fellow-feeling. This one sometimes does and sometimes does not. It would obviously be far too simple to assume that the old residents comprise one tightly integrated community, and to see all the newcomers simply as a disruptive invasion. Yet even these rudimentary inquiries showed quite clearly that there are some serious frictions between the recent settlers in the area, and the long-established host community. Again and again we heard loud complaints about the new arrivals. Sometimes they were flatly blamed for lowering the tone of the area, or 'bringing the district down'. Sometimes their presence was merely mentioned, as though the information would speak for itself. It is perfectly apparent that such feelings constitute an important element in the moral chemistry of the neighbourhood. It was for this reason that we became increasingly anxious to discover the elements of population movement in St Ann's.

Although this sounds easy, it is in fact a very difficult task to obtain reliable and precise information on mobility, particularly in the house-by-house, street-by-street detail that we required. In the end we decided to compare the register of electors for the years 1961 and 1965. This is certainly a less than perfect procedure. In the first place the registers only list those eligible to vote and exclude all those under twenty-one, all aliens and all other non-voters. Houses wholly occupied by aliens are considered, for the purposes of the register, to be empty. Moreover, despite strenuous efforts to keep them up to date, the registers vary enormously in accuracy: the more movement of population there is in a district, at any given time, the more inaccurate they will be. Nonetheless, the registers are published annually and are a systematic attempt at a full list of adults. By taking two lists, separated by four years, we hoped to be able to get some rudimentary estimate of the overall rate of mobility and, perhaps more importantly, to discover whether or not there were striking variations in movement from one street to another.

We found that 29 per cent of the adults in the households listed on the 1961 registers were not to be found in 1965 registers; or, looking at movement from the other end, that just over 30 per cent of the 1965 voters had not been registered in 1961. There were, however, striking differences between streets. Some few had a turnover rate of well over 40 per cent while others showed less than a 20 per cent change in population. In general, owner-occupied houses are more steadily occupied than rented houses. If there were any truth in the persistent rumour that the corporation uses its property in St Ann's to accommodate what it calls 'problem families' (those who cannot or will not meet rent payments on the council house estates and so on), it might be expected that, in an area like St Ann's, privately rented houses would be more permanently let than those owned by the corporation. Certainly streets with a high proportion of corporation-owned property tend to have a considerably higher rate of population turnover.

But there are other reasons why a street may have a high rate of population movement. The basic demography of the street clearly plays an important part. Some 'elderly' streets, now amongst the most stable, will become more turbulent as the old people die, leaving property vacant. As each property falls empty, unless it is immediately taken over for demolition, it will be occupied by new people, who are not only very likely to be younger than their neighbours, but who might be strangers to the town or even to the country and who may well have young children. Very easily, without having ill intentions themselves, these unfortunates can come to be seen by their neighbours as disrupting the established pattern of relationships in the street. One or two newcomers in a street can perhaps be assimilated into its patterns. A whole host of new people, however, can, without easily being able to form firm social ties for themselves, unwittingly be held responsible for shattering those which already existed among the older inhabitants.

Residents on those streets with a high degree of population continuity have had an opportunity to establish themselves, to identify themselves with the street and with one another and to develop community responses to common problems. This is obviously more difficult on streets with a continual turnover of people, where a withdrawal from intimate social contacts, a reticence, a shyness amounting almost to mistrust can be quite widespread. If a high rate of population turnover will normally make it harder for people to put down healthy social roots within the street, community sentiment is even more gravely corroded when there is a widespread and deliberate antagonism towards the newcomers. A most frequently encountered complaint is that St Ann's is being destroyed, both physically and socially, by the arrival of numbers of 'problem families'. Many people go so far as to allege that the corporation follows a policy of moving such families into the property it owns in St Ann's, in order to clear them from the outlying council estates which border the city. Needless to say, if the corporation had such a policy it would not publicly admit to it. At the same time, it is perfectly plain that a movement of population from the estates to the city centre is not necessarily a movement of delinquents or of difficult people. Not everyone who moves from expensive to cheaper corporation property is a rogue or villain; people can make such a move because they are short of money, and this may very well not be 'their own fault'.

On the other hand we do have certain other evidence about problem families, although we did not gather it ourselves. The publication of our preliminary report provoked at least one informed comment from an official of the corporation, Mr R. B. Woodings, the children's officer. In a private commentary on our report circulated to members of the Children's Committee, but withheld from the press, he said:

In all, exactly 100 families in the St Ann's Redevelopment Area have been reported from various sources as being 'problem families' from a total of 423 families so reported in the whole City of Nottingham. That is, 21.1% of all the families live in St Ann's area.

In the area of the St Ann's Study Group Report, 38 'problem families' have been reported. ... It will have been noted from the Report that the area surveyed ... contained about one-fifth of the houses and families of the whole of the St Ann's area ...

Of 400 corporation tenants (with rent arrears in the City of Nottingham) 50 tenants were in the Redevelopment Area and they had some 140 children in these families. That is, 12·5% of all such cases in this City were in the St Ann's area ... of 44 families where there was danger of eviction ... 10 families (22·7%) came from ... St Ann's.

It can hardly be a coincidence that a fifth of the 'problem families' in Nottingham have found their way to St Ann's, while half the total of such families reported in the district owed the corporation rent. It seems quite clear that such families are being concentrated into a ghetto, no doubt for sound administrative reasons. Part at least of the intense movement of population in corporation-owned properties of St Ann's can be explained in this way. That there would be 'problem families' in this area, whether the corporation moved them in or not, is not denied. It would, indeed, be remarkable if there were none: the area is full of problems, some of which are bound to rub off on at least some families.

Another group of 'problem' people are also coming to St Ann's in increasing numbers as it is made ready for the bull-dozers. These are the growing body of vagrants who doss down for a little while in empty houses before moving on to other places. On Monday, 3 July 1967, the *Nottingham Guardian-Journal* carried this alarming front-page story:

The partially-clothed body of a 19-year-old girl was found doubled up and half-hidden under the staircase of a derelict house in Union Terrace, Nottingham, yesterday by two Irishmen who had been 'dossing down' in a neighbouring empty house. She had been battered to death. The Irishmen ... were on their way to a cafe for a cup of tea when they saw a navy blue reefer jacket lying in an alley behind the row of derelict houses, and a trail of blood leading into one of them. ... It was about 10.00 a.m. ... that they left one of the derelict cottages known as Union Cottages where they had slept rough. Passing up the path alongside the former yards of the cottages, now dumping places for rubbish, they spotted a jacket ... following the blood spots into one of the 26 derelict cottages, they found more blood stains ... the ... body ... was ... under the old staircase.

While the two men were on their way to police headquarters, the body was seen again by two children playing in the area.

As more and more houses are allowed to stand empty, vagrants become a more familiar sight. The authorities attempt to ex-clude them by boarding up the ground-floor doors and win-dows of the unoccupied houses. One small shop on the St Ann's Well Road was boarded up in this way several times in one month, as residents repeatedly complained that young men 'sleeping rough', were shouting somewhat lewd invita-tions to local girls from the upstairs windows. Since wooden boards are so ineffective as barricades, one begins to see more and more houses bricked in solid, with all windows and doors sealed.

All of these complaints and fears, even when they are quite unjustified, nonetheless contribute to a breakdown of com-munity feeling. The people next door, or down the street, how-ever, are only one element in a community, and not neces-sarily the most important. Family and chosen friends are certainly as important. Many of the beliefs which are widely current about working-class community rest on a series of assumptions about the existence of extended family systems, in which the mother-in-law, far from figuring simply as a music-hall butt, plays a crucial role in a developed social network. A number of studies, of which the best-known is Michael Young and Peter Willmott's classic work on family links in Bethnal Green,[3] all make essentially the same point. In working-class communities, the continuing and close links between a mother and her daughters become the cornerstone of family life.

Mum-centredness is particularly a function of that period of the life-cycle where her children have grown up and married, leaving Mum, if she is still young enough, and hale enough after the strains of bringing up her own family, as an active and useful centre of family life, extremely influential because of her experience, and strongly motivated to keep her children around her. Where separation of conjugal roles has left her little in common with her husband, this tendency is enhanced. As one Bethnal Green dustman said, with unconscious poetry, 'Mum's is the central depot in this family.'

Following the publication of Young and Willmott's first study in the mid-fifties, a somewhat dogmatic argument broke out about these assumptions. There were those who challenged the view that 'mum' was a combination of advice bureau, welfare service, and benevolent leader, and instead wished to present a picture in which she was to be construed as a petty-minded tyrant. At that time, according to which prejudice they embraced, sociologists tended to align themselves into opposing groups, some welcoming, others attacking the disruptive development of slum-clearance and council-housing schemes, which were assumed to break up the extended family, and with it, mother-in-law sovereignty. Looking back on this controversy, it seems to us that in this case, as in many others, the crucial question to be asked is, what do people actually *want*? This ought, surely, to be of greater importance in the determination of planning policy than the opinions of professional re-

3. *Family and Kinship in East London,* Penguin Books, 1962.

searchers or theorists. If this view is accepted, the principal difficulty which will remain is not theoretical, but eminently practical: different people want different things, and some are not sure what they want.

It is not, therefore, in order to judge the virtue or otherwise of St Ann's in relation to some pre-established norm of family contact, that we interest ourselves in this question. If people want to be near their mother-in-law, they ought to have that privilege. If not, then they ought also to have that privilege. In fact, such liberty will not really be fully open to most people until there are marginally more houses available to them than can immediately be occupied, and at rents they can afford. A world with humane concerns at its heart might be persuaded to accept such a goal as having slightly higher priority than, say, the dredging of minute quantities of useless muck from the surface of the moon. Up to now, however, our society cannot even be prevailed upon to accept that limited degree of priority for housing which would entitle everyone to live *somewhere*, near or far from mother, at an acceptable standard. Since we live here, now, close to several places like St Ann's, we have to accept as a fact that, whatever ought to happen, there is considerable evidence that the extended family is an important part of the institutions of many working-class districts.

However, of the people we interviewed in St Ann's, only 15 per cent had their parents living nearby, while no more than 12 per cent had grown-up sons and daughters living in the neighbourhood. The importance of this pattern becomes clearer if it is compared with research in other cities, or indeed with our own investigation of another Nottingham working-class district. In their study of Bethnal Green, Michael Young and Peter Willmott interviewed 933 people [4] of whom 369 [5] were married and had at least one of their parents still living. Of the 369, exactly half the men, and 59 per cent of the women, had parents living in Bethnal Green itself. An additional 18 per cent and 16 per cent respectively had parents living in

4. *Family and Kinship in East London*, p. 208.
5. ibid., p. 36, Table 4.

adjacent boroughs, yielding a total of 68 per cent and 75 per cent in each case who had parents living 'nearby'. Calculating from Young and Willmott's figures, this gives a total of 263 (28·1 per cent) people out of 933 whose parents lived 'nearby'. It seems quite fair to say that, with a figure close to half this, the St Ann's population has a much weaker family network than that which exists in Bethnal Green. Of course, this comparison is weaker than it seems at first sight because we deliberately did not press our respondents to give a precise answer as to exactly how near 'nearby' was, yet it seems very unlikely that this will be a narrower term than that involved in Bethnal Green. In 1955, at the beginning of Young and Willmott's investigation, Bethnal Green had a predominantly working-class population of 54,000, and seems in other ways to be comparable with St Ann's, with its dense working-class concentration.

The relative weakness of family ties in St Ann's is confirmed by our inquiry on the Edwards' Lane council-housing estate. Whereas in St Ann's six out of ten of the people we talked to had relations of some description living nearby, the comparable figure on the estate was eight out of ten. About the same number in both areas (15 per cent) had parents close at hand, but on the estate over a third of the householders had grown-up sons or daughters within range, three times the figure for St Ann's. Certainly, this gives a picture of the estate as being both closer-knit than St Ann's and, at the same time, less close-knit than Bethnal Green. The most interesting fact to emerge from the comparison of the conditions in the two Nottingham districts is that the sons and daughters of St Ann's seem very much more likely to get out, to move completely away, than do those on the estate.[6] Naturally, statistics like these must be interpreted with considerable caution: but they

6. For a more detailed discussion of these figures, and the other results of this inquiry, see 'The Morale of the Poor', pp. 19ff. There are some parts of St Ann's in which these contrasts reveal themselves more starkly. Our original area of investigation was such a one: see 'Poverty, Deprivation and Morale', Chapter 3, p. 53.

reveal the differences in social life which result from the greater instability of the population in St Ann's. Whatever allowances are made, the clear impression remains that in St Ann's the traditions of family dependence have become considerably weaker than is common in more firmly rooted working-class communities.

Has the frailty of the extended family encouraged the formation of other close associations between people who are not related to one another? Apparently not. Certainly the pattern of friendships which exists could hardly be seen as fully compensatory. Nearly four people out of ten in St Ann's said they had no friends at all in the vicinity. Of the 250 people who *did* have friends nearby, 155 were friendly with their neighbours. Apart from their immediate neighbours, the largest single group of friends cited were drinking companions (53 or 12 per cent). Of course, the word 'friend' is capable of different interpretations, and it may be that people in St Ann's do not spend it over-lightly. Even so, there is a largish number of people who are, apparently, without close ties with others in the district. When we asked the same questions on the council estate, we found a higher proportion of people (nearly 70 per cent) had friends nearby, a large proportion of whom were actually neighbours.

Having no relatives nearby may be unavoidable, and having no friends at hand may be a matter either of choice or of misfortune. But nearly everyone will have neighbours, and in a district like St Ann's having neighbours (and in turn, being a neighbour) involves some degree of contact, no matter how unsought or how unwelcome that contact may be. Living next door to someone provides an extremely arbitrary but largely unavoidable introduction to them, yet it is not one which necessarily leads to harmony and mutual help. Of course, in St Ann's, as anywhere else, some people get on well with their neighbours and in terms of mutual aid, of favours given and received, they may have found an adequate substitute for the extended family. Others do not enjoy such harmonious relationships, while some go so far as to minimize their contacts with their neighbours as much as possible and are surrounded by an atmosphere of acrimonious mistrust. To some extent it appears that unfamiliarity breeds contempt, as the amount and character of 'neighbouring' seem in part to depend upon the length of time that families have lived next door to one another. Some of the most acid comments about neighbours came from, and were directed at, newcomers. Although there were great variations in 'neighbouring' habits, some sort of a pattern does emerge, and just as was the case with the shape of its family networks, in this matter also the council estate contrasts quite sharply with St Ann's. When we asked people how frequently they called upon, or were visited by, their neighbours, over half of the total St Ann's survey sample told us that they *never* called upon their neighbours. On the council estate this rather large total shrunk to 46 per cent. On the other hand, a quarter of the St Ann's residents popped in to see their neighbours once a week or more, while a third of them said they received visits *from* neighbours as frequently. The estate proved to be more sociable than St Ann's, especially in regard to willingness to *initiate* visits. What seems beyond doubt is that in St Ann's a very large part of the population is upon fairly formal terms with its neighbours.

To assess the attitudes underlying this pattern of behaviour we asked two further questions. First, did people think it better to try to 'get on well' with their neighbours, or to 'keep themselves to themselves'? Second, did they think that their fellow-residents were like themselves, or in some way 'different'? This second question was deleted from the questionnaire of our second survey, so the 'identification' figures only refer to our first findings:

Table 5.

Sociability	No.	%	Identification	No.	%
Try to get on well	199	48·2	'People are like me'	93	52·8
Keep to self	194	47·0	'People are different'	48	27·2
Don't know	16	3·9	Don't know	33	18·8
No answer	4	0·9	No answer	2	1·2
	413	100		176	100

That under half the people tried to 'get on well', and that almost the same number 'keep to themselves' might be taken as a mark of some alienation, of a withdrawal of sociability. Whether this is a fair assumption or not, it indicates that attitudes associated with the cultivation of privacy are, at least at the level of verbal acceptance, widespread. Of course, the category of people 'trying to get on well' does not overlap with the rather similar proportion of people in our first sample claiming that 'people round here are like us'. This last grouping made it clear that as often as not its response was descriptive, amounting only to recognition of a common social status. It was often accompanied by some such remark as 'They're all working people'. Of course the simple recognition of a common social status does not always imply any active effort to ingratiate oneself with one's peers. But this general picture ought not to be interpreted too rigidly to mean that in St Ann's *homo homini lupus est*'. Nothing could be more misleading. Again and again we have to allow for the fact that people have mixed feelings. A resounding indication of this, strongly counterbalancing these replies, comes in the answers to the question 'Do you feel that you could expect your neighbours to help you if you were in a jam?' 274 said 'yes': exactly two thirds. Only 101, or just under a quarter, were prepared to give a flat 'no' in reply. Perhaps this response might be taken as some measure of the positive feeling of St Ann's people towards their neighbourhood.

All these sentiments contribute to a distinct impression of widespread dissatisfaction with the neighbourhood. That there was a general, diffuse dissatisfaction has already been mentioned as a key difference between St Ann's and Deeplish. But the details of the conversations we had with people in St Ann's brings this dissatisfaction into an altogether sharper focus. It is very plain that there are sharp reactions, not only to the state of the bricks and mortar and to the condition of the housing and amenities, but to the habits of other people as well. Indeed, there are a whole series of social tensions which are at least as deeply felt by many people as is the lack of physical amenities.

The by now familiar objections to the corporation's new tenants: 'they bring in rubbish: jailbirds and idlers'; gossipy objections to the neighbours: 'they are nosy', 'they can't be trusted', 'turn your back and they'll steal your purse', 'make a friend here and you'll get three or four enemies'; distressing frictions between generations or ethnic groupings; complaints about teenage vandalism, about broken windows, noises and fighting: all these were painfully frequent complaints, even though they tended to be clustered around a number of spots within the area. But many people who complained showed themselves to be deeply ambivalent about the area, being torn between an obvious involvement in and identification with the neighbourhood, and a resentment towards those who are thought to disturb it. Of course by no means all disturbances are necessarily occasioned by inhabitants, as one graphic instance among many will serve to reveal. An old lady told us that she liked the area, because 'everyone is friendly, including the coloured people. None of the neighbours are "wranglesome".' But she also disliked it, because of the 'noise from the cafe and Bingo hall round the corner, especially from the cars. People are regularly sick in front of my house, and they are always using the front doorway and the cellar-grating as a toilet, because it is in the dark part of the street, away from the street lights.'

If people can find themselves so deeply at odds with themselves in their attitudes to their home territory, there is more than one possible kind of ambivalence. While there is a fairly large grouping of people who like their neighbours but resent either newcomers or drunken invaders from other districts, or 'vandals' among the young people, there are also those whose liking for the area springs from a quite different source. There was the sad young woman, a divorcee, to whom we have already referred, who summed up some of the most depressing features of the neighbourhood when she told us 'You can lose yourself in an area like this.' She had, she said, 'come to get away from my husband and my past life'. Yet even for this woman the advantages were not unmixed. She also strongly disliked the area, because 'I had all my children's clothing stolen from the line at the back: now I never feel secure from break-ins'. Several other women complained of pilfering from their clothes-lines, while a good many others complained of breaking and entry offences. Gas meters, in particular, are frequently rifled by thieves. In between these examples of devotion to the neighbourhood against overwhelming odds, and acceptance of its disadvantages *because* of what is felt to be its lack of community concern, it is naturally possible to find responses mixed in a thousand different ways. But if many of these may be the result of less grievous tensions between conflicting values, they are, for all that, likely to contain their own measure of ambivalence. For example, although people in St Ann's can be quite seriously torn between their feeling that the area is running down and their memory of its happier days, they may well, at a more instrumental level, weigh its nearness to the shops against its manifest inconveniences in a hundred other respects. However, despite considerations of this kind, their overall dissatisfaction with the place is perfectly clear. It is altogether apparent that, in so far as we were able to explore the informal community responses of people in St Ann's, we found, for all its sketchiness, a picture which is very different from the convenient assumption that very poor housing standards and a high degree of physical deprivation necessarily go hand in hand with unreserved social intercourse and warm brotherly feeling. They do not.

The network of informal social relationships in St Ann's is comparatively neat and raw community ties are more feeble than they are in many other working-class areas.

But what about formal organizations? It is important to find out how far people participate in organized activities of various kinds, not simply because this knowledge is helpful to people who seek to understand the nature of slum life, but far more because any work of self-defence and mutual improvement among poorer people must begin by taking stock of their existing voluntary associations and by assessing the degree of organized social activity in which they already engage.

It is possible to draw some picture of the state of organized social activity in any given area from its public records. For example, the City of Nottingham Education Committee has published a handbook which lists all the various youth groups which are registered with the local authority. Although this list is now several years old and youth groups are constantly forming (and dissolving), it does give some idea of the scale and character of provision for youth in the city in general and in St Ann's in particular. There are, for example, thirty-three registered youth clubs in the city; twenty of these are sponsored by the Education Department, the others are voluntary. Only one of these clubs is in St Ann's. There are fifty-two registered youth groups attached to religious organizations, only one of which is within the area. There are ten registered specialist groups; one of these, an Amateur Theatre Club, has a Youth Theatre and is situated within the area. But this group is based on the intensive work of a group of amateur players and drama enthusiasts, who have enterprisingly converted a small warehouse into a miniature theatre. It is an exciting project. Nevertheless, its situation in St Ann's is virtually its only point of contact with the neighbourhood. The rows of cars outside the little theatre bring its members in, and take them out again by closing-time at the latest. None of the youngsters who live nearby are members of the Youth Theatre, nor do their parents significantly swell the audience when a production is staged. The only youth groups which seem to have any significant role to play in St Ann's are the uniformed ones; there are two detachments of the Boys' Brigade and one of the Girls' Life Brigade, three Boy Scout troops, four companies of Girl Guides and one of the city's three Ranger groups. Finally there are two St John's Ambulance or Nursing Cadet groups.

There are, then, very few straightforward recreational groups. There are some quasi-military, mildly disciplinarian, or service groups, which will no doubt both interest and absorb some small number of St Ann's youth. There is, however, neither the scale nor the variety of provision to come anywhere near satisfying the needs of the young, let alone enough to offer any slight compensation for the multifold disadvantages and frustrations of slum life.

The state of the youth movement prefigures that of adult voluntary associations in St Ann's. 45 per cent of the people we spoke to told us that they were not members of *any* organizations at all. 54 per cent did belong to something and, of course, some people belonged to more than one voluntary body. Thus we found that slightly over a fifth of the people belonged to a church, while slightly under a fifth were members of trade unions. Less than 3 per cent were members of any political party. 8 per cent adhered to some other type of grouping.

The church members included a number of people who stated that they were Roman Catholics while some other people stated that they belonged to the smaller sects. The Elim tabernacle is situated in the middle of our first survey area, and there are a number of revivalist churches bordering the district. One, on the main road to the north, which lies just outside St Ann's, attracts a very lively and sizeable congregation, as polyglot and cosmopolitan as any group of people who could be met with in St Ann's itself. The Church of England groups, which are loudly protesting against the rationalization of their structure which will be brought about by the redevelopment scheme, did not have very many adherents among the people we talked to. It seems that when they seek religious comfort, people in St Ann's are prone to gravitate to the more colourful and dramatic forms of worship. Probably the hard-pressed representatives of the established Church look enviously at the crowds of people who flock into the fundamentalist chapels to sing their hearts out, and who punctuate the direct and rather strident utterances of their preachers with loud cries of 'alleluiah!'. Alleluiah indeed: there is little enough to sing in praise of whatever god it was who made St Ann's and left it to its fate. The cries which go up from these strange and ugly tabernacles are scarcely shouts of unalloyed joy. They are desperate affirmations that life was meant to be richer than the drab round it is. No one could form or grow a human soul in order to calculate that its experience would end at the boundaries of these grim streets, at the limits of aspiration possible here. Yet the striking thing is, that with all the labour of secular agitation which remains to be done in St Ann's, the churches, particularly the little churches, are at the top of the organizational league in the district. There is a clear tendency for poorer people to be more devout than their less deprived neighbours. It is tempting to speculate that the poor are in greater need of divine comfort than the rest of the population and that in St Ann's churches are of greater importance as doorways to slum clearance in eternity than they are in this troubled world. However, it is only fair to add that a high proportion of church members are to be found among the elderly, who, of course, are predominantly poor. The elderly may also well share their preoccupation with the next world with many other old people, more affluent, but no less convinced of the inadequacy of the poor little lives they have been enabled to lead in the here and now.

In the secular field, the picture is one of unrelieved apathy. Because of their obvious importance in relation to the proportion of poverty attributable to low pay, we will return to the role of the trade unions in Chapter 10. It is enough here to say that only 18·4 per cent of the breadwinners in our St Ann's population belonged to unions, compared to a national figure of roughly 50 per cent of the male working-class population. Not only is union membership weak in the district, but it seems that it is less likely than average to become involved in leadership. When we examined the local Trades Council Directory for 1968, we found some two hundred local trade-union branches listed as affiliates. Of these only five had branch secretaries who lived in St Ann's which has a population of 30,000, almost entirely working class. The Greater Nottingham area, from which the Trades Council draws its representation, has a total population of 460,000: this figure is drawn from all classes. Thus St Ann's accounts for more than one fifteenth of the total population of the area, but provides only one fortieth of the local union leadership. In terms of committed participation the political groups run nowhere. There are three fairly energetic Conservative councillors for the main St Ann's ward and the Labour Party maintains a struggling group of loyalists who do their utmost to win recruits but with very scant results. It would be eccentric to try to explain this lack of commitment to existing public organizations by assuming that people in St Ann's are in some way 'lazy' or indifferent to their fate. In this field, as in many others, there are no bad soldiers, only bad generals. It is difficult to find any plausible reasons why anyone in St Ann's should believe that the organizations to which they could conceivably adhere might in some way assist them in solving any of their actual problems. The reason why less than three per cent of the people in St Ann's even trouble to hold membership cards in the political organizations was tellingly expressed in an interview with a lorry driver, a young ex-serviceman, who was intelligently interested in political questions, and indeed spent some considerable time in expressing his somewhat scathing opinions about the leaders of both major political parties. When our interviewer asked him to what he attributed the neglect of the area, he replied:

'Why? Because as far as I can see, we're not important. The people that they're going for are the people that are in the estates. Why? Because they think, "if we can keep them happy, we're all right". Admittedly, there are more people in the estates than there are in St Ann's. So who are we compared to Broxtowe, Aspley estate, Clifton estate and all the rest of them? They outnumber us, so if they keep them happy, they don't have to bother with us.

'The people that's in now, it's all take and no give. They want this, they want that, they promise you this, they promise you that. As long as we are the idiots that's coughing up for them, they're not bothered with us. They're not bothered one little bit about us.'

So our interviewer asked, 'Do you ever say this to your councillor?' 'I don't know who he is,' came the answer.

Another young worker, married with two young children, graphically summed up his reactions:

'The reason I got a car was to get out of Nottingham, to get out of St Ann's. Why? Because it makes me bad. To be able to walk round my own town and think "I don't like this" and go out somewhere else. When it boils down to it, what is St Ann's? It's just nothing but a load of dung. I know the barrow boys. They've been born and bred round here. But you never see them in Nottingham over the week-end. When it's a week-end you won't find them in Nottingham, they're out. There's nothing in Nottingham, not now. They're knocking all these buildings down and building car parks. What do you want a car park for? I want a house where I can turn round and say, "Right, get in that back garden or backyard and play to your heart's content", and I've no worry about anything. To be able to walk out on the street and be proud to walk about and say, "I live at Nottingham, I live at St Ann's, I live around that area." But you can't. People say to me, when I go to different places, "Where do you come from?" I say Nottingham. "What part?" "St Ann's." "Ugh!" This disheartens you from the start.'

This represents a fairly clear statement of what most people understand by apathy. Of course apathy, so often blisteringly excoriated, is often 'a private solution to public problems', in the apt words of E. P. Thompson.[7] It can, indeed, be an active and rational response to overwhelming difficulties. If it is unlikely to be a successful response, then it is surely proper to add that many more favoured citizens than those of St Ann's have tried to solve their problems by recourse to inappropriate means. The private solution to the problem of a leaking roof is to stick a bucket under it. The public solution is to raise hell and make the landlord repair it, together with all the other derelict properties he owns: or, beyond this, to agitate for the provision of decent living accommodation as a right. If people do not pursue the public solution, it is not necessarily because they are 'lazy'. You cannot be lazy in seeking to answer a leaky roof with a bucket: you have to be alive to every change in the weather, and when it rains you have to rush up and down

7. *Out of Apathy*, Stevens, 1960.

stairs to empty the pail. The plain truth is that the private answer in such a case is proven and effective in the short run. The public solution is all too theoretical and abstract, and the established organizations are all too willing to leave things that way. For this reason, the comparative weaknesses of the public organizations of the area should hardly be blamed on the indolence of the people, and left at that. A few intelligent and generous initiatives in the district might produce a response which would surprise many of the people who are responsible for the leadership and conduct of those organizations. But intelligence in such a context requires an ability to see the connexions between the manifest want and neglect which are raging through it and the whole social outgrowth of privilege and comfort which sucks its nourishment from such an unlikely subsoil. And generosity requires more than kindness: it needs the ability to draw a line of implacable hostility between the men and women who are subjected to such conditions, and those people who draw their influence and power from a willingness to impose such a way of life on others.

There is no housing problem in St Ann's; there is no poverty problem in all the squalid corners of the conurbations of Great Britain; there is no problem of cultural deprivation and educational starvation in all our larger cities; what there is, is a problem, and a vast problem at that, of the arousal of self-confident joint action among the poor. There is lack of compassion and it is, as always, ugly. But it is not the crucial element in the situation. Comfortable people may well only discover their common humanity with the forgotten Englishmen in all their big towns when these towns are brought to life by the clamant demands of the poor themselves. The growing crisis of British politics is, in great measure, revealed in this situation. Not only do people not know how the other half lives: they scarcely know that the other half exists. Things accordingly get worse. As conditions become more acute, the 'remedies' advanced appear more piddling and more irrelevant. In the interests of humane polity even more than in the interests of sheer economic survival, vast structural changes are long overdue in the political economy of this country. Such changes will never be approached until the means are found to voice and organize the unrepresented interests whose silent and amorphous shadow hangs over us all.

6 Learning to Live in St Ann's

In 1876 they built a school in St Ann's. Perhaps in those days it was an imposing building, with its tall neo-gothic windows. Now it is dirty and the soot-dampened rays of whatever sun gets through to St Ann's find it difficult to make their way to the children. The children, of course, are still there, packed in the warrened corridors and classrooms, or loosed into the minuscule playgrounds which were scalloped out on two distinct and unconnectable levels. Eight or ten minutes walk away is the nearest green patch, the one recreation ground which serves the margins of St Ann's: and the top forms of the school have to crocodile down to the park in order to do their physical jerks, unless it rains or is too cold, in which case they are marched into the local Church Hall. It is a junior school, and rather than take the smallest children across busy main roads, they are exercised in the tiny playgrounds. The big kids are taken swimming in the Victoria Baths and to get there they have to be shepherded in a convoy for twenty minutes.

This school contains ten useable classrooms, one of which has a sink, because it once passed as a biology laboratory at a time when the school also served to teach seniors. Through two classrooms there is an all-day stream of traffic to and from the cloakrooms, which are so situated as to cause the maximum social interaction, since they straddle the only entrance. Life is interesting for the teachers in these rooms, not only because of the processions which need to come and go through them, but also because of the noise that filters in from the playground while the first and second years are doing P.T. School dinners, until a year ago, were served in a dining centre, which involved another set of pilgrimages, across two hectic main roads. Now a small dining-room has been provided, and the children can be fed in two sittings. In the Assembly Hall it is hard to keep order because the room is too small to pack in the children in any civilized way. As is general in St Ann's the lavatories are out in the rain; perhaps this encourages control of the natural functions. The cloakrooms have stone floors and intermittent supplies of hot water. The Director of Education describes this as 'the worst school in the city'.

Another school is comparatively modern. It was finished in 1892, stowed away in a sidestreet and neatly laid out with six of its eight classrooms converging on to its central hall. In this the infants who use the building do their music lessons, learn to dance and do exercises, and are also taught to pray thankfully to God for all the blessings he has showered upon them. Although this is a lot more convenient than the junior school's arrangements, the accumulated effect of all this dancing, knees-bending, singing and praying is, as our observer put it, 'rather disturbing for the other classes'. Other classes can get their own back by maintaining a constant through traffic for everything they need to fetch and carry. Our observer wrote, charitably, that this 'has its advantages, for it helps to maintain a family atmosphere'. There is the same dearth of cloakrooms, storage space, sinks, as in the junior school. Since the new dinner centre has been erected in the playground, the children have been spared the daily trek across two perilously busy streets.

What of the children who are put through these slum prisons? They are not well developed. They are on average smaller and less hardy than the middle-class kids from the suburbs. They don't win at the inter-school games. They lack stamina, fall ill easily and are often absent from school. Every epidemic which hits the city booms in St Ann's. The school health service reports that fresh starters are often in need of attention for complaints which would ordinarily have been under care for some time. In one school a fifth of the children are treated each year for nits, as compared with just over a twentieth of the children at a school on a council estate, and none of the commuter-suburb schoolchildren. They catch all sorts of other things, which are then shared around. Impetigo is common. They are not starving, but they frequently suffer from ill-balanced diets. Some of them come to school without breakfast, either because mother went off to work before them, or perhaps because the family got up late. A third of them get free school meals, as against a thirtieth of the children on the housing estate. Approximately 6,000 children in Nottingham are entitled to free meals. The Education Committee has also budgeted to spend £11,100 on ordinary clothing and about £2,000 on school uniforms for needy children in the city. Since a very large proportion of those people whose incomes were low enough to entitle their children to free meals at school were, at the time of our inquiry, not claiming such benefits (and almost certainly even today a smaller but significant proportion of those entitled to free school milk and meals will not, for a variety of reasons, avail themselves of the opportunity), these figures are an obvious pointer to widespread deprivation.

If St Ann's produces children who are often physically stunted, delicate or retarded, it also provides its quota of emotional problems for the young. As many as two fifths of the school population investigated came from broken homes and 16 per cent were educationally subnormal. Eccentric behaviour was, not surprisingly, common in class. The fact that so many children were obviously disturbed or insecure had an unsettling effect on some of those who had otherwise stable backgrounds. It should not be thought that St Ann's is altogether exceptional in this respect, even in Nottingham. In a separate project of investigation into Educational Priority Areas (as defined in the *Plowden Report*) we found, in one school in the Meadows, another extensive Nottingham slum for which no plans exist for serious redevelopment in the next decade or more, the following picture: 90 per cent of the children were considered by their teachers to be to some extent emotionally disturbed; 65 per cent lived in homes in which their families shared accommodation with other families; 55 children out of 96 taking school meals received them free. To these figures should be added the teachers' impressions that probably all the children lived in substandard houses, that very many children lived in conditions of gross overcrowding, that many also lived in homes without high standards of cleanliness, in split families, in unstable houses, in unsettled families which moved house often or in homes which lacked books and in which parents did not take any great interest in the education of their children. Among immigrant children there were the familiar difficulties of language. 8 children spoke very poor English. Another 8 were considered to be severely retarded. About 50 children had both parents working. 16 lacked a father living at home, one lacked a mother, and two lacked both parents. The social-class composition of the school was as follows:

Table 6.

Fathers' Occupation	Number of children
Professional and managerial	Nil
Clerical	3
Skilled workers	16
Unskilled workers	263

As a direct correlative of these kinds of circumstance, the children of St Ann's are intellectually handicapped. Our investigator found that many lacked range and scope: not only were they little used to conditional modes of thought, but on joining the schools they seldom had any idea about play with paints, water, sand or clay. They had almost no experience of pencils, pictures or books. Consequently they lacked the prerequisites of reading ability. Shape discrimination was very imperfectly developed among them, although it can very easily be perfected by play with jigsaw puzzles, not to mention the variety of toy-apparatus which is common in middle-class homes. Their word stock was small. In a word, they were backward. Arriving as retarded children in the infant classes, all too often they rose to the junior grades in the same condition. Very many of them could not read when they passed into the junior school. Over a third of them were still retarded when they left that level. In addition to those children who were manifestly educationally subnormal, many more were borderline cases. Few found their way into special schools: there were not many places. Some 16 per cent are tested each year for educational subnormality. All of them, their teachers believe, would benefit from some kind of specialized teaching. However, a mere handful are allotted places in the special schools. The rest remain behind, and are not notable either for their ability to concentrate, or for their conformity to those norms of behaviour which most teachers take for granted. Our reporter claimed that this 'drags down the general level of class attainment'.

There is a strong case for suggesting that such a lowering of attainment is by no means inevitable in places like St Ann's, if both modern teaching methods *and adequate amenities* are made available. However it seems likely that given the present woefully inadequate material provision and a teaching staff which, while it is imbued with the most self-sacrificing ethos and the highest possible goodwill, has little sociological understanding, in this case our reporter may well be right. Modern pedagogy has little scope effectively to put out its wings in such thin air. It would be crass to blame the harassed teachers for the results: a quarter of the children of St Ann's cannot read by the time they are seven: nearly half the seven-year-olds have reading ages of between four and five; a further third, between five and six: less than a tenth are average readers for their own age, and only 4 per cent are up to two years ahead of their peer-group.[1] This compares with almost 60 per cent of the children aged seven in a commuter suburb on the outskirts of Nottingham, who had reading ages between one and five years in advance of the normal standards.

1. The difficulties which underline these figures are summed up by one of St Ann's headmistresses, Mrs N. Heyes: 'We begin by setting up what we think is a satisfactory environment: we try to give these children emotional security and establish a contact between teacher and child. Any teacher who can write in her daily report "Today William smiled at me" has probably achieved as much as a teacher somewhere else who could write "Today Johnny did five pages of sums".'

In Nottingham, in spite of thirteen years of protest by the local Labour Party and other reformers, comprehensive schooling is still a long way off. Successive councils, under the sway of leaders of either party, have stonewalled on this issue with inspired doggedness. One of the results is that Nottingham children are still tested at eleven plus, and sorted either into grammar or modern schools, or equivalent streams in bilateral schools. The touchstone of such selection is a verbal reasoning test in which, obviously, past reading performance greatly affects the resultant score. Presented with a modest fanfare as 'the abolition of the eleven plus', this rather shady substitution possibly worked long enough to win a few votes for someone in one local election and certainly a temporary lull in inner-party conflict. What it did not do was to improve the life-expectations of any of the poor children of St Ann's.

When we took a count of the number of children who obtained grammar-school places from St Ann's, it was so small that we could not believe our results. Accordingly, we approached the local education office, and several members of our study group, who worked in the probation service, were kindly allowed to go through the local records and compile, street by street, a full count of the grammar-school places held by St Ann's children. We found that they were 1·5 per cent of the school population. In the residential suburb which our original investigation had taken as a control, 60 per cent of the children were allocated grammar-school places in the year in question. We published these figures and local officials were quick to comment on them. We were accused of distortion. Less gently, one alderman, a prominent member of the Conservative group on the council, declaimed that we ought to 'stay out of St Ann's' and that 'bearded nits' from the University ought to concentrate their investigations on the problems raised within the University itself. The Director of Education produced some figures which purported to disprove the results of our research. We were barred from prosecuting further inquiries in the files of the education office and teachers became reluctant to talk to us.

Of course, whether social investigators are allowed to report the matter or not, the fact remains that only 1·5 per cent of the child population of St Ann's gets into grammar school. This is more worrying than the indecently secretive responses of the local authority, which might well be forgiven a slight flush of shame.[2] It can, of course, be argued that aptitude for grammar-schooling is a characteristic which is determined by physical inheritance, and that substandard genes are to blame for the educational record of places like St Ann's. Although this type of explanation is now universally discounted by enlightened educators, it is still current among certain educational administrators who seem largely to base their resistance to such reforms as the introduction of comprehensive schooling on the (nowadays usually unstated) assumption that intelligence is transmitted through the penis at the moment of conception rather than developed in the social interaction of human beings. Mercifully, such whimsies are not now current either in the majority of teachers' training colleges, or in the majority of public offices concerned with education.

2. We have already explained in 'Adult Education and Social Research – A Case Paper', (Occasional Papers in Social Research, No. 2) published by Nottingham University Department of Adult Education, 1968, how the Director of Education was able to arrive at a much more comforting figure than ours. If you add up all the grammar-school places which are allotted to the *schools* of St Ann's, you get a much higher figure than the one we revealed, which applies to the *children* of St Ann's. The reason is plain : some of the schools in St Ann's draw into their catchment areas children from outside it, including some from much wealthier middle-class districts. These kids go to grammar school. When we pointed this out, it did not stop the Director from continuing to quote his original figures. When journalists from the *Observer* interviewed the officers of the Education Department, they quoted us on this matter : they were told that there was no way in which the Department could define an area other than by taking the schools within it as primary units. This would be a more reasonable reply if the whole of this particular area had not been scheduled for demolition : and it would have assisted us if such definitional problems had been made plainer in the official pronouncements, instead of their claim that our figures were 'false', as if we had invented them.

A fair statement of what are basic assumptions in modern pedagogy runs like this:

'Learning to learn' should not be confused with the early teaching of the child to read, to spell, and even to do simple arithmetic. Such coaching in the home is merely trying to do the school's task before the child enters public education. 'Learning to learn' is a far more basic type of learning than coaching the child on school learning. It includes motivating the child to find pleasure in learning. It involves developing the child's ability to attend to others and to engage in purposive action. It includes training the child to delay the gratification of his desires and wishes and to work for rewards and goals which are more distant. It includes developing the child's view of adults as sources of information and ideas. ... Through such development the child changes his self-expectations and his expectations of others.[3]

The American research workers who have advocated this view, which represents a widely consensual statement, continue:

While all of this is not absent in the culturally deprived home, it does not play such a central role in child rearing in such homes. The size of the family, the concern of the parents with the basic necessities of life, the low level of educational development of the parents, the frequent absence of a male parent, and the lack of a great deal of interaction between children and adults all conspire to reduce the stimulation, language development, and intellectual development of such children. If the home does not and cannot provide these basic developments, the child is likely to be handicapped in much of his later learning and the prognosis for his educational development is poor. Such a child is likely to have difficulty and to be constantly frustrated by the demands of the typical elementary-school programme. His frustrations and disappointments in school are likely to have an adverse effect on his view of himself and his main desire must be to escape from the virtual imprisonment which school comes to represent for him.

Since it has been clear for a very long time that measured in-

3. B. S. Bloom, A. Davis, and R. Hess, *Compensatory Education for Cultural Deprivation*, Holt, Rinehart & Winston, 1965, pp. 15–16.

telligence can be considerably increased by environmental changes, it is immediately obvious that an understanding of such environmental handicaps to learning as these *should* lead to real possibilities of remedial action. In fact, a vast research industry has been at work,[4] but it has produced all too little direct and active response by the authorities. It is increasingly plain that what slum children lack is not native wit, nor abstract intelligence, but adequate social investment. Dr J. W. B. Douglas has stated the problem with admirable economy:

When housing conditions are unsatisfactory, children make relatively low scores in the tests. This is so in each social class but whereas the middle-class children, as they get older, reduce this handicap, the manual working-class children from unsatisfactory homes fall even further behind; for them, overcrowding and other deficiencies at home have a progressive and depressive influence on their test performance.[5]

Careful study of the evidence on this score leads Douglas to this conclusion:

The pool of talent found at the end of the secondary school period is likely to be only a portion of that which would be found if it were possible to draw fully on potential rather than realized ability. *Over a period of three years in the primary schools, there is a substantial loss of ability in the manual working-class children which could be prevented, it seems, by better teaching, even if the attitude of working-class parents towards education does not change* [our italics].[6]

Such evidence has become too strong to allow continued official credence for genetic explanations of educational inequality. Certainly the most advanced statement to come from an official quarter on these issues is to be found in the Plowden Committee's *Report*[7], which marks a breakthrough in that it

4. For documentation on some of this work, see A. H. Halsey, J. Floud, and C. A. Anderson, *Education, Economy, and Society*, Free Press, New York, 1961, Parts III and IV.

5. *The Home and the School*, Panther Books, 1967, p. 67.

6. ibid., p. 160.

7. *Children and Their Primary Schools:* A Report of the Central Advisory Council for Education, H.M.S.O., 1967.

registers the problem in a manner which demands attention from the policy-makers. The heart of the *Report*, in so far as our work has been concerned, is to be found in its treatment of Educational Priority Areas:

In our cities there are whole districts which have been scarcely touched by the advances made in more fortunate places. Yet such conditions have been overcome and striking progress has been achieved where sufficiently determined and comprehensive attack has been made on the problem. In the most deprived areas, one of H.M. Inspectors reported, 'Some heads approach magnificence, but they cannot do everything. . . . The demands on them as welfare agents are never ending.' Many children with parents in the least skilled jobs do outstandingly well in school. The educational aspirations of parents and the support and encouragement given to children in some of the poorest neighbourhoods are impressive. Over half of the unskilled workers in our National Survey want their children to be given homework to do after school hours; over half want their children to stay at school beyond the minimum leaving age. One third of them hoped their children would go to a grammar school or one with similar opportunities. The educational aspirations of unskilled workers for their children have risen year by year. It has been stressed to us that the range of ability in all social classes is so wide that there is a great reservoir of unrealized potential in families dependent on the least skilled and lowest paid work. A larger part of the housing programme than ever before is to be devoted to rebuilding and renewing obsolete and decaying neighbourhoods. The opportunity must be seized to re-build the schools as well as the houses, and to see that both schools and houses serve families from every social class. It will be possible to make some progress in reducing the size of classes in primary schools in these areas as well as elsewhere. Colleges of education which have taken a special interest in deprived areas report that their students respond in an encouraging fashion to the challenge of working in these neighbourhoods. Most important of all, there is a growing awareness in the nation at large, greatly stimulated, we believe, by our predecessors' Reports, of the complex social handicaps afflicting such areas and the need for a more radical assault on their problems. These are the strengths on which we can build. How can they be brought to bear ?

We propose a nation-wide scheme for helping those schools

and neighbourhoods in which children are most severely handicapped. This policy will have an influence over the whole educational system, and it colours all the subsequent recommendations in our Report. It must not be put into practice simply by robbing more fortunate areas of all the opportunities for progress to which they have been looking forward; it can only succeed if a larger share of the nation's resources is devoted to education.

Impressive evidence was marshalled in the *Report*, to show how great is the growing division between the social and educational expectations of the deprived groups and those of the rest of society. While the *Crowther Report* [8], published in 1959, had emphasized 'how sharply the average standard of living has risen' since the war, and insisted that full employment, with 'the combined effect of inflation, of progressive taxation, and of the social-security schemes of the Welfare State has been to direct the larger part of the rise in the national standard of consumption to the lower income groups', Plowden, on the other hand, insists 'there has not been any appreciable narrowing of the gap between the least well off and the rest of the population'. After considering the evidence about class differences in health, perinatal mortality, stillbirth rates and living conditions, and looking at the implications of the Milner Holland Committee's study of London housing conditions, the Plowden Committee went on to recommend differential treatment for the schools in especially deprived areas, as an attempt to begin remedial work within them. They recommended the designation of 'Educational Priority Areas' to discriminate in favour of deprived populations in the allocation of resources.

The many teachers who do so well in face of adversity cannot manage without cost to themselves. They carry the burdens of parents, probation officers, and welfare officers on top of their classroom duties. It is time the nation came to their aid. The principle, already accepted, that special need calls for special help, should be given a new cutting edge. We ask for 'positive discrimination' in favour of such schools and the children in them, going

8. *A Report of the Central Advisory Council for Education* (*The Crowther Report*), H.M.S.O., 1959, pp. 45–7.

well beyond an attempt to equalize resources. Schools in deprived areas should be given priority in many respects. The first step must be to raise the schools with low standards to the national average; the second, quite deliberately, to make them better. The justification is that the homes and neighbourhoods from which many of their children come provide little support and stimulus for learning. The schools must supply a compensating environment. The attempts so far made within the educational system to do this have not been sufficiently generous or sustained, because the handicaps imposed by the environment have not been explicitly and sufficiently allowed for – they should be.

The proposition that good schools should make up for a poor environment is far from new. It derives from the notion that there should be equality of opportunity for all, but recognizes that children in some districts will only get the same opportunity as those who live elsewhere if they have unequally generous treatment. It was accepted before the First World War that some children could not be effectively taught until they had been properly fed. Hence free meals were provided. Today their need is for enriched intellectual nourishment. Planned and positive discrimination in favour of deprived areas could bring about an advance in the education of children in the 1970s as great as the advance in their nutrition to which school meals and milk contributed so much.

Every authority where deprivation is found should be asked to adopt 'positive discrimination' within its own area, and to report from time to time on the progress made. Some authorities control schools or even one school of this kind where deprivation is so serious that they need special help. Most of these schools and areas are already well known to teachers, administrators, local Inspectors, and H.M. Inspectors. Local knowledge will not be sufficient to justify decisions which are bound on occasion to be controversial. Objective criteria for the selection of 'educational priority schools and areas' will be needed to identify those schools which need special help and to determine how much assistance should be given by the government. Our national survey showed the prime importance of parental attitudes, and it might be thought that a measure of these attitudes could be devised. But the data for the selection of priority schools and areas must be readily available, without additional surveys, and in any event the validity of answers given by parents with the education of their children at stake might fairly be questioned. The criteria required must identify those places where educational handicaps are reinforced by social handicaps. Some of the main criteria which could be used in an assessment of deprivation are given below. They are not placed in order of importance, nor is any formula suggested by which they should be combined. They may require further study. The criteria are:

(a) *Occupation*. The National Census can report on occupations within quite small areas, and, for particular schools, the data can be supplemented without too much difficulty. The analyses would show the proportions of unskilled and semi-skilled manual workers.

(b) *Size of Families*. The larger the family, the more likely are the children to be in poverty. Wages are no larger for a married man with young children than they are for a single man with none. Family size is still associated with social class, and men with four or more children tend to be amongst the lowest wage earners. Family size also correlates with the results of intelligence tests – the larger the family, the lower the scores of the children. The children are liable to suffer from a double handicap, both genetic and environmental – the latter because, it is suggested, they have less encouragement and stimulus from parents who have more children amongst whom to divide their attention. Those earning the lowest wages often make up their incomes by working longer hours. Often too, their wives have less time and energy to devote to their children. Family size likewise correlates with nutrition, with physical growth, and with overcrowding, and is therefore an apt indicator (when allowance is made for the age structure of the local population, and particularly the number of mothers of child-bearing age) of the poor home conditions for which schools should compensate. The National Census, supplemented by the schools censuses made by the education authorities, would provide the information required.

(c) *Supplements in Cash or Kind from the State* are of various kinds. Where the parents are needy, children are allowed school meals free. The proportions so benefiting vary greatly from school to school, and afford a reasonably good guide to relative need. The procedures laid down are designed to give free meals according to scales similar to those used by the Ministry of Social Security. Another criterion of the same type is the number of families depending on National Assistance, or its future equivalent, in a particular locality. The weakness of these criteria taken by themselves is that some people do not know their rights or are unwilling to seek them.

(d) *Overcrowding and Sharing of Houses* should certainly be included amongst the criteria. It will identify families in cramped accommodation in central and run-down areas of our cities. It is a less sure guide than some others because it may miss the educational needs of some housing estates and other areas which can also be severe.

(e) *Poor Attendance and Truancy* are a pointer to home conditions, and to what Burt long ago singled out as a determinant of school progress, the 'efficiency of the mother'. Truancy is also related to delinquency. The National Survey showed that four per cent of the children in the sample were absent, on their teachers' assessment, for unsatisfactory reasons. (Appendix 5, paragraph 27.)

(f) *Proportions of Retarded, Disturbed, or Handicapped Pupils* in ordinary schools. These vary from authority to authority according to the special schools available and the policies governing their use. But, everywhere, the proportions tend to be highest in deprived districts. It is accepted that special schools need additional staff, and the same advantages should be extended to normal schools with many pupils of a similar kind.

(g) *Incomplete Families* where one or other of the parents is dead, or not living at home for whatever reason, are often unable to provide a satisfactory upbringing for their children without special help.

(h) *Children Unable to Speak English* need much extra attention if they are to find their feet in England. This is already recognized in arranging teachers' quotas, but should also be used as a general criterion.

All authorities would be asked to consider which of their schools should qualify, to rank them according to criteria such as those we have listed, and to submit supporting data. Advice would also be available from H.M. Inspectors of Schools. In this way the Department of Education and Science would have full information both about the social and the educational needs of the school and areas. Many of the criteria would be closely correlated. With experience the data required could be simplified so as to ease administration; but meanwhile, a wide variety of criteria should be employed. The schools near the bottom of the resulting rankings would be entitled to priority. We envisage a formal procedure enabling the Secretary of State for Education and Science to designate particular schools or groups of schools as priority schools or areas. Those so designated would qualify for the favourable treatment. Local education authorities would submit regular reports on these schools to the Secretary of State for the purpose of determining what progress was being made, how long their designation should continue, which aspects of the programme were proving most effective, and what further steps should be taken.

This prescription was a bold and imaginative one, on the whole. But to be effectively applied it needed immediate and expensive action. Such action has not been forthcoming, on anything like the required scale. On 29 August 1967, it was announced by the Department of Education and Science that £16 million was to be allocated for school building in Educational Priority Areas. The Secretary of State declined to designate E.P.A.s himself, on the grounds that local education authorities 'are well placed to judge which districts suffer from the deficiences which the Plowden Council had in mind'.[9] The allocation was to be made for both major and minor works, and to be spread over the two years 1968–70. On 19 November 1968, Mr Crosland's successor, Mr Short, announced that some 5,000 teachers in 500 schools were to get increments of £75 on their salaries, in consonance with the Plowden recommendations.[10] Plowden had recommended increments of £120 as a 'first step' and L.E.A.s had submitted a list of at least 1,500 schools which they felt to be qualified for such aid.

The Plowden Committee itself has not been satisfied with the subsequent actions of the Department of Education: it issued a statement on 10 January 1969, saying that 'piecemeal progress' had been made, but that the Department 'has not for-

9. D.E.S. Press Release, 29 August 1967.
10. *The Times*, 19 November 1968.

mulated a systematic policy' in response to its *Report*.[11] Of course, the general economic stringency can be cited as the major reason for the very modest efforts which have been made to implement the most important recommendations of the *Report*. The question is one which involves, like all other problems of poverty, a determination of priorities. By leaving the designation of E.P.A.s to local authorities, the Government does something to minimize the claims which are made upon it. Not every local council is as quick as it might be to take advantage of such facilities as are offered. An inquiry we made into this problem revealed a surprisingly large number of L.E.A.s which had never asked for any assistance under this dispensation. Many of them governed industrial cities in which it seems unlikely that there are no deprived areas. Of those which do make claims, many are disappointed. The Nottingham authority designated seventeen schools as, in its view, qualifying for these allowances, but only eight were approved by the Department. Nottingham teachers were considerably dissatisfied with this result, which resulted in a number of anomalies: for instance, the Douglas Infants School received the increments, while the adjacent Douglas Junior School did not.

But all this is part of a general crisis. The Plowden Committee recommended very modest steps to meet an extremely serious problem. Obviously, 'positive discrimination' would need to discriminate *very* positively even to begin to meet the kinds of problem we have been describing. Such a beginning in education would mean a very long-term, slow-moving reform in relation to the whole social problem in all its complexity and depth. But even this beginning is applied hesitantly, too little, too late, and in too random a fashion. To rejuvenate the schools as a means to enlivening the society as a whole sounds an attractive strategy for reform. But the balance-sheet of achievement, since Lady Plowden's Committee published its findings, indicates that a more difficult, but doubtless more effective strategy will involve the improvement of the schools

11. *Daily Telegraph*, 10 January 1969.

as a result of an awakening of the poor themselves. It seems increasingly clear that 'social justice', in this field as in most others, requires energetic advocates among its would-be beneficiaries. You get the rights you fight for. Tell it in St Ann's.

7 A Culture of Poverty?

Anyone who seeks, seriously, to understand how a deprived community lives, will quickly come to appreciate that the different threads and strands of life down-town are ravelled together to form a knot of great complexity. In our case, what began as a straighforward, almost naïve, curiosity about the extent of material poverty rapidly developed into a much clearer understanding of the complex dimensions of the many different deprivations which are experienced in a district like St Ann's. To begin with, there was the substantial proportion of the population actually living below the poverty line. This was by no means a uniform group, but a most heterogeneous and varied sample of people whose circumstances differed almost as markedly as did their abilities to cope with those circumstances. Secondly, there was the gross environmental deprivation: the poor housing, the density of population, the dirt, the lack of privacy: all crucial aspects of life in St Ann's, which affected everyone who lived there, irrespective of their personal circumstances. Thirdly, there was the social deprivation, reflected in the poverty of public facilities, the gaunt Victorian school-buildings, and the absence of parks and open spaces. Just as their environmental and social deprivations affected everyone who lived in the neighbourhood, so somehow, nearly everyone seemed to be caught up in a characteristic and distinctive set of social and political attitudes. This is not to suggest that everyone in a district like St Ann's thinks alike; such a suggestion would be manifestly absurd. But there seems to be a common context or 'atmosphere' from which individual views emerge. In nearly every interview we under-took, we detected a basic sense of hopelessness, or powerless-ness, underlying, and at the same time reinforced by, people's fatalistic acceptance of their situation. Although the degree of resignation or despair may vary from one man or woman to another, and although it is possible to nourish greater hopes and wider expectations in some families than in others, there are still very few people (even among the young) who express unqualified self-confidence or optimism. This is not to say that people in St Ann's are perpetually gloomy or lugubrious; far from it. One is constantly aware of a warmth, generosity, and humour – so often more characteristic of the poor than of those with more to lose. The difference we would emphasize is that cheerfulness and optimism find an almost exclusively private expression, and are not reflected in any sense of public or political optimism. The overwhelming majority fail to have any broad social expectations, almost as though they have learned that such expectations are beyond their reach or con-trol. When cheerful optimism is felt, it is not because things are getting any better, but because they are not getting much worse. Many of those interviewed were only too conscious of their discomforts and deprivations, but this consciousness did not generally find a purposive expression. All too often complaints were made in the same tone that one might adopt when com-plaining of the weather, and while grievances were frequently expressed in a mood of justifiable irritation, this seemed to represent some kind of attempt to come to terms with what we outsiders felt to be an unbearable situation, rather than any idea of changing it.

W. G. Runciman has lucidly stated the core of this problem in his study on *Relative Deprivation and Social Justice*:

Political theorists of many different persuasions have wondered at the acquiescence of the underprivileged in the inequalities to which they are subjected, and have explained this acquiescence in terms of ignorance, or habit, or traditionally restricted expectation. If the least fortunate strata of society – Saint Simon's *'classe la plus nombreuse ou la plus pauvre'* – were fully aware of how unequally they were being treated, would not all societies break out into revolution? 'What is needed,' said Durkheim, 'if social order is to reign is that the mass of men be content with their lot. But what is needed for them to be content, is not that they have more or less but that they be convinced that they have no right to more.' In stable societies with a long and unbroken history of customary inequalities, it is not difficult to see how the aspirations of the underprivileged could be kept low enough for the pattern to remain undisturbed. But once the possibility of improvement has been disclosed, it becomes more remarkable that inequalities should continue to be passively accepted by the great majority of those at the lower levels of society. We must beware of confusing acquiescence with contentment; the impossibility of remedy can inhibit action without inhibiting the sense of grievance. But even in societies which are no longer 'traditional', it is only rarely that egalitarian resentments are as militant or as widespread as the actual structure of inequalities would suggest to be plausible.[1]

The aptness of these observations was at once apparent to us: one has only to stroll up the hill from St Ann's, out of the cobbled and grimy streets into the green and spacious avenues of Mapperley, to look at the rose-gardens in bloom, or to admire the solidly constructed houses, to wonder whether either at the top or the bottom of the ridge there is any conception of common humanity.

That there is an enormous disparity in living standards between the richer and the poorer people in our society is self-evident: but to find, as we did, some of the relatively wealthy living cheek-by-jowl with some of the poorest, separated by little more than a main road, at once brings the whole problem into a sharper and more urgent focus. Needless to say, elaborate discussion about such differences in living standards, even among near-neighbours, figures prominently in the academic literature on the subject. There are two predominant themes in the discussions, two approaches to the same question which are, in important respects, not consonant with one another.

The first theme can be called the 'culture of poverty' approach. This argues that the poor constitute a distinctive cul-

1. Routledge & Kegan Paul, 1966, pp. 25–6.

ture or community within society; that the experiences, attitudes, and values generated in poor communities are passed on from one generation to the next in a never-ending cycle; that the life of the poor proceeds at a different rhythm, with different preoccupations from those of society at large, and involves different conceptions of what is and what might be: all of these separate the poor from the rest of society – not only economically, but also intellectually and emotionally.

The most distinguished spokesman of the 'culture of poverty' argument is the American anthropologist Oscar Lewis; in a series of books he has evoked with great detail and vivid insight the tempo and quality of life among the poor of Mexico and Central America. In his most recent study,[2] he has tersely and vividly outlined the basic characteristics of the culture of poverty and the circumstances in which such a culture develops. It is, he says, 'both an adaptation and a reaction of the poor to their marginal position in a class-stratified, highly individuated, capitalistic society. It represents an effort to cope with feelings of hopelessness and despair which develop from the realization of the improbability of achieving success in terms of the values and goals of the larger society.' ... It is able 'to perpetuate itself from generation to generation because of its effect on the children. By the time slum children are age six or seven they have usually absorbed the basic attitudes and values of their subculture, and are not psychologically geared to take full advantage of changing conditions or increased opportunities which may occur in their lifetime.' At the same time 'it is also something positive and provides some rewards without which the poor could hardly carry on', such as 'local solutions for problems not met by existing institutions and agencies because the people are not eligible for them, cannot afford them, or are ignorant of or suspicious of them'. Among the characteristics of those living in the culture of poverty, Lewis stresses

the lack of effective participation ... in the major institutions of the larger society ... they have a low level of literacy and education,

2. *La Vida*, Panther Books, 1968.

usually do not belong to labour unions, are not members of political parties, generally do not participate in the national welfare agencies, and make very little use of banks, hospitals, department stores, museums, or art galleries. They have a critical attitude towards some of the basic institutions of the dominant classes, hatred of the police, mistrust of government and those in high position, and a cynicism which extends over to the church ... [they] are aware of middle-class values, talk about them, and even claim some of them as their own, but on the whole they do not live by them ... on the local community level, we find poor housing conditions, crowding, gregariousness, but above all a minimum of organization beyond the level of the nuclear and extended family ... [although] there may be a sense of community and *esprit de corps* ... people with a culture of poverty are provincial and locally oriented and have very little sense of history. They know only their own troubles, their own local conditions, their own neighbourhood, their own way of life.

In *The Other America* Michael Harrington uses the term 'culture of poverty' to describe the situation of the poor in the United States:

Taken as a whole, poverty is a culture. Taken on the family level, it has the same quality. These are people who lack education and skill, who have bad health, poor housing, low levels of aspiration, and high levels of mental distress. They are, in the language of sociology, 'multi-problem' families. Each disability is the more intense because it exists within a web of disabilities. And if one problem is solved, and the others are left constant, there is little gain.

Harrington goes on to claim that 'there is a language of the poor, a psychology of the poor, a world view of the poor. To be impoverished is to be an internal alien, to grow up in a culture which is radically different from the one that dominates the society.' [3]

3. Macmillan, 1962. We should beware, however, of attempting to explain as 'cultural', behaviour which may well have a simple physiological or environmental root. Alvin Schorr has pointed out that depression, loss of ambition, apathy and lethargy are characteristic symptoms of malnutrition, or deficiences of diet. Similarly he has stressed that living in overcrowded and insanitary housing, apart from the obvious health hazards, often means a lack of sleep, or disturbed sleep, with

These notions of the culture of poverty have been developed out of field-research in the villages and urban slums of Mexico, Puerto Rico, and the United States; clearly they have their roots in a complex of circumstances, traditions, and expectations far removed from what we know in this country. Nevertheless, in a number of important respects there seems to be a parallel between the descriptions of Lewis and Harrington, and our own first impressions of slum life in Nottingham. Certainly we observed the hopelessness and despair, we saw that our respondents did not participate to any significant degree in the 'major institutions' of the larger society, even in such organizations as trade unions where a basic self-interest might be assumed. (In highly deprived areas even such institutions as the schools, which all children must by law attend, fail to make much of an impression, as is clear from the *Plowden Report*.) However, it seems to us that the really crucial difficulty involved in this approach is to determine exactly what is meant by the poor being 'aware of middle-class values, even claiming some of them as their own' and in exactly what ways such people 'do not live by' these values. If 'middle-class values' means simply certain conventions of family life, or Calvinist attitudes to work and thrift, or standards of sexual morality, then it is possible to find evidence for the existence of certain subcultural groupings; however these are not co-extensive with the whole communities we studied. Rather, there are clusters of subcriminal groups, colonies of problem families, which, as we have shown, are among the heaviest crosses which their respectable but equally poor neighbours feel themselves unjustly called upon to bear. Indeed, where the

---

consequent sluggishness and lethargy. Overcrowding may also, he suggests, produce other social patterns, such as 'children freed or freeing themselves early from parental control; a good deal of disorganization in everyday routines; little studying, poor work habits and poor self-discipline and little communication between parents and children'. It may be revealing to discuss such observations in terms of a culture-pattern, 'but, perhaps the link, simpler and less esoteric, lies in the stark facts of the way they live'. (Alvin Schorr, 'The Non-Culture of Poverty', *American Journal of Orthopsychiatry*, Vol. xxxiv, No. 5, October 1964.)

'respectable' poor are affected by the syndromes of hopelessness and despair, it is as often as not because they feel they are being 'dragged down' by the encroachment of the fringes of these groups. The evidence we have already cited about the attitudes of long-established residents in St Ann's to some of the newcomers who have either been parachuted into local-authority-owned cheap houses, or who have gravitated into relatively low-rent privately owned accommodation, graphically sustains this view.

But if 'middle-class values' are to be interpreted in the wider sense, as meaning the dominant socio-political assumptions, then the whole story is somewhat different. The extent to which the poor both are, and are not, of society hinges on the degree of their own ambivalence towards these assumptions. There are probably more reproductions of Annigoni's portrait of the Queen in St Ann's' pubs than there are in all the commuter gin-palaces of Nottingham put together. Does this mean that St Ann's is politically committed to the *status quo*? Indeed, does it even mean that St Ann's is more royalist than the dormitory estates? This is surely doubtful. At a deeper, and far more significant, level, to what extent do St Ann's residents accept the value-system which has grown up as a function of the received economic structure? How far do they regard working as employees, as wage-slaves, as inevitable? How far do they see the given distribution of income within society as 'natural'? How far do they see the power-structure under which they live as 'normal'? The sociological concept which enables us to come to grips with this problem most adequately is that elaborated by Marx: to what extent does 'commodity-fetishism' or more general 'false consciousness' determine the attitudes of the people in St Ann's, and is that extent greater or lesser than we find elsewhere in society? In short, are the people we studied more, or less, capable of visualizing an alternative structure of society than their contemporaries?

It is of course possible to reject these 'middle-class values' in more than one way. One can offer one's rejection in various forms of 'deviance', culminating in what will be called 'criminality': or one can begin to evolve positive forms of rejection, based from the start upon cooperative, collective action, beginning with the development of such organizations as trade unions and moving on to various forms of overall political activity.

But in so far as such forms of activity come to seem plausible, and an alternative social structure appears to be a realizable option, then the fatalism and atomization so tellingly described by Oscar Lewis will inevitably begin to give place to new attitudes. Indeed, Lewis himself has made this point: when he looked at a slum district of Havana, after the Cuban Revolution, and compared his impressions with those he had received in the same district a few years earlier, he came to the conclusion that although poverty remained in that area, the 'culture of poverty' did not. Hope had come into people's lives. If a revolution can dissolve the culture of poverty even before appreciably improving the physical condition of the poor, it is not entirely implausible to suggest that effective political organization might begin to do the same thing, even before such organization could prove itself capable of reconstituting social life as a whole. Conversely, in so far as existing organizations are felt to be irrelevant or retrogressive, we can expect the degree of hopelessness and estrangement to intensify.

A variation on the theme of sub-cultures, perhaps more easily subject to empirical investigation than that of Oscar Lewis, has been elaborated by Runciman. He explores the acceptance of different or even divergent standards in what is ostensibly an open society by making use of the concept of 'reference groups'. People can protect themselves from the effects of recognizing the extent of inequality by restricting their own identification, narrowing the social range through which they are prepared to make comparisons with their own position.

If there is some truth in this picture, it needs to be seen in a certain light: buttressed though a sub-group may be against the outer social world, it must, in the modern division of labour, be in some sort of communication with it. Such communication will not simply involve the constant commerce of information, which, indeed, may not flow with any great speed or accuracy; more important is the diffusion of basic systems of values and attitudes – and these gain force for being unstated, implied, assumed.

The distinction between the two approaches, although they are both concerned with the value-systems of the poor, is that one sees their value-system as in significant respects different and detached from that of the more affluent, whereas the other sees it as essentially similar, albeit modified, weakened or neutralized by the critical contexts within which judgements and comparisons are made.

This is more than a nice academic quibble. It is important to a proper understanding of poverty and its effects upon people, and once we recognized it as such it became an increasingly absorbing part of our inquiry. Our basic aim was to see what differences there were between the answers given by the poorer households and those of their more affluent neighbours; but an equally interesting contrast emerged between the answers of the poorer respondents, and those of the declared trade unionists in our sample. (These two groups were, in fact, almost entirely separate, with only a handful of trade unionists among the poorest households.) The trade unionists seemed to resemble least the profile suggested by the description of the culture of poverty; not only were they among the more affluent, but they were integrated into organizations and associations which gave them at least some sort of voice and even certain possibilities of exercising power – if only defensively – within society. The contrast between their attitudes and aspirations and those of their poorer, more isolated and under-represented neighbours might, we thought, throw some light on the problems raised by the 'culture of poverty' argument.

Needless to say, it is not easy to explore the depth and permanence of any person's commitment to a given value-system. In many cases, although there may be a highly developed immediate sense of justice and fair play in any specific and concrete instance, there is a less well-defined, and certainly less consistent, abstract notion of social justice as such. Nonetheless, it is possible to ask a range of linked questions, whose combined answers build up a powerful, though impressionistic, image – first of all, of people's view of the sort of world we are supposed to live in, and secondly, of whether they consider that it represents a fair, equitable, and ultimately acceptable order of things. It is possible, for example, to explore a person's notions of the actual and desirable distribution of income, the limits of his economic expectations, and what he feels about his own place in the economic system. One can ask, for instance, 'How much does a man have to earn to be wealthy?' in order to establish what, for the respondent, constitutes 'wealth' (a condition to which many aspire, though not in a particularly hopeful or expectant way). Or one can ask a person to describe his own economic position (is he, for example, wealthy, comfortably off, hard-pressed, or does he think of himself as poor?). One can inquire how much larger a weekly income a person thinks he would need to live comfortably, to get some idea of the modesty or otherwise of his immediate demands.

Then there is a whole range of questions concerned with the fairness of the present distribution of economic rewards. 'Do you receive a fair wage?'; 'Should there be a minimum wage? If so, what should it be?'; 'Should there be a top limit to wages or salaries?'; 'Are some people paid too much?'; 'Should wage-rates be more equal than they are?'; 'Is the wage you receive a true indication of the contribution you make, or does the employer make a great deal of money out of you?'

The answers to all these questions tell us something about people's understanding of, and commitment to, the present economic system. But our understanding becomes greater when the answers to all these questions are examined together; when the constellation of answers is seen to reveal a pattern, sometimes clear and unambiguous, sometimes bewildering and confused. Interpretation of this sort of data is not easy, and there is ample scope for discussion and disagreement about details. The complete picture which emerges, however, is in outline fairly clear, and goes some way to establishing the limits of consensus about the contemporary economy.

What then, given that some people have more than others, is 'wealth'? The first and most obvious fact about the replies we got to this query is that the people of St Ann's do not think about wealth as being primarily a matter of ownership. Almost everybody answered in terms of a sum of money stated as a weekly income. Very few named an annual income. Hardly anyone named a capital sum, although a few people named objects: 'a car and a house', for instance, figure several times in the replies. Secondly, a surprisingly large number of people regarded 'wealth' as a figure little larger than the average earnings of an adult male worker.

In October 1966, at the time of our first survey, the average weekly wage of an adult man was £20 6s. 0d. Taking a sum a little less than £5 more than this for convenience, we estimate that one household in every six we interviewed thought that £25 (in some cases an even smaller sum) was 'wealth', and of those who could suggest a figure at all nearly three quarters chose a sum no greater than £50 a week. It is safe to say that a large proportion of the people in St Ann's regard as riches (beyond the dreams of their avarice at any rate) an income which many middle-class people would think as penury.

There were some differences between the answers given on the one hand in the poorer households, and on the other in the houses of trade unionists. Predictably, perhaps, the poorer households gave consistently more modest estimates than the trade unionists, who tended to nominate larger weekly sums as representing 'wealth'. Even so, it is both surprising and revealing that so many should have so low an estimate of what constitutes wealth. One probable reason is sheer ignorance of the very substantial incomes that are taken for granted in more favoured sections of society.

Of course, everyone knows of the astronomical earnings of a handful of pop stars, and other entertainers, and most have a shrewd suspicion that, say, property-speculators, or brothel-keepers, manage to scrape a few pennies together. But most of us, who have to earn our living by honest toil, are felt to be in a different league, where, though differentials undoubtedly exist, they are less extreme. This became strikingly apparent to us on one occasion when we overheard a conversation between two lorry-drivers who were employed by the local Cooperative Society. They were talking about one of the professors at the University who was, it seems, a nodding acquaintance and an occasional drinking partner. Agreement was quickly reached that the Prof. was 'a good bloke', and also that he obviously earned good money. 'Why,' exclaimed one of the drivers, 'I'll bet he's dragging a score a week.' At the time, professorial salaries in fact averaged £80 a week.

Though there may be uncertainty about abstract notions of wealth, there should be no such difficulty with self-description. When asked if they are wealthy, quite well off, comfortably off, hard-pressed, or poor, most people can give a ready answer. We encountered only one person who described himself as 'wealthy', and a further five who admitted to being well-off. Six out of ten of the people we spoke to described themselves as comfortably off, and the others as hard-pressed or, occasionally, poor. At the same time more than one in five of those who described themselves as comfortably off, and two fifths of the total sample (including the one self-confessedly wealthy person) admitted later that their income was not enough to live on comfortably. This may suggest that a certain amount of penny-pinching may be considered so normal as to be quite compatible with being 'comfortably off'.

Most of the poorer households described themselves as 'hard-pressed' or 'poor', although as many as two fifths of them were, apparently, 'comfortably off'. Here again, many of these later said that their incomes were not large enough to live on comfortably. It need hardly be said that the self-assignments which people make when catechized in this way can be unreliable to the extent that they may wish to put a bold front on their conditions. It is certainly possible that some people may

159

feel poverty without thinking it a desirable thing to confess to social investigators, or even, perhaps, to themselves.

If their incomes are felt by so many people to be inadequate, how much larger a wage do they think they need? Not a great deal, apparently, although here again the poorest group is more modest in its demands than the trade unionists. This, despite the fact that trade unionists already tend to draw larger wages than non-unionists, and in many cases have incomes quite substantially larger than those of the poorer households. Yet over a third of the poorer people said they would be satisfied with an additional £5 per week, as compared with only a fifth of the trade unionists. Clearly the aspirations and demands of trade unionists are pitched somewhat higher than those of poorer households. In this connexion, a number of obvious points should perhaps be made. The poorer you are, the more an extra £5 is likely to mean to you. As a percentage increase, £5 is much greater to a poor man than it is to a rich man. If you have never developed expensive tastes, you are easier to satisfy than you might otherwise be. Such banalities are frequently cited to justify deprivation as being, in some way, a humane and civilized condition. An old witticism is current in the hosiery industry in Nottingham: 'Our dog don't like pork chops' they will say to you. Surprised, you ask, 'why?' and are triumphantly told: 'because he's never had none!' There are a lot of things that people living near the social-security level don't need, because they've never had them. It is, perhaps, this simple fact which explains the low level of personal aspiration, or personal greed, displayed by so many of the poorer families.

Now, although more than half our sample said that their incomes were sufficient, this does not exclude the possibility that the relativity of aspirations which we have been discussing might involve *collective* hopes or standards a little more adventurous than *individual* ones. Assuming that people identify with their peers, and limit their expectations to the level of those of their workmates and neighbours, then it is possible that they might be satisfied with their personal standards *vis-à-vis* this reference group, yet dissatisfied with the overall standards of the group as a whole. This of course thrusts us into a complex confusion of attitudes about differences in wealth, social equality, the justification of differentials – and also about a guaranteed minimum, enforceable at law, below which no one should be allowed to sink, and its converse, a maximum above which no one should be able to climb. When discussing these themes, there is never complete uniformity of opinion among people sharing similar conditions, and seldom any real consistency underlying individual attitudes. Nonetheless, taken in sum, a fairly clear pattern emerges from our 400 conversations, giving quite a vivid profile of this one community's response.

For a start, four people out of five think that there should be a national minimum wage; moreover four out of five of these think that such a minimum should be a sum larger than £15 per week. This certainly means that a great many would welcome a national minimum established at a higher level, in some cases considerably higher, than their own current earnings. There was a very slight tendency for the poorer people to nominate a sum nearer to £15 as the desirable figure, and a marked tendency for trade unionists to support considerably more ambitious demands. The answers of the trade unionists tended to be pitched higher than the rest. Not only were more of them in favour of the minimum rate being above £15, but also they chose much higher figures by which the £15 should be exceeded. The discussion about a £15 minimum wage which has been raging in the trade unions, following on the initiative of the Transport and General Workers' Union, may have had an influence on the general tendency to choose a figure at or above that level, but the apparently sharper appetites of trade-union members as a group is certainly connected with the fact that they were in fact among the best-paid people in our sample. There can be little doubt from these figures, however, that Mr Frank Cousins and his successor, Mr Jack Jones, will find large numbers of supporters for their claim among non-unionists and unionists alike. Further, the estimate of £15 per week as a realistic minimum, whatever economists may say about it from the point of view of their estimate of the 'national interest', accurately reflects the needs felt by a wide section of lower-paid working people, while falling well short of the sum nominated by many of the better-paid, and better-organized.

This certainly suggests that people can be satisfied with their condition *vis-à-vis* their neighbours or their workmates, while still being discontented about their joint, collective, over-all social position.

Dissatisfaction with the overall position of one's own social group may, of course, be based upon nothing more than crude self-interest, and the widespread desire to improve one's group's relative position. It may be, on the other hand, part of a broader concern with questions of social equality and justice. Of course, for very many of the people to whom we spoke, the pursuit of either narrow self-interest or abstract social equality would, in the short run, amount to the same thing. We judged that the assumption that there should be a guaranteed mini-mum level of living was only one aspect of a totality of attitudes and desires, and we therefore sought also to discover what was felt about equality of incomes, or what range of income-differ-ences should be allowed. As before, this involved two separate queries. The first concerned the respondent's own social group; should there be greater equality of wages – in this case, hourly pay rates – so that the differential between higher-paid and lower-paid workers would be reduced? The second question tried to break out of the reference group, to grasp the attitudes towards the higher-paid salariat; are the top people in the country paid too little or too much: indeed, should there be a top limit to earnings?

As far as hourly wage rates are concerned, there was a wide-spread, though by no means universal, feeling that they should be more equal. About half the people we spoke to in the second survey (where these detailed inquiries were made) thought that there should be greater equality, while about a third thought there should not. The others were not sure. The poorer fami-lies, many of whom stood to gain from this suggestion, were slightly more enthusiastically egalitarian than the others, but not enormously so. Indeed while it is broadly true that there was an increasingly anti-egalitarian tendency as one climbed the income ladder, it is also true that up to the £25 a week mark, there was a two to one majority of egalitarians over declared non-egalitarians. Among those with incomes greater than £25, many of whom, in terms of the distribution of income within the reference group, stood to lose by greater equality of wage rates, there was an equal split between those in favour and those against.

Much the same egalitarian undercurrent can be detected in the attitudes towards salary levels. Although a handful of people said that top people were paid too little, and about one person in six thought that top salaries were enough, over half the population thought that they were too high. This particular view was even more widespread among the households which were themselves better-off than among the poor.

All in all, these answers indicate a fairly marked and general egalitarian sentiment, even if there is no evidence that it is very militant or aggressive. According to this sentiment, both wages and salaries should become more equal than they are, and the bottom level of wages should be raised substantially. Although this opinion is by no means unanimously held, it is nonetheless sufficiently widespread in this particular working-class community (which is quite unremarkable in its political commitments, to judge by its election results), to cast some considerable doubt on those theories (of various eminent sociologists) which assume that traditional working-class consciousness and solidarity are everywhere and rapidly disintegrating, and being replaced by an outlook more akin to the individualistic and acquisitive values of the middle class.

It is one thing to feel that a more equitable distribution of income would be desirable. It is quite another, however, to regard the existing distribution as positively undesirable. Durkheim, as we have already seen, argued that '... what is needed for them to be content, is not that they have more or less, but that they be convinced they have no right to more'. How far

163

then do people accept their lot as unavoidable, as in some way 'natural'? Is there any positive discontent, any feeling that things are decidedly not as they should be; any real sense of unfairness? Of course, there is a clear case for the view that 'fairness' is not just an elusive, but a positively illusory, quality in wage-fixing agreements. Yet however contentious statements about 'fair' rates of pay may be, the assumptions of wage-earners themselves, whether well- or ill-grounded, tell us a good deal about the state of social consciousness – and this plays a key role in determining the degree of disquiet or of conflict that exists about the distribution of income. But this consciousness is itself a variable quality, which is extremely difficult to measure with any precision, as is amply demonstrated by the significantly large numbers of respondents who found these questions very difficult to answer. Only the trade unionists seemed able, in most cases, to give ready answers. The number of 'don't knows' among non-unionists was larger, and among the poorer households was larger again. On the question of fair wages, however, most employed people had a view, and while over half of all our respondents thought they did in fact receive a fair wage, there were some important variations among different groups. A larger proportion of the poorer people thought their wages were 'unfair' than any other group, although the trade unionists were not far behind.

Workers who feel their wages are unfair must assume that their employers are paying them less than their worth. Yet not everyone who thinks he is paid less than the value of his produce is prepared to go on to say that this is an 'unfair' situation. Many regard it as inevitable, and some as 'normal'. In these respects, the different groups with whom we are concerned gave rather different answers. The poorer families are less likely to think that their employers are making money out of them than the general population, and considerably less likely to think so than trade unionists. And even when the poorer people *do* think their employers make money out of them, they are more likely to estimate the amount involved as a small one than are their better-off workmates, and much more likely to do so than their trade-union colleagues. That is to say, the poor are less likely to feel 'exploited' than the non-poor; and even when they do feel themselves to be exploited, they estimate the degree of exploitation as being lower than do their better-off neighbours.

At the same time, trade-union members seem marginally more prone to think of themselves as exploited than non-unionists: and certainly when they *do* think of themselves as being exploited, they tend to assume the amount involved to be greater.

Although it would be misleading to assume that all trade unionists are among the higher-paid wage-earners (although they do tend to earn more), or that all the poor are necessarily earning smaller than average wages (although they do tend to earn less), there is some evidence to suggest that aggressive dissatisfaction with the level of earnings and a keen sense of being paid less than one is worth are more commonly encountered among the relatively higher-paid workers than among those with the lowest wages.

In general, it seems that the more you earn, the more you think your employer is making out of you. Of course, this could quite easily be an objective estimate, in the sense that in high-wage, high-productivity enterprises, workpeople may well not only produce more, but also produce a greater surplus, than their opposite numbers in low-wage, low-productivity enterprises. Moreover many of the lowest-paid workers are employed in the service industries: here there is often no very obvious product in terms of which one can evaluate one's labour. Again, the service industries have never developed the same convictions about the value of labour that can readily be found in the 'productive' industries. Without such convictions it may be particularly hard for a worker, especially if he is one of a mere handful of workers employed in a small firm, so to assess matters as to make large claims about his own contribution.

It is, then, possible to detect not only a widespread undercurrent of egalitarian sentiment, but also a parallel undercurrent of dissatisfaction with the *status quo*. Although this dissatisfaction was only overtly expressed by a minority of those interviewed, we found it more unambiguously and frequently stated by the better-paid participants in organizational life than among the poorer and more isolated workers. The poorer and more isolated are not, however, a homogeneous group. Rather there are two main groups (if 'groups' is the right word to describe very loose categories of people). One shares more or less fully in the attitudes and criticisms we have discussed; the other, whom we encountered in substantial numbers in our first survey, does not. They reveal a complex of aspirations which are noticeably more modest, of attitudes considerably more complacent, a resigned, 'that's how it goes' approach to family and social life. Although we encountered a substantial number of families with a broadly similar outlook, they do not constitute a group in any more meaningful sense than that they embody certain similar attitudes. If anything, they are more of an 'anti-group' than a group. They certainly find formal association of any kind more difficult than other people, and they tend to live at some distance, morally speaking, from their fellows. Reviled by many residents as the cause of all St Ann's difficulties, labelled by the authorities as 'multi-problem' families, not only do they not accept any common identity, but will frequently express the most caustic of opinions about one another. They are, each, all too prone to agree that the other is a 'problem'. Living more or less from day to day, from one crisis to another, they have few hopes or expectations, and hence fewer systematic demands and complaints. Life is taken as it is found.

All in all, one is forced to conclude that the poorer section of the community is somewhat more modest, ambivalent and self-effacing in its attitudes and aspirations than its more affluent working-class neighbours, and markedly more modest than those of its neighbours who are paid-up members of trade unions. However, it would be an over-simplification to attribute this modesty to a distinctive cultural pattern. While it is true that in many cases we found a lower level of expectation among the poor, there was nonetheless some expectation; although there were variations in the scale of demands and the intensity of their expression, there certainly were demands, and indeed they were, at bottom, the same demands. Excepting the so-called 'problem families' the poorer households could not be said to be culturally distinct from the richer; they appeared to respond to the same values, to share the same basic assumptions, to accept similar restraints. Far from the lower pitch of their stated aspirations being evidence of a detachment from the accepted value-system, it could simply be the expression of a 'realistic' appraisal of their possibilities, given that they had so little power at their disposal to change them. It is considerably easier for a trade unionist, conscious of the organized power to which he contributes and from which he gains protection, to conceive of a statutory minimum wage far beyond anything that could be dreamt of by a non-unionist, perhaps insecure in his employment and almost certainly lacking confidence in any collective strength among his workmates.

Again it seems clear that consciousness of a possible improvement in one's circumstances automatically increases dissatisfaction with one's present lot. We should therefore expect to find (as we do) the most ambitious demands, most militantly expressed and pursued, among those trade unionists (or for that matter, outside St Ann's, among professional people) most successfully organized, and most determined in the pursuit of their goals.

There are of course structural differences between the poorer population and the trade-union population, which may account for some of the observed differences in attitudes. For example, a number of the poorer households were, as we have seen, composed of retirement pensioners, and attitudes might well vary from one generation to another, particularly as regards income-expectation. Many of the older pensioners, particularly those who at no time commanded a high wage, must have, by contemporary standards, an exceptionally humble opinion of their economic worth, and an extremely hazy idea of what wage levels actually are, let alone what they might become. Again there may well be, in broad terms, a difference in attitudes and morale between those employed in manufacturing or extractive industries, and those in service industries. The latter are not only often more difficult to organize into trade unions but have never developed the same sense of solidarity as many of their counterparts in manufacturing. In any event, as has already been observed, it is somewhat more difficult in many of the service industries to establish standards of relative worth and hence of equitable payment, as the product is often more indeterminate and hence harder to measure.

Differences in the age composition of the population or its industrial classification may thus have a marked effect upon the individual's social attitudes, unrelated to any specific subcultural pattern basic to the value-system. One must suppose that in any population, no matter how homogeneous in composition, there will be some variations between individuals in their commitment to the value-system; such variations may arise out of differences in personality and temperament, or again, as we have argued, out of structural rather than purely cultural causes.

From our knowledge of this one urban community, it would be very hard to maintain with any assurance that the poor constitute a single subcultural entity. There seems little doubt that our sample population, poor and non-poor alike, has some sense of common social identity, and shared purpose. There is also very little doubt that the general 'middle-class' conviction that the possible world already exists, for better or (in this case) worse, and that our received institutions are 'natural' even when they affront nature, and 'normal' even when they parody insanity, is all too widely prevalent among the poor. In this sense, they are more than able to 'live up to' these degrading standards. Their condition will not change until they can develop meaningful institutions for joint action, in which they can form new values and larger hopes. We can be confident that such values will be richer and more humane than the ones to which they are now subject.

PART THREE

Why Poverty?
Can it be Fought?
Who will Fight it?

You have, through your knowledge, powers, which man never had before. You can use these powers well or you can use them ill. You will use them well if you realize that mankind is all one family and that we can all be happy or we can all be miserable. The time is passed when you could have a happy minority living upon the misery of the great mass. That time is passed. People won't acquiesce in it . . .

Bertrand Russell Speaks His Mind
World Publishing, New York, 1960, pp. 172–3

8 Why?

Why has such poverty recurred in Britain? Why, indeed, is it a growing problem in all the advanced countries? Why has all the effort at redistribution of wealth apparently been so fruitless? Isn't this truly a wealthy country?

Some people in it are certainly wealthy. These people wield power, but it is power of a very special and peculiar type. They are able to dispose of great resources (which have been socially earned) without subjecting themselves to serious social control; but they are also, themselves, subject to innumerable capricious pressures, before which they may well be impotent, which positively *prevent* any real attempt to make humane public policies.

Aneurin Bevan, who is frequently quoted by our present political leaders, and who, it might be added, cannot from his present habitation readily comment upon the purposes for which his words are sometimes used, had a clear view of this matter:

What are the most worthy objects on which to spend surplus productive capacity? ... After providing for the kind of life we have been leading as a social aggregate, there is an increment left over that we can use as we wish. What would we like to do with it? Now the first thing to notice is that in a competitive society this question is never asked. It is not a public question at all. It cannot be publicly asked with any advantage because it is not capable of a public decision which can be carried out. Therefore in this most vital sphere, the shaping of the kind of future we would like to lead, we are disfranchised at the very outset. We are unable to discuss it because the disposal of the economic surplus is not ours to command. ... The surplus is merely a figure of speech. Its reality consists of a million and one surpluses in the possession of as many individuals. ... If we reduce the question to the realm where we have brought it, that is to say, to the individual possessor of the surplus, the economist will provide us with a ready answer. He will tell us that the surplus owner will invest it in the goods for which he thinks there will be a profitable sale. The choice will lie with those able to buy the goods the owner of the surplus will proceed to produce. This means that those who have been most successful for the time being, the money owners, will in the sum of their individual decisions determine the character of the economy of the future. ... But ... the kind of society which emerges from the sum of individual choices is not one which commends itself to the generality of men and women. It must be borne in mind that the successful were not choosing a type of society. They were only deciding what they thought could be bought and sold profitably.[1]

In a word, social priorities should not be left for the market place to determine. A later socialist writer has put the same problem, of social priorities, rather more trenchantly:

How many businessmen resolutely decide that they must leave schools and offices to rot, and press on with doubling their TV commercials and lacquering their reception rooms with the money saved? Do any at all? On the contrary, how many mightn't even feel a stealthy susurrus of dismay if they learnt that this was the end outcome of their harmless, familiar routines?[2]

Perry Anderson, in pressing home this attack on the market system as the arbiter of men's lives, goes still further:

What finally defines the whole system is that it utterly expunges men from its place of essential working. These decisions are not taken in the board-room or in the bank-manager's suite or even in the exclusive club or the pleasure yacht. They are taken *nowhere*. They are *not taken*, they are not decisions: fatalities. Nobody calculates them and enacts them, they happen unmeant. Our callous and malformed priorities are the prodigious obverse of a thousand discreet, blameless gestures.[3]

But the market does not merely fail to provide for public needs.

1. *In Place of Fear*, MacGibbon & Kee, 1961, pp. 58–9.
2. Perry Anderson, 'Sweden – Mr Crosland's Dreamland', *New Left Review*, No. 7, 1961, p. 10.   3. ibid.

The indictment of St Ann's in this respect is plain: one passes the dingy schools and regards the hoardings, those evidences of million-pound campaigns to persuade the populace to do what it may well be going to do anyway: drink milk, eat cheese, clean its teeth, wash its clothes. One struggles down Alfred Street Central, a busy shopping street, packed with immobile motor cars and leisurely van-drivers unloading their deliveries, no one able to move except on foot. In this, the poor share the total social condition: it is profitable to sell identical soaps in expensive competition with one another, or to pour out an unending stream of motor vehicles. Schools and roads, on the other hand, must be provided from a stingy public purse. Houses are plentiful on the market, if you want to buy a river-side penthouse. But if you want simply to get out of a slum, houses for you must be especially created, away from the market, out of the same strained public resources. You can only buy from the market what is for sale on the market: you cannot buy clean air, or safe roads, or parks for the children to play in, unless you are rich enough to opt right out of the normal conditions of life in and around the slum centres of our cities. For the many who are not so rich, there is no market solution for these deficiencies. To get such amenities in St Ann's, you have to persuade other people to join you in lobbying for them, and your lobby will only be effective if it is prepared for a protracted and difficult struggle.

But in another respect, the market enforces a double penalty upon the poor. Not only the money-centred priorities of production, but, from this point of view more immediately felt, the distribution of rewards itself is determined in the same callous, blind fashion, in the market place. Competition invariably results in inequalities. Someone wins. Someone loses. The winners in economic competition amass monopoly powers over whole products and industries, with all the people in them. The losers, in the worst cases, fall upon public relief, or in the better ones, scrabble away for the barest of livings in the increasingly hard-pressed conditions of the uncompetitive trades. In such a moral wilderness, the very drive to economic growth is a drive to intensified inequality. Since the achievement of maximized rewards is the only acceptable criterion of success in such a system, more growth will take place where more profit is to be found. Concentration of wealth and power flows inevitably from such 'success'. But at the opposite pole, 'inefficient' employers, who may indeed make perfectly good chairs or print perfectly good tote tickets, find that they must, in order to stay in the race with their intensively capitalized betters, increasingly sweat their workpeople. It is an old story. It has, of course, been ameliorated during the post-war years by the extension of social insurance, but at the same time even this has provided its own brake upon the development of true security for the less privileged. Today, the fact that unemployed workers draw a dole, and redundant workers are compensated, means not only that they escape the worst torments of nineteenth-century poverty, but also that their capacity to consume maintains itself, albeit in grossly restricted form, and exerts its own regenerative effect upon the economy in times of recession. But this fact, and the allied fact of extensive military expenditure, combine to replace the rigours of old slumps by a new malady: that of permanent inflation. And permanent inflation is a savage attack upon the already meagre standards of the poor, whether they are on public relief or at work. Even this is not the whole story of the effect of the market upon poor people as consumers. Under monopoly conditions, there is a strong tendency for companies to concentrate on selling small quantities of their products at a high price, rather than large quantities at a low price. More, in Michael Barratt Brown's words:

Not only are there more shops in the West End of the town than the East, but the prices of the basic goods are more easily raised than the prices of the goods and services on which we spend our discretionary income. Bread, potatoes, public transport, fuel and power are such a small part of the spending of the one third of the population with two thirds of the money, that they will still pay if the price goes up. The poor pensioner families have as a result seen the prices of their household budgets rise twice as fast in the last twenty years as the prices in the budget of those with £40 a week or more.

In his 1964 election campaign, Mr Harold Wilson said a great deal about the poor:

At every level of our national life, talent and ability are wasted; our children do not get equal opportunities or our citizens equal chances to develop their qualities and energies. In an age of great potential plenty, we are still in this country cursed by indefensible pockets of shameful poverty and injustice which twelve years of so-called affluence have not removed.[4]

This was only one of very many similar invocations. But at the same time he also had a great deal to say about economic growth. More of it: that was what he wanted.

This could have been a rational mixture of aims. But one thing is abundantly plain. It is quite impossible to pursue growth through the mechanisms of the market, and at the same time secure redistribution of income. There is a respectable school of Fabian thought which is not averse to establishing norms to which men in the street might be compelled to conform. This approach to equality is unimaginative, at best, and falls far short of the liberal goal of a society in which every man can develop to the limits of his capacity. Indeed, unkind people have been known to draw comparisons between this type of crude egalitarianism and the efforts of Procrustes, who beguiled wayfarers to pass a night in a bed of his own design, a bed which lopped bits off the tall, and stretched out the short until every occupant assumed a uniform, if arbitrary shape. But crude though it may be, the Procrustean approach to equality is at least logically consistent. Mr Wilson has inherited a whole variety of slogans from his forbears, which he has been adept at repeating with all the signs of conviction. Procrustes Wilson, the leveller, was, a large body of electors were once persuaded, about to apply all the spectacular resources of science-based technology to his rack. But the trouble is that a rack is a rack. It can stretch people, and perhaps it can shrink them. What it cannot do is to stretch them and shrink them at the same time. The effort to perform such a dubious assignment is calculated to cause the maximum possible pain simultaneously with the

4. *The New Britain: Labour's Plan*, Penguin Books, 1964, p. 11.

minimum detectable actual change. On the scale of the political economy, growth follows inequality and prefigures greater inequality, unless it is socially initiated and controlled. Rapid economic expansion, in a market economy, means an increase in private investment which can only be stimulated by the prospect of rewards. The effective stimulation of growth on such premises is the effective further polarization of society, in which the poor wage-earners will drop further and further behind their 'betters'.

In another context, Mr Wilson inveighed, in his campaigning days, against the irresponsible power of monopolies. By the same implacable logic, however, his administration has not merely witnessed, but positively encouraged, the greatest concentration of industrial forces ever known in this country. Such aggregates are even less amenable to public, social control than their precursors – so disturbing to the prime minister a few years ago.

Let it be clearly understood what we are not saying. We are not saying that 'nothing has been done' for the poor. Doles have gone up. Some, though not enough, slums have been cleared. A little, a very little, money has gone to Educational Priority Areas. But essentially, all these ameliorative measures are derisory compared to the central problem, which is that of the overall distribution of income as it is shaped by the market (and predominantly the market within the productive, which is to say, profitable, heartlands of the economy), and the aggravated indetermination of wholesale social priorities. It is, in Michael Barratt Brown's words, 'money, not numbers, which pulls in the market'. People come second. Poor people come way, way back. Growth without social control is not merely *not* the answer to this problem: to the extent that it could be achieved, it would exacerbate matters.

So the problem is that of social control of the economy, community determination of social policies. In a word, it relates to the regeneration of socialist ideals and the crystallization of an effective movement to realize them.

Just what are the growth points to look to, in this work? First of all we must see what they are not.

9 The Decline of the Welfare State

I

The 'rediscovery' of poverty in the sixties has been a slow and contentious business. To assert that there remained a widespread problem of poverty was to challenge an integrated set of myths and pieties which had become so widely accepted as to be taken, by many people, as axiomatic. Poverty among substantial sections of the working class was supposed to be non-existent. There were ample job opportunities at all levels of skill. Working-class wage rates and incomes were rising, at a rate which was seen as prodigious by previous standards. Extrapolation from some widely reported cases enabled people to believe that the wages of even unskilled labourers were generally more than favourably comparable with the incomes of non-manual, clerical and administrative grades. The deterioration of the traditional middle-class differentials was, supposedly, considerably worsened by the imposition of swingeing rates of income taxation. The revenues of such taxes were used to provide an endless array of expensive social services, in cash and in kind, which primarily benefited the already overpaid working classes, to the great detriment of their moral fibre. Many learned authorities were convinced that there had been a substantial redistribution of incomes and wealth, which was assumed to have abolished both the poor and the rich; moreover this transformation of the economic order had apparently happened extremely rapidly. As early as the spring of 1946, two years before the most important pieces of welfare legislation took effect, and while thousands of men and women were still in the Armed Forces, the *Economist* entered 'a plea for mercy on behalf of the middle range of the earned incomes', a plea which it reiterated at frequent intervals in the following months and years. Again, in January 1948, the *Economist* claimed that 'the total amount paid out in wages in 1946 ... was 60 per cent higher than before the war ... while the average salary, in real net purchasing power, has fallen by anything from 20 to 30 per cent ... At least 10 per cent of the national consuming power has been forcefully transferred from the middle classes and the rich to the wage-earners.'[1]

In 1949 the Board of Inland Revenue itself spoke of 'a very considerable redistribution of incomes' between 1938 and 1948; another year later the *Economist*, never exactly the most audacious of conservative publications, referred to 'a vast redistribution of incomes'. Throughout the fifties, further studies, some by distinguished academic economists, seemed to confirm this conclusion. Harold Lydall, of the Oxford Institute of Statistics, not only sought to demonstrate the striking difference in income distribution between pre- and post-war Britain, but argued that this reflected a permanent tendency in the economy which was biased towards a continual redistribution in favour of wage-earners. In 1955 Professor Robbins wrote, somewhat lugubriously, of a relentless pressure towards 'collectivism and propertyless uniformity'.

Naturally enough, among the middle classes, at whose expense this economic revolution had apparently been achieved, considerable frustration and resentment were registered at this supposed erosion of their time-honoured differentials. This resentment frequently found expression in a sharply hostile attitude towards the social services and the Welfare State. The systematic development of a wide range of new or radically reorganized social-service agencies between 1944 and 1948, some distributing cash benefits, other providing services, usually without any direct charge, came increasingly to be interpreted as a grossly profligate exercise, lavishing assistance upon those very sections of the population who were prospering as a

1. Quoted in John Saville, 'Labour and Income Redistribution', the *Socialist Register*, 1965, pp. 151 ff. (Merlin Press, 1965.)

result of the redistribution of income. Many of those taking advantage of the new services were felt to be taking unfair advantage, to be exploiting the services not because they were in need, but because they could not resist 'something for nothing'. Thus in the early fifties much was heard of doctors' surgeries crowded out with applicants in search of unneeded spectacles, false teeth, wigs, even cosmetics. Foreigners were alleged to be flocking in to have their superfluous organs removed, while an army of malingerers was quite generally supposed to be rattling with unnecessary pills. Since the mid-fifties we have heard less of this kind of complaint, but more of the hitherto unnoticed legions of the work-shy and feckless, who foxily dedicate their developed cunning to the systematic deception of the staff of the Supplementary Benefits Commission, specially selected as they are, to the last man, for their gullibility and naïvety.

At the same time there developed an altogether more informed and considered critique of the Welfare State; this concentrated its attack on the universality of provision. It was, so the argument ran, grossly inefficient to distribute social-service benefits to all, including many who had no need of them, being quite capable of providing for themselves. In recent years this theme has found two expressions; one in the discussion about selectivity, the concentration of resources on those whose need is greatest (sometimes called 'positive discrimination'), the other in the 'Choice in Welfare' debate. These discussions need not concern us here, except in as much as they have had, whatever their principal protagonists may have intended, a tendency to confirm the prejudice that welfare expenditure is a woefully wasteful expenditure of the tax-payer's money, spent primarily on improving working-class living standards and constituting a dolorous public burden, inimical to both personal incentives and economic growth.

Now if it were true that incomes had been dramatically redistributed, to the distinct advantage of the poorer sections of the community, and if it were true that scalding income taxation was concentrated with the malignant force of a laser on the middle-income groups, and, indeed, if it were true that the Welfare State poured out its services exclusively upon the wage-earners, then any assertion of the continued existence of wide-spread poverty in the working class would certainly be rather implausible. On the contrary, it would be among the indigent, pauperized salariat that we should expect to find hardship. Unfortunately none of these assumptions are true, and the existence of poverty is a demonstrable fact, which has even impinged upon the libraries. There, if only in the shape of footnotes, it begins to attract an attention which the brute facts have been all too slow to command. First of all, one can refer to the work of J. L. Nicholson.

Nicholson is concerned, first of all, with what has happened in the post-war period, and he is constrained by his data to begin with 1953. His analysis suggests that pre-redistribution income showed much the same degree of inequality in 1953 and 1959; and although the total effect of Government taxes and benefits was a reduction of inequality, again it was of the same order of magnitude in the two years. Nicholson estimates that in those two years the total effect of Government redistributive activity was to reduce the measure of inequality by one fifth of what it was originally. In the process of doing this he makes some interesting estimates of the power of various types of tax or benefit in contributing to a reduction of inequality. In an appendix he also makes a comparison between his measures of post-war inequality and those made in 1937 by Barna. He stresses the fact that because of differences of method this can only be a very rough comparison, but he arrives at the interesting conclusion that 'There appears to have been little increase in the amount of vertical redistribution between 1937 and 1959.'[2]

When one then considers the vast extension of industrial and commercial fringe benefits that has taken place in recent years, the relevance of declared cash-income as an index of the distribution of real wealth is further questioned. Professor Titmuss, who has produced the most detailed and convincing study of

2. Dorothy Wedderburn, 'Facts and Theories of the Welfare State', the *Socialist Register*, 1965, p. 133.

these matters, observes that 'in the United Kingdom as in other modern economies there has been a marked growth in the provision of benefits in kind during the last twenty years or so, and ... that for many groups in the occupied population the receipt of such benefits rises sharply with income'.[3] These benefits extend from meal vouchers or subsidized canteens which are often available to all employees, to a network of benefits confined in the main to higher executives. These may include 'housing, the underwriting of bank overdrafts, direct loans, educational trusts and scholarships, non-contributory pensions, tax-free lump sums on retirement, access to shooting and fishing rights ... most of which are allowable as legitimate business expenses and none of which find their way into the calculation of income statistics'. In this way, although a person's stated (and taxed) income may seem relatively modest, the standard at which he lives may be considerably more exalted.

Secondly, our tax system has certain features which substantially reduce the levelling effect which a progressive tax system might otherwise have. First of all there is an elaborate system of tax allowances, which reduce the tax liability of those entitled to them. Everyone who has filled up the Inland Revenue's forms will know of some of these; they include the allowances for children (which, incidentally, are considerably more valuable to the beneficiaries, and more costly to the Exchequer than the universal Family Allowance), and tax relief on interest charges on mortgages or bank loans (which, in most cases, represent a substantial housing subsidy). But, these official allowances apart, there are more sophisticated methods of tax avoidance:

Deferred payments of various kinds, the redistribution of income within families, and the conversion of income into capital gains, are all legal devices which are likely to operate only for the benefit of the higher range of earners, and certainly not for manual workers and their families. The more notorious manipulations, such as the ploughing back of large earnings into private companies, or heavy investment in farms organized as private companies with

3. Richard M. Titmuss, *Income Distribution and Social Change*, Allen & Unwin, 1962, p. 171.

children as major shareholders, are probably common only among the very small number of people in the higher range of surtax income.[4]

That certain minor changes have been made in the system of taxation since these plaints were published does not change the basic situation: as Mr Wilson told the T.U.C. in 1964: 'If you borrow from some of the World bankers you will quickly find that you lose ... independence, because of the deflationary policies and the cuts in Social Services that will be imposed on a Government that has got itself into that position.'[5] If bankers are not too keen on social services, they are not notoriously in favour of income redistribution, either.

If one looks, not at the distribution of income, but at the distribution of wealth itself, then the degree of inequality is truly amazing. Professor J. E. Meade found that at the end of the fifties.

no less than 75% of personal property was owned by the wealthiest 5% of the population. Moreover the rich obtain a higher yield on their property than do the poor. ... The result is that the concentration of income from property is even more marked than the concentration of property ownership itself, and in 1959 no less than 92% of income from property went to 5% of the population.[6]

These diverse pieces of evidence all point to one general conclusion; that the period since the end of the war has seen no substantial vertical redistribution of income. Such vertical redistribution as has occurred has been very modest in scale, and far from being evidence of a permanent equalizing tendency in the post-war economy or the result of social-welfare policies, is more likely to be 'the result of war-time changes and the once and for all achievement of a higher level of employment in the post-war period'.[7]

4. W. G. Runciman, *Relative Deprivation and Social Justice*, Routledge & Kegan Paul, 1966, p. 86.

5. The *T.U.C. Annual Report*, 1964, p. 383.

6. *Efficiency, Equality, and the Ownership of Property*, Allen & Unwin, 1964, p. 17.

7. D. Wedderburn, 'Facts and Theories of the Welfare State'; 'once for all' may be a hopeful way of describing what has taken place *up to now*.

The Welfare State, then, has been no Robin Hood. It has taken little from the rich and given less to the poor. Income has not been redistributed vertically between classes, but rather horizontally within them. The main redistribution has been between specific groups in the population. Thus the National Health Service benefits the sick, at the expense of the healthy; Family Allowances help the fecund at the expense of the childless; old-age pensions benefit the elderly at the expense of the young. The overwhelming majority of healthy, childless, young people are, of course, situated in the working and lower middle classes. The same classes also produce the majority of illness, children and senility. When Peter is not paying Paul, Paul is paying Peter. This is, for some, a convenient arrangement: it combines the advantages of diverting attention from other possible payers whilst at the same time provoking a politically useful animus between the actual donors and recipients. From time to time public issue can be taken on behalf of one or the other group, thus arousing a real frenzy of back-biting animadversion within the ranks of the subject population.

II

Quite clearly then, the Welfare State has not made a revolutionary change in the order of society. Nor has it even succeeded in more modest targets. William Beveridge, whose famous report on Social Insurance and Allied Services was a blueprint for post-war social policies, was not primarily concerned with bringing about a vertical redistribution of wealth at all. He was convinced that provided there was full employment (destroying one of his five giants, Idleness) then the Giant Want would, for most people, be destroyed automatically.[8] Social-security programmes were necessary to cover those pre-

8. Of course, Beveridge's commitment to full employment represents a striking development in his own thought: some years earlier he wrote: 'To guarantee work on honourable conditions is to demoralize the people by making the lot of the less efficient, less steady, less industrious man

185

dictable, unavoidable contingencies when earnings were likely to be interrupted, while a modest programme of National Assistance would protect the few misfits who for one reason or another were protected by neither employment nor social security. In essence, this was not an 'unreasonable' programme. It seemed to offer the necessary safeguards both to the weak and to the less weak. In Beveridge's proposals, however, there were two flaws; flaws which ensured that, even by Beveridge's own standards, the Giant Want would survive – somewhat shrunken, perhaps, but still menacingly large.

First of all the *Beveridge Report* recommended that the rates of benefit of the social-security services should be calculated to support life at subsistence level only. For Beveridge, this was more than just an administrative decision, but a point of principle discussed at some length in the *Report* which bears his name. To pay more than a subsistence payment would be to discourage personal savings, and would deprive people of a necessary incentive to make appropriate provision for themselves. An appropriate subsistence level he thought, could be scientifically calculated by 'impartial expert authorities'. At the same time he acknowledged that such calculations are fundamentally a matter of judgement, and that such judgements change with time. This suggests that our 'impartial expert authorities' are by no means making a straightforward 'scien-

---

who is the first to lose his employment as pleasant as that of his more efficient, or steady or industrious fellow, who retains his employment. . . . The line between independence and dependence, between the efficient and the unemployable has to be made clearer and broader. . . . Those men who through general defects are unable to fill such a "whole" place in industry must be recognized as "unemployable". They must become the acknowledged dependants of the State, removed from free industry and maintained adequately in public institutions, but with complete and permanent loss of all citizen rights – including not only the franchise, but civil freedom and fatherhood. To those, moreover, if any, who may be born personally efficient, but in excess of the number for whom the country can provide, a clear choice will be offered: loss of independence by entering a public institution, emigration, or immediate starvation.' William Beveridge, *Sociological Papers* (ed. the Webbs), Vol. I, pp. 326–7. Cited in the *Black Dwarf*, 14 March 1969.

tific' calculation, but are engaged in a much more problematic and speculative exercise.

Be that as it may, the rates of benefit which were introduced with the establishment of the National Insurance Scheme, were, broadly speaking, consistent with Beveridge's recommendations. Beveridge calculated the cost, at 1938 prices, of 'necessaries', and added 25 per cent to allow for the war-time rise in the cost of living. In the 1946 National Insurance Act a rather greater allowance was made for the rise in living costs, so that the level of benefits was somewhat more generous; however, it established the principle of flat-rate benefits at a minimum acceptable, rather than maximum possible, level. These rates of benefit can be criticized on two grounds. Firstly, accepting for a moment the basic validity of the subsistence principle, were the calculated benefit rates based upon an accurate and valid assessment of subsistence needs? Secondly, and more fundamentally, was the subsistence principle itself valid?

To deal with the first question. In calculating his benefit rates Beveridge relied heavily upon a 1937–8 Ministry of Labour survey of working-class household expenditure, which provided him with fairly detailed information on spending patterns. In general, however, Beveridge calculated a figure for each item of household expenditure that was smaller than the figure in the Ministry's survey, on the grounds that 'subsistence expenditure can clearly be put below these figures, which relate to households living on an average well above the minimum'. The final benefit rate was thus arrived at by a process of stringent calculation on a very narrow range of supposedly necessary commodities bearing no marked relationship to actual spending patterns.

From the outset, the rates of benefit were too low to guarantee, even by Beveridge's own declared standards, security from want. This initial inadequacy was aggravated by the developments of the post-war economy. The forties and fifties were a period of economic growth, during which time the relative value of the social-security benefits fell sharply as they came to represent an ever-smaller sum in comparison with earned income. Similarly, changes in the cost of living, particularly during the years of inflation in the mid-fifties, eroded the value of the flat-rate benefits. During the discussions that preceded the establishment of the National Insurance Scheme, there had been talk of pegging benefit rates to the cost-of-living index, so that an increase in living costs would have entailed an automatic increase in the scale rates. However, this suggestion was not implemented. So the scale rates, inadequate to begin with, fell further and further behind.

One indication of this inadequacy was the ever-growing number of people who found it necessary to apply to the National Assistance Board for extra relief. In Beveridge's original proposals, as we have already remarked, the National Assistance Board was to be a temporary device, acting as a 'safety-net' to relieve those who failed to qualify for National Insurance benefits. As the Insurance Scheme became established, it was thought, those applying for National Assistance would become fewer and fewer. In practice, the reverse was the case. Every year the numbers of people requiring help grew, despite the supposed stigma attached to such help, which in fact deterred many people from availing themselves of the service offered. Thus, at the end of 1949 just over a million weekly allowances were being paid by the National Assistance Board, while at the end of 1966 the figure had reached over $2\frac{1}{2}$ million. Had the benefits available through the National Insurance Scheme been adequate, presumably such widespread recourse to the National Assistance Board would have been unnecessary. The large, and ever-increasing, number of applicants is striking proof of the original inadequacy of benefit rates, and of their aggravated deterioration in value as inflation took its toll, while living standards in general rose further and further above the 'net'.

By the end of the fifties, the flat-rate subsistence principle itself was abandoned with the introduction of the Graduated Pensions Scheme. This departed from the principle of uniformity of contribution and benefit, in favour of a system of graduated contributions related to earnings, and appropriately differentiated benefits. In this scheme it was publicly acknowledged that needs might vary from family to family, and that provision for periods of interrupted earnings should take some account of the amount normally earned. Whatever the merits of this view, it is an obvious departure from the subsistence principle, for it is by no means apparent that the requirements for bare physical survival vary significantly between one income group and another. The principle of graduated and earnings-related benefit has since been extended to include sickness and unemployment benefits, and all recent developments and proposals for the reform of the social-security system have assumed the continued extension of the earnings-related principle, moving towards some such target as half-pay on retirement. Now, although for many people such a scheme will provide a more generous pension than was available under the old flat-rate principle, it is also apparent that a scheme which relates benefits to levels of earnings is hardly likely to relieve the poverty of those whose earnings are low. It would be optimistic to suppose an earnings-related pension scheme (whether it be at the rate of half-pay or even more) will represent freedom from poverty in retirement for those whose earnings never allowed such freedom during their working life. Until social security is considered as part and parcel of the total distribution of income within society – and this must involve a critical study of the initial distribution of wealth – it will offer scant relief to those whose earnings (and entitlements) are lowest.

Whatever its limitations, however, for the aged and the sick, there is a social-security system of some sort. But for the largest poverty group, the families of men who are at work but who receive incomes inadequate to meet their needs, there is no such security. This is the second fatal flaw in Beveridge's plan: social welfare is conceived as a system ancillary to, but separate from, the market system. Indeed it is seen as essentially subordinate to the market system, covering only those few situations which the market cannot adequately cope with itself. Thus, all benefits paid out under the National Insurance

Scheme apply only to situations such as unemployment or sickness, situations where there is an interruption of earnings. The allowances paid by the Supplementary Benefits Commission (née National Assistance Board), are available on proof of need, but the Commission is not permitted to make payments to households where the breadwinner is at work, no matter how pressing the family need may be. Thus the low wage-earner can find relief neither as of right nor on demonstration of need, but must reconcile himself and his family to living at whatever standard his low wage permits. This large group, who cannot escape poverty while at work, can expect no improvement in their circumstances in the event of a period of sickness or unemployment, which would make them eligible for both social-security benefits and Supplementary Benefits. Precisely in order to avoid the situation where a family might receive more in welfare payments than it would in earnings, the Ministry operates its 'wage-stop'; that is to say, whatever level of benefits a family may be eligible to receive according to the Ministry's scales, the actual sum paid out shall not exceed the amount that was being earned before the interruption occurred. No matter how inadequate a family's earned income; no matter how far short of that family's needs the income may fall (needs are measured here, of course, by reference to the Ministry's own fixed scales), in the event of such low earnings being interrupted, the Ministry will fastidiously maintain such a family in its accustomed poverty: in no event can Authority allow its resources to be used actually to *raise* anyone's living standards, even as far as the level of the Ministry's own estimate of minimum requirements.

The one benefit to which a working family is in all cases entitled is the Family Allowance; the payment of non-contributory weekly cash allowances to all families with two or more children is the closest that our social-security programme has got to a conception of security that is universal, embracing every family, working or otherwise. And yet, until recently, the Family Allowance was the most neglected of all benefits. No allowance at all is paid for the first child, and the allowance paid on second and subsequent children from 1946 onward was little more than half the amount that Beveridge reckoned to be the subsistence cost of a child. The effects of inflation, and subsequent increases in the scale-rates of other benefits, made the value of Family Allowances increasingly marginal, so that their contribution to the solution of family poverty was very small. Despite this, it must be acknowledged that the Family Allowance is unique, in that it is universal in scope, in no way dependent on proof of need or a contribution record, and that it is an immediate and direct response to changes in family needs. It has flexibility and immediate relevance to family poverty that give it an especially significant role.[9]

In short then, the social-security system was designed as a desirable adjunct to a (presumably) efficiently operating market system, on the assumption that those able to take a place in the market would be able to maintain themselves at a satisfactory standard of living. Only Family Allowances were thought of as a truly universal service, but these have always played a minor role in our social-security system. In such a system, many of the lower-paid workers have remained at constant risk of relative poverty. For those outside the market system, social security offered an alternative; for dogmatic reasons, however, this alternative was to be available only at the most parsimonious of levels. In an age of constantly elevated expectations, those dependent upon social security became increasingly underprivileged, their relative deprivation increasingly marked.

III

At this point it is useful to inquire what welfare legislation has as its fundamental purpose. An important clue is to be found in

9. In 1967 and again in 1968 the Allowances were substantially increased, so that today they are more important than ever before; even so, if we compare our rates of Allowance with the very much more generous rates paid in some continental countries, our system is seen to be deplorably half-hearted.

the opening phrases of Professor Asa Briggs' definition of a Welfare State: this, he asserts, is 'a state in which organized power is deliberately used ... in an effort to modify the play of market forces'.[10] This dictum quite rightly locates welfare policy squarely in the context of the market economy and obliges us to evaluate the impact of social-service institutions upon the workings of the free market. However, while most people would agree that welfare policies are one attempt to modify the play of market forces, there is no agreement over the legitimate extent of such modifications, or their permanence.

Professor Briggs himself indicates three directions in which the Welfare State intervenes in the market:

First, by guaranteeing individuals and families a minimum income irrespective of the market value of their work or their property; second, by narrowing the extent of insecurity by enabling individuals and families to meet certain 'social contingencies' (for example, sickness, old age, and unemployment) which lead otherwise to individual and family crises; and third, by ensuring that all citizens without distinction of status or class are offered the best standards available in relation to a certain agreed range of social services.[11]

In the same volume of essays, Professor T. H. Marshall would extend the notion further to 'include all the measures adopted either to influence, or to interfere with, or to supersede the free play of market forces in the interests of welfare',[12] while in a third essay a German commentator, Professor Boettscher, distinguishes between a Social Market Economy, which combines an essentially free market system with measures designed to preserve an 'acceptable' social balance, and a Welfare State which supersedes the market altogether.

10. Asa Briggs, 'The Welfare State in Historical Perspective', *Archives Européennes de Sociologie*, Vol. 2, 1961, p. 228.

11. Asa Briggs, op. cit.

12. T. H. Marshall, 'The Welfare State – A Sociological Interpretation'. *Archives Européennes de Sociologie*, Vol. 2, 1961, p. 288.

All of these differing views are in sharp contrast with those of a group of economists closely associated with the Institute of Economic Affairs. They feel that all attempts to interfere with the operation of the free market are inherently undesirable, leading to waste, inefficiency, and loss of output. Rather grudgingly they will concede that some of the welfare measures adopted after the Second World War were, at the time, appropriate, but would claim that they had only a temporary justification until capitalism could overcome the shortcomings so apparent in the thirties. Given steady economic growth, however, 'the true object of the Welfare State ... is to teach people how to do without it'.[13] Whatever temporary benefits may have accrued from welfare interventions may now, it seems, flow from the workings of unimpeded market forces, and the Welfare State should be allowed to wither away as speedily as possible.

This particular point of view is coloured by the social and political values of a hundred years ago; it is naïvely convinced of the primary importance of material incentives as a stimulus to activity, and fearful of the effects of welfare policies upon their recipient's moral fibre (with particular reference to his will to work). This quite extraordinarily crude assessment of the role (or non-role) of welfare is, of course, shared only by a handful of serious commentators; moreover its exponents distract attention from a much more important, but equally divisive, discussion which concerns the relationship that does, or should, exist between the play of market forces and welfare considerations. Clearly one's attitude to this relationship depends upon one's view of the purpose of welfare policy. For example, there are those who hold Professor Boettscher's Social Market Economy view: they argue that market forces give the economy a unique drive and direction (which they prize highly) but that in the process social situations and personal contingencies are precipitated with which the market itself cannot adequately cope; these, if ignored,

13. A. Peacock, 'The Welfare Society', *Unservile State Papers* (Liberal Party, 1961).

would ultimately generate such tensions and conflicts within the body politic that its stability would be threatened by unrest or rebellion. The function of welfare policy is seen, in such a framework, as being to create appropriate institutions which will reduce such tensions to an acceptable level – though without, presumably, fundamentally distorting the processes of the market.

This point of view has some subtlety: it conceives of a delicate and flexible relationship between market and welfare requirements, a relationship which would change and adapt as the developing economic and social situation dictated. Nonetheless, welfare considerations are seen as basically subordinate to the play of the market; they are not seen as an independent category, involving a unique expression of human rights with an integrity and ethos separate from the market, but as a narrowly functional adjunct of the dominant market situation.

The notion of welfare rights is, however, central to the view represented by Professor T. H. Marshall. He argues that in modern times we have witnessed the gradual establishment of national equality of status; this is reflected first of all in the achievement of civil equality before the law (an eighteenth-century struggle), then in the winning of political rights, in particular voting rights (essentially a nineteenth-century achievement), and most recently in the recognition of social rights of citizenship, symbolized by welfare legislation guaranteeing certain minimum social entitlements. While the latter at least may involve a modification of the play of market forces, it is a necessary modification, if only because without such rights of citizenship the modern market mechanisms cannot function adequately. In this view, welfare legislation is certainly functional – ultimately it assists the market – but it is not purely functional. Welfare policy can be rooted in a social philosophy, and is seen as complementary to the market, rather than subordinate to it.

In all these different assessments of the role of social welfare there is one implicit assumption: that welfare forces and market forces are fundamentally in opposition to one another. The more we extend the scope and character of welfare provision, the more we are encroaching on what was hitherto the province of the market. The feature which distinguishes the different theories of the Welfare State is the relative significance each gives to welfare, and hence the extent to which they anticipate public and planned controls over market forces. As we have observed, some see any welfare intervention as being in the long term undesirable, others as being necessary but to be kept to a minimum, others again as being both necessary and desirable, as it were in partnership with the market.

All these viewpoints share the same fundamental weakness, however: they tend to interpret the situation in a static way, as though the passing of a particular piece of welfare legislation marks a decisive and permanent alteration in the relationship between market and welfare forces. In fact, of course, such alterations, if they are to be decisive and permanent, require a preceding, equally decisive and equally permanent, alteration in the power relationships in society. That such alterations in power relationships can occur is undeniable: indeed the truism that the most significant advances in welfare legislation take place in the aftermath of major wars is borne out by a whole history of significant (though not necessarily decisive) alterations in the power structure that have been seen to occur in or immediately after wartime.

The trite observation that some of the most important enactments of the Welfare State, such as the 1944 Education Act, were passed by the war-time Coalition Government (as though this demonstrated a timely, if tardy, conversion to welfare policies of all hitherto reluctant politicians) has combined with the post-war vogue for what is called 'consensus politics'[14], to convince many normally sensible commentators

14. A view of politics that is based upon the assumption that widespread almost bi-partisan political assent can be achieved by the pursuit of 'pragmatic' programmes, based apparently on nothing but the sound common sense of the floating voter, and in reality simply echoing Aristotle's preconceptions about the virtue of the mean.

that an end has been made to 'ideological' politics, or indeed to any politics that acknowledged continued opposition and conflict within the social system. Apparently, we are all Fabians now, and are expected to endorse the recurrent and time-honoured theme in Fabian thought that fundamental social change can be achieved by a gradual process of reformist legislation, each new enactment contributing to the greater and more rational control of the blind forces of the market, and representing, as it were, a foretaste of the Socialist Commonwealth to come. This conception of a coexistence between private and public enterprise was described by Bernard Shaw, in a characteristically brilliant and witty manner:

The making of city streets through which everyone may walk without direct payment is flat Communism; but the making of the boots in which men walk along them can be left to private business. In the country the roads and bridges can be made by private enterprise and paid for by their users at toll-gates and turnpikes. The two systems soon get mixed. Tolls and turnpikes are a nuisance to people who do not like to be delayed by repeated stoppages and payments at closed gates and are useless to proletarians who, their pockets being empty, must evade the tolls by trespassing into the fields and breaking the hedges. Therefore toll bridges and turnpikes are 'freed': that is, paid for out of the rates and taxes: communized, in fact, as a necessary measure of convenience, in spite of their profitableness, when the State is sufficiently organized to undertake such public services. How serious this limitation may be is shown by the fact that it is hardly an exaggeration to say that from the time when the ancient Romans, who were great road-makers and bridge-builders, left Britain in the fifth century until the nineteenth century, no new public bridges were built in England. Our rivers are still grievously under-bridged. Even in the middle of the city of Dublin one of my father's eccentricities was to shout 'This infernal bridge will break me' when he crossed the river Liffey at the cost of a halfpenny by a toll bridge which was near his office.

But in spite of the cases in which private enterprise reduced itself to absurdity in practice as the turnpikes and toll bridges did, the world that I was born into held it as a sacred principle that the Government must not do anything that private profiteering enter-

196

prise could and would tackle. When I reached the age which was in my particular case the age of indiscretion, I was ripe for the discussion of the question why my father should pay a halfpenny to cross a cheap metal footbridge and yet be allowed to use the much more expensive and handsome stone bridges, with their roadways for horse and foot, for nothing. On reflection it became clear that my father did not enjoy the use of the public bridge for nothing: he was rated by the City Corporation for the cost of its maintenance; but his share of that cost was much less than a halfpenny a crossing, and less troublesomely collected. Thus there was Capitalism on one bridge and Communism on others a few hundred yards off, with Communism providing very superior accommodation at a lower price.[15]

What Shaw in this passage underestimated was the resilience of market forces, and he would no doubt be both surprised and amused if he were to know that the biggest and handsomest 'public' bridges built in the past decade now cost all those who wish to cross them, not a halfpenny, but the substantial toll of half a crown.

The truth is that welfare and market principles are irreconcilably in conflict with one another, and at no point in time is there a declared truce; there is no gentleman's agreement as to the proper province of each, no honourable observation of agreed demarcation boundaries. On the contrary, the two methods of distribution remain in a perpetual and dynamic state of opposition.

In the case of Britain, welfare legislation has failed to humanize the economic and social system because it has been a strategy of people who have avoided a confrontation with the forces of the market on at least two crucial issues. The first of these concerns the distribution of income. Welfare-oriented measures have never been intended to produce an initial distribution of income sensitive to individual and family need. (Although it seemed at first as though the Incomes Policy might have some redistributive purpose favouring the lower-paid workers, this has now been officially denied.) Then, as we

15. G. B. Shaw, *Everybody's Political What's What?*, Constable, 1944, pp. 260–61.

have already documented, the success of welfare interventions in securing a post-income redistribution through progressive taxation, subsidies, and social benefits has been, at best, marginal. On this vital issue, then, which determines the extremes of wealth, which in turn determine the limits and character of aspirations, and in large measure the exercise of effective social power, welfare considerations have always abdicated in favour of the market place.

The second confrontation so far avoided concerns the allocation of national resources. The institutions of a Welfare State require massive capitalization no less than modern industry does; the development of ever more sophisticated and expensive technology is as important to medical care as it is to the production of motor-cars or aeroplanes; the need for highly trained staff is as pressing in social work as it is in advertising. But crucial decisions about capital investment, technological expansion, and manpower recruitment in the welfare sector have always deferred to the prior claims of the market. That this was taken for granted was underlined already even in the National Plan, when it was still hoped that a growth rate of 4 per cent would be achieved. It was also in the National Plan that the criteria for choosing items on which expenditure was to be made were clearly spelled out. The criterion was to be not social need but 'contribution to economic growth'.[16]

The context in which these acts of default have become possible, even inevitable, has been one of total failure to attack, or even to see the need to attack, the concentration of economic power in the hands of irresponsible caucuses, and the subordination of social production to private control.

A detailed examination of the tortuous shifts of the changing power structure of post-war Britain is far beyond our present scope; but it is pretty clear that the sense of national consensus which evolved during the war, and which informed the reformist legislation of both the Coalition and the Labour Government which succeeded it, began to dissipate before the

16. *May Day Manifesto, 1968,* ed. Raymond Williams, Penguin Books, 1968, p. 28.

end of the forties, as public expenditure in the welfare sector attracted increasing criticism. Such expenditure was increasingly frequently depicted by some conservative thinkers as a spendthrift misallocation of scarce resources, as inimical to economic growth and incompatible with individual freedom. The reformist forces, particularly the forces of the Labour Movement, while they have never self-consciously or explicitly renounced their commitment to welfare, have, under the fire of their conventional adversaries, allowed their priorities to be modified. Full employment, rising living standards, and the push for economic growth (desirable though these are in the abstract) came to be seen by more and more putative radicals as a credible alternative to policies of social welfare or of redistribution: security from want, and expectations of a steadily improving standard of living, became increasingly associated with the most orthodox of economic policies, and the development and extension of welfare policies became an increasingly marginal concern, little more than the window-dressing of party political debate. Without constant vigilance in the defence of welfare, and vigour in its extension, in other words, without a permanent political commitment, both the scope and the effectiveness of welfare policies must be systematically threatened.

Today, as welfare policies themselves are increasingly brought into question, so are the other ingredients of the 'Welfare State': full employment, rising standards of living, and so on. An all-round devaluation has set in in the parity of political expectations.

There is a constant and unremitting pressure upon welfare policies and institutions, a pressure which aims first of all to minimize the extent of their effect on market forces; this pressure is widely acknowledged, and its operation can be witnessed daily in the continuing clamour that people should be 'liberated' from compulsory participation in State-sponsored welfare schemes (a liberation that is usually confined to those sections of the population whose subsequent – and often compulsory – participation in a privately sponsored alternative scheme will considerably strengthen the market). What has not been so widely acknowledged, although its effect upon the welfare system is even more corrosive, is the way in which the welfare system is not only challenged from without by market alternatives, but changed from within, as continually intensifying pressures to have the welfare system approximate ever more closely to the market system itself take their effect. In this way, the welfare purposes which inspired their originators' efforts are so diverted or reshaped that, far from modifying the play of market forces in the interests of welfare, the encroachments of welfare are continuously met, contained, and reversed in the interests of the market. Ultimately, the welfare system comes to assume the shape and the values of the market, to identify itself increasingly with the purposes of the market, and to be seen not as an alternative to market methods of distribution, but as a buttress to them. Such a transformation of the welfare system will, of course, be hailed by exponents of the market as 'rational', 'realistic', and even 'progressive'. Thus the White Paper on the envisaged reform of the social-security system is claimed, by its authors, to be a more 'radical' document than the *Beveridge Report*, although in fact it finally sabotages the few remaining traces of the Beveridge principles (some of which, let it be said, well merited sabotage), while introducing nothing more radical than a logical extension of the Macmillan Government's Graduated Pensions Scheme. The assumption upon which such claims are based is that fourpence is twice as 'radical' as tuppence, and that any cash benefit uplifts the soul. It is an assumption worthy of Jeremy Bentham, but it has nothing to do with real radicalism, which must attack all attempts to measure people and their creative activities in cash.

One is reminded here of Tawney's wise advice that 'you can skin an onion leaf by leaf, but you can't skin a tiger claw by claw'. The market-tiger, is, however, not merely a brawny, but also a subtle beast, which has learned well that it is both easier, and ultimately more satisfactory, to nurse its prey before eating it. Today's controllers know how to subvert the purposes of welfare legislation from within. 'You can no more have a partly Socialist economy,' Ernest Mandel has written, 'than you can have a partly pregnant woman.' Welfare subversion of the norms of the market is inevitably contained and out-manoeuvred if it does not lead directly on to a radical and irreversible social transformation in which the relationships of *power* over the economy are reversed.

The dismal catalogue of retreat and withdrawal from the relatively whole-hearted post-war principles of welfare distribution could be given at depressing length. We watched the introduction of prescription charges (presumably, on the dubious grounds that those who really need drugs can afford to pay for them – a basic conviction of the market in all fields) and have now seen their recent reintroduction, a matter of months after the re-election of the Government which assumed office with a mandate to secure their abolition. This apostasy has merely been the most noted amid a host of increasinly market-oriented alterations of the welfare system.[17]

One example must suffice to demonstrate the persistent pressure to reintroduce market elements into the social-welfare system: a study of the twenty-year development of the social-security system, culminating in the White Paper of 28 January 1969, shows how carefully the bath water has been preserved, while distant wailing can be heard from Ministerial drains.

The *Beveridge Report*, nothing if not a Liberal document, readily accepted that welfare provision should not interfere too much with the market. We have already criticized at length Beveridge's restrictive assumptions about the virtue of the subsistence principle, his desire to goad people into improving their position through self-help, the accumulation of savings and other laudable bourgeois virtues, and his enthusiasm for insisting, even at the heart of a social-security programme, on doing nothing to impede what lovers of the *status quo* call indi-

17. Among which could be cited the restrictions on free school milk and school meals, increasing reliance on means-tested Supplementary Benefits, and the gradual but perceptible move towards selectivity in many areas of social welfare.

vidual initiative – known to the heretically disposed more simply as 'the rat-race'. At the same time, we should acknowledge that Beveridge was equally insistent upon a number of other principles of a far more truly radical nature. He was convinced that provision should be universal (that is that provision should not be confined to the demonstrably poor and needy, but should be made for everyone, rich and poor alike); in addition, provision should be uniform, that is that everyone should be equally assured, contributing and benefiting equally. Nowadays these latter provisions are all too often patronizingly interpreted as an understandable, if euphoric, reaction to the unifying trauma of a major war, almost as though the social ideals of unity and fellowship are irrelevant, if not actually undesirable, in peace time.[18]

In its operation, however, the National Insurance Scheme quickly departed from these original principles. Under the stress of inflation, and the erosion in the real value of the National Insurance rates of benefit, successive Governments came to rely increasingly upon developing the role of the National Assistance Board, rather than contemplate an increase in the universal rates of benefit. Needless to say, entitlement to relief from the N.A.B. rested firmly on stringently enforced demonstration of need by the applicant, a test which is represented by some people as a 'channelling of resources to those in greatest need', but seen by others as a revival of the discriminating, inevitably stigmatizing, practices of the last years of the Poor Law.

The initial departure from the principle of universal entitlement, was greatly extended by the 1959 Graduated Pensions Act. This Act made two renewed and major onslaughts on the Beveridge principles. To begin with it introduced the notion of graduation, of contribution and benefit, into the social-security system. In so far as this indicated a disenchantment

18. Such a jaundiced attitude to our shared and communal needs would be more plausible had not our more recent peace-time leaders so insistently urged us to rediscover the Dunkirk spirit as a means of reviving our flagging national efforts.

with the subsistence notion of need, it could be welcomed; but in so far as it was introduced without any associated policies to rationalize the market distribution of incomes, it not only acknowledged, but endorsed (within the modest limitations of the Scheme) the existing pattern of income distribution. Far from modifying this aspect of the play of market forces, it actually carried it into the heart of the welfare sector itself.

More than this, though: the 1959 Act established the right to contract out of the Graduated Pensions Scheme, in favour of any approved alternative superannuation schemes offered by private insurance companies. Since 1959, the proportion of the population which has been contracted out in this way has grown considerably: by the end of 1967 about 25 per cent of employees were contributing to privately organized occupational schemes, although such schemes cater more for administrative and managerial grades than for normal workers. In Professor Townsend's words

... Beveridge's scheme of flat-rate pensions has been destroyed by the acquisition of occupational pensions of a generous kind on the part of large numbers in the population, particularly salary-earners. We have in fact two emerging nations in old age. There are state pensioners whose incomes are supplemented by Means Test, and there are state pensioners who have occupational pensions as well, which are worked out on very different principles and are usually supplemented by the taxpayer. The question is whether to try to integrate the two systems in the interests of obtaining national unity and equalizing resources, which was implicit rather than carefully worked through in the Labour Party's 1957 scheme, or whether to accept two systems in perpetuity, which appears to be the conclusion the Government has now reached.[19]

In this way, the joint principles of graduation and contracting out have both contributed to the creation of a social-security system which sinuously perpetuates in retirement some of the basic inequalities which people experience in their working lives. In this sense, the social-security system has come increasingly not only to resemble but indeed to support, the

19. The *Guardian*, 29 January 1969.

'free market'. Contracting out has, of course, done more than merely support the market; the social-security contributions now constitute the largest single source of investment capital and have apparently become an indispensible prop to the sustained development of the market. But this particular investment capital is levied as a form of compulsory savings from a substantial proportion of the employed population; savings which are turned over to a series of private companies who invest them in equities on the Stock Exchange. At no point in these transactions does the contributor or the State have any control over these investments; this gives the companies concerned an unprecedented power of investment (and ultimately control) over crucial sectors of the market, a power which carries with it no responsibility or accountability to either the contributor or the community at large, other than a contractual commitment to honour pension pledges:

We do not know how this power is being used in terms of social welfare priorities or how far these massive investment funds are being or will be used to restore the outworn, mid-Victorian social capital of Britain. What we can only call 'social policy decisions' are, however, continually being made, without any proper awareness or public discussion of what is involved in terms of the common good, and what consequences may flow from the choices made. It all goes on in what Weber described as 'the secret sessions' of private bureaucratic power. 'The "secret",' he added, 'as a means of power, is, after all, more safely hidden in the books of an enterpriser than it is in the files of public authorities.' [20]

Of course, since Titmuss first wrote these words, the extension of the occupational pension schemes, and with it, the growth of the power and influence of the insurance companies, have only made his criticisms more relevant, and his general conclusion is more apt ten years later than it was at its first publication:

... as the power of the insurance interests (in combination with other financial and commercial interests) continues to grow they will,

20. Richard M. Titmuss 'The Irresponsible Society'. Reprinted in *Essays on the Welfare State*, 2nd ed., Allen & Unwin, 1963.

whether they consciously welcome it or no, increasingly become the arbiters of welfare and amenity for larger sections of the community. Their directors, managers and professionally trained advisers will be making, in their own eyes and in the eyes of many other people, sober, profitable and responsible decisions. But ultimately and in the aggregate they will not lead to a more rational and balanced disposition of social resources in relation to the needs of the nation and the problems of social organization in a new age. These office-holders of power will not see – for it is not, after all, their purpose or business to see – that one of the most important problems of the future will centre round the socially effective use of rising national incomes and not the technical running of this or that part of the economic system. A wrong sense of proportion in attitudes to the 'economic surplus' – to the savings of the community – for example, may well be one of the more serious dangers to public morality in the 1960s.

Nevertheless, these men will be driven, not as wicked men but as sober, responsible decision-makers, to intensify the contradictions which are distorting the economy and blurring the moral values of society. Social policies will be imposed without democratic discussion; without consideration of the moral consequences which may result from them. In this sense they will be irresponsible decisions.[21]

The phrase 'the socially effective use of rising national incomes' would, of course, be used by some to justify the use of pension funds as investment capital in this way. After all, is it not both convenient and desirable that in addition to guaranteeing pension rights, the contributions should be used to stimulate further economic growth? The rational view, of course, would be that it depends which parts of the economy are growing. We are back where we started this argument. Socially, most people would choose to have growth in a number of vital sectors, though they might well disagree over priorities. But if the market alone determines growth, then there is nothing whatever rational about it. What will sell will grow. So we have the spectacle of more and more motor-cars being produced to be driven on less and less adequate roads;

21. Richard M. Titmuss, op. cit., p. 216.

of ever more frenzied competition to occupy larger sectors of a shrinking market in a favoured handful of prosperous nations, while two thirds of the world's population hovers on the brink of starvation for the want of cheap agricultural machinery; or within the 'advanced' countries themselves, the sight of the evolution of a continuously widening gap between the comfortable majority and the deprived and growing minority. The real catch-phrase to describe such a landscape is 'private affluence and public squalor, with private squalor seeding in every crevice'.

Left to itself, welfare intervention by the State can never break this vicious circle, and indeed, normally, will not be intended to try. If the problem is to be mastered, a structural revolution is required, to abrogate the private control of public resources, and to settle priorities by rational democratic debate rather than the alchemy of the market. That such a system has never yet been adequately tried makes it the more important to begin to experiment with it.

Let us briefly examine what sort of forces might be interested in beginning such a change.

10 The Fight Against Low Pay

About 2½ million males and about 5 million females, including juveniles and part-time workers, habitually earn less than £15 a week, whilst 1¼ million adult male full-time workers take home less than £15 a week. ... Most women are low-paid, and ... workers in ill-health or over 50 are often low-paid. The majority are low-paid either because they live in the less prosperous regions or work in the more inefficient industries, or both.[1]

It was with these words that Mr Donnet, of the General and Municipal Workers' Union, presented a resolution on low pay to the 1968 T.U.C. The resolution was carried by such a large assent that no call was made for a card vote. This Centenary Congress followed a whole succession of impassioned debates within the affiliated unions, in which the Government's Incomes Policy was scrutinized by delegate after delegate. Again and again it was alleged that the low-paid were at least as badly situated, and often even worse off, as a result of this policy, than they have been hitherto.

As Miss V. Parker, a York representative at the U.S.D.A.W. (shop workers') conference, put it: 'I am very sorry indeed to say that two years ago I went to the rostrum in support of the prices and incomes policy because of what Mr George Brown said: "we shall look after the lower-paid worker". I am afraid I have also been very disillusioned, very disillusioned indeed.' Miss Parker spoke from experience. She never takes home more than £11 a week.

1. *T.U.C. Report*, 1968, p. 577.

In answer to a delegate who had raised the problem 'how do you define a low-paid worker?' she retorted: 'Has our friend from Birmingham never heard of the three card trick? Has he never been asked to "find the lady"? Because that is where the lower-paid workers are.'

Of course, it is generally conceded that women's wages are often disgracefully low. But at the fifty-third congress of the General and Municipal Workers' Union, there were plenty of men who came forward to show that they and their workmates were almost as badly off. Evidence of this trend is to be got from a host of other unions.

Ever since Townsend and Abel-Smith published the results of their investigation in 'The Poor and the Poorest' it has been increasingly understood that low pay is a prime cause of poverty. Townsend and Abel-Smith's calculations received striking confirmation from the Ministry of Social Security's *Report on the Circumstances of Families*. According to this report, in the summer of 1966, no less than 125,000 families with two or more children, in which the father was working full-time, had total resources below the level of the provisions of public relief (Supplementary Benefit). 65,000 of these had less than £12 10s. 0d. a week.

In both our surveys of the St Ann's district of Nottingham, we found very clear evidence that it was not the legendary fertility of the poor which explained their condition, since, for most families living on the borderline of poverty, it was the second or third child, rather than the fifth or sixth, who plunged them below it. When we said, in the report on the findings of our first survey, that low wages were an important cause of poverty, the *Times Educational Supplement* thought this was so obvious a point that it qualified as the 'funny of the week'. But the picture which is now emerging is one in which not only the sick, the unemployed, or the bereaved sink below acceptable standards: there is also a staggering number of working people, who put in a full week's work to earn less money than they might, in other circumstances, be able to draw as a dole. Perhaps all this does seem obvious. But when one is constantly met by angry citizens who claim that modern

poverty, unlike poverty in the old days, is a just reward for indolence, vice, and general lassitude, it becomes important to
say the obvious, and if necessary, to say it loud.

A general study of the problem of low wages has been made
by Judith Marquand.[2] She analysed Ministry of Labour statistics, collected in 1960, about the earnings of adult male
workers, to produce a shattering account of the concentration
of low-paid workers in various industries. This showed that,
while the low-paid manufacturing industries are, quite predictably, mainly contracting industries, there are two serious
exceptions to the trend which correlates poor wages with an
adverse market. Five out of six low-paid non-manufacturing
industries had expanded in the period she reviewed. Further,
a key place in the league table of low-paid industries is occupied by local and national Government service.

Judith Marquand also showed that 'there is a strong tendency
for industries employing many women to have particularly low
rates of pay for the low-paid men employed in the industry.'

The conditions of working women represent a scandal in
their own right, quite apart from the adverse pressure which
their reduced rates of pay exert, in all too many cases, on the
earnings of the male workers employed alongside them. Over
half the employed women in this country are paid less than five
shillings an hour, while only 4% get more than ten shillings an
hour. Over a third of the jobs currently filled by women are
routine: non-manual jobs, almost completely devoid of responsibility. Yet it appears that most of the married women who
return to work, even of this kind, do so primarily in order to
escape the even greater boredom of domestic life. The class of
women workers is, truly, a twice-exploited class, which is even
more alienated from control over the conditions of its life than
are the male workers.[3]

2. 'Which are the low-paid Workers?', *British Journal of Industrial
Relations*, November 1967.
3. The trade-union campaign for equal pay has been stronger in resolu-
tionary fervour than in practical results. There are two basic definitions
of equal pay: equal pay for equal work, which has come to mean that
if a woman strays onto a job which would normally be done by a man,
she must be paid the same rate; and equal pay for work *of equal value*,

Here again, the tendency for local and national Government services to set a bad example to the rest of industry is as marked as it is in the case of male workers. In spite of the fact that the Government has conceded the principle of equal pay in the civil service, there are still, according to the *Incomes Data Service*, over '600,000 women industrial workers in national local-government service, and public sector industries such as forestry, the Atomic Energy Authority and the Health Service, who are not entitled to equal pay'.

In mid-1967, a family consisting of a man, his wife, and one child, could, assuming that they had previously been living above that level, when they came in need of public relief, draw from the Ministry of Social Security benefit to the extent of £14 a week. Calculating that a man in work would have additional expenses for travelling, and for standard stoppages, the

---

which means that equivalent grades of work should be equally paid, whether or not they are mainly female occupations. The effect of the implementation of the second definition, would be to put all women on at least the same basic rates of pay as apply to men throughout industry, unless the unions were asleep at the time.

Working on the first definition, which has, not unnaturally, been accepted by the Confederation of British Industry as a basis for dis-cussion, some 3 million women would get wage-increases. On the second definition put forward by the T.U.C. and the I.L.O., 7 million would be affected. An I.L.O. Convention, number 100, outlines this principle. Like the famous convention on the forty-hour week, established before the war, it has never been ratified by the Government. That the present Government has failed to ratify either of these conventions is yet another instance of its failure to use its power to protect trade unionism. To leave the convention on equal pay unratified is, of course, to make a com-plete mockery of all the claims that the incomes policy is designed to help meet the needs of the low-paid workers, in whose interests many unions misguidedly agreed to surrender powers.

Trade unions have by no means solved the problem of female recruit-ment, and the proportion of women trade unionists is still deplorably low in many industries. This unpalatable fact minimizes the possibilities of equalization of wages through bargaining machinery alone. At the same time, the legislative approach is not being actively pushed by many trade unionists, who have come to expect more kicks than halfpence from the political wing of their movement during the last few lamentable years.

T.U.C. has argued that the minimum income of such a man should be £15 a week. Those earning less than this amount are officially defined by the T.U.C. as 'low paid'. The statistics concerning industrial earnings are unsatisfactory, and precise information is very difficult to come by.[4] The 1960 Survey of the Distribution of Earnings, for example, covered only 73 per cent of manual workers, leaving out such important, and often ill-paid, groups as clerks, farm workers and hotel workers, and also under-representing the low-paid workers in those industries it *did* cover.[5] The T.U.C. have calculated the number of low-paid men as being in the region of 1,800,000.

In our inquiry into St Ann's, we found plenty of confirming evidence on these matters. A list of the occupations of the people we interviewed who were receiving incomes between 120 per cent and 140 per cent of their social-security entitlement will make this perfectly plain. We found only two self-employed men, a general dealer and a window cleaner. We found one deaf rehabilitation trainee. After that, we ran into a variety of occupations we might expect to find listed in a count of people in poverty; the Wages Council sectors of people working in, for instance, catering. Some of these are on any count grossly exploited, and we are not sure if some may not be illegally exploited.[6] But after this, we came across a list,

4. Hence the call of the N.U.G.M.W. for an up-to-date comprehensive survey. This has been taken up by the T.U.C.: cf. *N.U.G.M.W. Annual Conference Report*, 1968, pp. 327–49 and *T.U.C. Annual Conference Report*, 1968, pp. 567ff.

5. See Edmunds and Radice, 'Low Pay', Fabian Research Series, No. 270, p. 5.

6. In his survey of 'Minimum Wages in a Fully Employed City', Mr E. G. A. Armstrong investigated the extent to which Wages Council rates were found to have been flouted, in Birmingham, over a period of three years. He presented a dismal picture: 'In only two weeks of the three years were no inspections carried out in Birmingham. In 137 of the remaining 154 weeks, arrears were recovered. Amounts recovered in any one week ranged from 10s. to £1,765 10s. while the weekly averages of arrears were 1962–£92, 1963–£121, 1964–£68. As already indicated, the bulk of these arrears were recovered through routine inspection. The inferences seem plain – the near certainty of a chronic condition of

not of people employed singly in the service trades, difficult to organize and isolated from others in the same bad conditions, nor even of declining and weakly competitive industries: but the very contrary. It is a list of people employed in most of the major industries of the Nottingham area, and indeed, in the very largest factories, some of which are household names. A pipemaker at Stanton Ironworks; a soap processor at Boots; even some coal-miners employed by the National Coal Board. These rather shocking instances indicate that there is real scope for energetic work by trade unions, not merely in organizing new and more difficult territory, but in servicing that already gained. We even found a number of people living below 120 per cent of the old N.A.B. rates and working for the bigger firms, in which there are relatively strong trade-union organizations. A painter's labourer at Howitt's, a Barton bus driver, a storekeeper at Raleigh cycles, and two more coal-miners were among these unfortunates.

In this context, our findings about low pay in St Ann's fit into and complement a dismal picture. The thing they emphasize above all is that the low-paid are not evenly spread, a thin layer of underprivilege across the nation, but are herded together into ghettoes, in which they share not only low wages, but a dozen other social deprivations, from slum houses, meagre public services, squalid urban surroundings, at the material level; to the accompanying moral sense that nothing can be done, that they are at the bottom of the pit.

Furthermore, a disproportionate number of the people in our survey area were temporarily unemployed. Four people whose households fell into the category of families living at between 120 per cent and 140 per cent of their social-security entitlement, and at least nine people living in households which existed exactly at, or below, those rates, were unemployed. In all, some fifteen households were in poverty because of tem-

---

infractions and of undetected arrears every week. Full, even over-full employment, is clearly no substitute for continuing, year-round inspection. On average, arrears were recovered for six workers every inspection week and three firms found to be in arrears.'

porary unemployment (this figure excludes the chronic sick, and people who were obviously not easily employable). This number is greater than should be expected in a sample of this size. On the most conservative count, leaving out the cases of which we are not sure, and exaggerating the size of the relevant population against which the unemployed group is to be compared, we have about 6 per cent of the breadwinners of the survey district among those registered as unemployed, as contrasted with the East Midlands Regional rate of 1·9 per cent on 10 April 1967.[7] This rate is itself, by previous standards, abnormally high, as a result of the effects of the 'freeze and squeeze' economic policies which had been in operation nationally since the preceding July. A hitherto more usual figure for the East Midlands is that for 18 April 1966, which was 0·9 per cent. It seems plausible that the figures of unemployment in St Ann's would be likely to register at least the same fluctuations as those in the rest of the region: and, indeed, to the extent that 'problem families' are concentrated in the area, it could be that unemployment has been more seriously augmented in St Ann's than elsewhere, since it could easily be assumed that unskilled, perhaps relatively unstable workers, might be among the first victims of retrenchment. If this is so, then our figures for poverty in the district as a whole will have been distorted by the pressures of the economic policies followed since July 1966 and, should the economic recovery which is widely, if not very convincingly, anticipated, ever materialize, there would then be a certain improvement in the position in St Ann's. The effects of such fluctuations in the rhythm of the economy are rather difficult to document precisely; it is widely assumed that the East Midlands is a sheltered area; and, in that its overall unemployment statistics are much less unfavourable than those of most other areas,[8] this would seem to be true. What is misleading

7. Ministry of Labour *Gazette*, May 1967, Table III, p. 421. This rate has since proved remarkably steady, and was at exactly the same level in December 1968.

8. 2·4 per cent in December 1968, for the United Kingdom, 2·7 per cent in the South Western Region, 2·3 per cent in the North West, 2·5 per

about such general abstractions as these percentage rates of unemployed is precisely their failure to reveal specific concentrations such as that which appears to exist in St Ann's. If 1·9 per cent of unemployment were distributed evenly throughout the whole population, it would not have quite the shock-effect which it has in the actual event, in which it strikes much harder at some areas, and at some classes of people, than at others. Indeed, during the time that our first survey was coming to its conclusion, the *Daily Mirror* ran a special series of articles throughout a whole week, on the theme of 'Nottingham as a Boom Town'. It can be imagined with what wry expressions these articles were read in parts of St Ann's.

The people who are unemployed and living at or below the old National Assistance rates are important for a rather different reason. They have been caught in the 'wage-stop', which is a ruling which determines that any unemployed man on Supplementary Benefit must not, as a result of his adversity, receive a greater payment than he would have done if he had remained in full-time employment. This ruling has generated a great deal of controversy, since it clearly penalizes low wage-earners and large families. Its object is to discourage people from curing what appears to be regarded as their personal problem of low wages by ceasing work in order to live at the public expense. Its critics feel that a more humane disincentive to such idleness would be to ensure that wages and Family Allowances were universally fixed at a level at least as high as that fixed by the State as its minimum subsistence level.[9] It should be emphasized that there are several grounds on which unemployed persons may appeal against the application of the

cent in Yorkshire and Humberside, 3·6 per cent and 4·8 per cent in Scotland and the North respectively, and 4·0 per cent in Wales: only London and the South East and Eastern and Southern had more favourable statistics. The West Midlands, however, shared the same rate of 1·9 per cent.

9. Foremost among these critics is the Child Poverty Action Group. See 'The Wage Stop' (*Poverty*, No. 2, 1967), an article by Tony Lynes who was the Group's secretary; see also the Group's Memorandum to the Chancellor of the Exchequer in the same issue.

wage-stop to their benefit, but that in most cases no such appeals are made. Trade unions and social workers can find significant scope for work in assisting people in this condition to claim their rights, and this is especially true in districts like St Ann's. Left to themselves, many people living in or on the verge of poverty are either reluctant or unable to avail themselves of services to which they are entitled. Thus, in a different but related field, in November 1965, only 4 per cent of the children under five, nationally, who were entitled to free welfare foods, including milk, actually received them; the Ministry of Social Security estimates in its recent survey of family circumstances that approximately one quarter of the schoolchildren whose fathers are in full-time work, and who are entitled to free school meals, actually receive them; and in St Ann's we found that only 23 people had applied for a rate rebate (5.5 per cent), although 156 families lived in poverty (37.7 per cent), many of whom would certainly have qualified. If rights such as those involved in these areas of welfare are not exercised, in a situation in which no reprisals are conceivable against the claimants, it is hardly surprising that people are still less prone to exercise their rights in more contentious areas, in which they may indeed feel vulnerable to reprisals. Thus, in St Ann's we only encountered seven people who had ever applied to a rent tribunal for a cut in rent, although there were a number of people who might have established their case, had they been prepared to try. (We did find several people who expressly said that while they thought their rent was unreasonable, they feared eviction or other counter-action if they complained.)

With all the scope there is in St Ann's for this kind of welfare assistance, it is the more remarkable that voluntary organizations are so comparatively weak. There is no great enthusiasm for the established political movements, even though a majority of people claim to have voted in both general and local elections. This claim is false, at any rate in regard to the local elections: although it may be said in mitigation of the favourable gloss which St Ann's voters put on their electoral turn-out, that many of them may not quite appreciate the frequency of local elections, and may accurately claim to have voted at some relatively recent time, even if they did not vote at the last possible opportunity. Certainly only a tiny handful are members of a political party, and very few people are active in support of one.

Trade unions are much stronger. About one householder in five belonged to a trade union, and in a district like St Ann's they are a key group. For a start they belong to something and feel less isolated and vulnerable. Secondly they are among the better-paid members of the community. Although they are obviously vigilant in defence of their own interests, they are not especially selfish. On the contrary, as we have seen, they are rather more egalitarian in outlook than most, rather more conscious than most of injustices and discriminations, rather more adventurous than most in the demands they make on behalf of themselves and their class.

Indeed they do not conform with any striking accuracy to the 'I'm-all-right-Jack' stereotype of trade-union mentality. Of course, trade-union activity is not invariably egalitarian: although unions have traditionally preoccupied themselves with 'fair' wages, and been actively concerned with the protection of those weaker than themselves, yet a crucial part of trade-union strategy has always hinged on the maintenance and development of 'differentials'. Nonetheless what is clear is that although trade unionists are, on the whole, richer than the other inhabitants of St Ann's, a majority of them are still not in favour of the present distribution of income. If the greater egalitarian response we got from the people living in poverty can be attributed at least in part to obvious self-interest, there are, nonetheless, strong grounds for thinking that at least some part of the similar trade-union concern is solidary in its nature, based upon concern for people less able to defend themselves.

Trade-union militants are often reproached for pursuing every possible opportunity for self-enrichment, and it has more than once been pointed out that the most strike-prone people are frequently among the better-paid, or at any rate among the best-paid in relation to effort exerted. The reply of the militants would probably be, with some considerable force of logic, that this combination of action and effect had, indeed, been understood, and for that reason, continually reapplied. But it is a mistake, frequently made in newspapers, to identify this developed reaction with a studied indifference to the fate of people who happen to be less fortunate. In a paradoxical sense, it appears, up to a point, to be true that the more people are aware of the collective power they can wield in their own immediate interest, the more real is the possibility that they will come to a generous understanding of the meaning of such abstractions as 'community' or 'social' welfare. Certainly, the assumption that low-paid workers are poor because well-paid workers are not, is false. Not only does it leave out of account the whole area of non-wage incomes, but also it ignores all that is known about the sociology of collective bargaining. Employers do not normally rush forward to offer wage increases to people who are unwilling to demand them. Trade unionists are apt to echo the words of Mr Frank Cousins: 'while there is a free-for-all, we are part of the all', and to assert what leverage they can if they find themselves in a favourable market situation. However, this behaviour does not by any means betoken indifference to the fate of those who are either well organized but in a bad market position, or simply badly organized.

There is every evidence that the clinching argument which secured initial trade-union acquiescence in the Government's Incomes Policy was that it would, in some way, guarantee 'social justice'. The Statement of Intent, signed under the auspices of Mr George Brown on 16 December 1964, declared its '... social objective is to ensure that the benefits of faster growth are distributed in a way that satisfies the claims of social need and justice'. The White Paper on Prices and Incomes Policy [10] said, further: 'It is necessary not only to create the conditions in which essential structural re-adjustments can be carried out smoothly, but also to promote social

10. Cmnd 2639, April 1965, Para. 17.

justice.' Even when it became clear that economic growth was no longer on offer, and the ill-fated National Plan, which was supposed to be the underpinning of the whole construction of Incomes Policy, had been jettisoned, the White Paper on 'severe restraint' [11] reaffirmed that 'Improvement of the standard of living of the worst-off members of the community is a primary social objective.' [12]

Manifestly, had the Trades Union Congress been split on the grounds of pure self-interest, between low-paid workers who

11. Cmnd 3150, November 1966, Para. 28.

12. How far the Prices and Incomes Board has allocated priority to such a 'primary' objective can be judged from its treatment of the farm workers' pay-claim. (Cmnd 3911, H.M.S.O.) While authorizing a 7·4 per cent increase to these workers, thus raising their wages to the munificent level of £12 8s. a week, th P.I.B. declared itself unable to discriminate in any positive way beyond this point, even though, in their own words, the farm workers 'are by a fair margin the lowest-paid body of workers of significant size in the country' (sic). In the apt words of *New Society* (6 February 1969):

'The prices and incomes white paper permits pay increases "where there is general recognition that existing wage and salary levels are too low to maintain a reasonable standard of living". Statistics of farm workers' earnings are published in sufficient detail to enable the proportion falling below the social security minimum for an average family to be calculated. Figures were submitted to the board by the Child Poverty Action Group showing that the £13 a week or less earned by one in four male general farm workers represents, with family allowances added, a net income below the supplementary benefit rate for a family with three children aged 5–10 and paying the average rural rent. There would surely be "general recognition" that a three-child family with the father in full-time work ought to have an income at or above supplementary benefit level.

'The P.I.B., however, argues that since needs are determined by family commitments, "it is not possible to lay down a particular earnings figure which divides workers who qualify for an increase in pay under the existing low pay criterion from the rest". All one can do, therefore, is to compare the earnings of a particular group of workers with those in other industries. This conclusion is clearly unsatisfactory. The wording of the white paper, cautious and unspecific though it is, clearly implies an accepted standard of adequacy. Sooner or later we shall have to decide what we mean when we say that wages are not only low but too low. The P.I.B. has missed an ideal opportunity of making a start towards such a definition.'

would expect to benefit from the policy, and better-paid workers who would not, the policy could never have secured support, if only because skilled, and relatively better-off, workers frequently dominate the effective power structures even of unions which organize many low-paid workers. The rhetoric of social justice had a powerful appeal. At every individual conference, and at the T.U.C.'s own Congresses and special Executive Conferences, the proponents of the incomes policy inevitably took it at its face value.

Experience, however, rapidly soured the enthusiasts who thought that a major new instrument of equity had been established in the Prices and Incomes Board. John Hughes has provided a close analysis of the effect of the incomes policy on low-paid workers.[13] After examining the lowest earnings recorded in the regional statistics of Incomes, Prices, Employment and Production, he reported:

For April 1967 I examined each regional industry group in which the average earnings of men manual workers were less than 320s. a week. At the time the 'all industries' average was 411s. 7d., so that the industries surveyed showed earnings at least 20% below the industrial average. Leaving aside Northern Ireland, there were 34 cases in Great Britain of such regional-industries. Of these 34 lowest-earning regional-industries in Great Britain: 6 showed more than the 'all-industries' percentage increase in earnings from April 1960 to April 1967; 2 showed the same percentage increase; but 26 showed less than the 'all industries' percentage increase. Thus, this approach suggests two things. One is that the earnings gap has widened *against* many of the lowest paid industries in the 1960s (in Great Britain; for Northern Ireland the majority of cases show some closing of the proportional gap). The second is that regional development may be an essential element in an incomes policy that is concerned to improve the lot of the lowest paid workers. This is something the T.U.C. has recognized, but it is far less clear that the Government has recognized it.

Hughes assembles other important evidence from the *Prices and Incomes Board Report* on the 'package deal' in the engineering industry, which shows that in the three-year period

13. *Poverty*, No. 7, pp. 12–16.

concerned 'the gap between minimum earnings levels and average earnings increased'.

If this evidence is taken in conjunction with the effect of other Government policies, such as employment programme, or taxation measures, the resultant balance sheet becomes even more unfavourable for the low-paid. Hughes argues that at any rate up to 1966, 'the incidence of all taxes and benefits had not shifted in favour of lower income households'; he shows that not only has unemployment risen in sheer numbers, but also that it has intensified in its rigours: '64.4 per cent of the men registered as unemployed have been unemployed *for over eight weeks*. I have made the approximate calculation that the figure for wholly unemployed in October 1967 (when 532,000 were unemployed) represented ... *10,000,000 weeks of unemployment.*' [14]

Hughes concludes, 'If incomes policy is viewed, as it should

14. Since John Hughes' research into this question, other investigations have been made. One such was completed by Mr R. F. Fowler, director of statistical research at the Department of Employment and Productivity. Commenting on this, Eric Wigham wrote in *The Times*, January 1969:

'. . . it is the extended period of transitional unemployment with which we are concerned. A comparison between October 1963, and October last year suggests that as high a proportion of men found new jobs within three weeks then as do within four weeks now.

'Why this has happened and why new vacancies are not filled as quickly as they used to be must be largely a matter of surmise. But redundancy pay can be only a minor factor.

'There are other possibilities. The number of skilled vacancies seems to form a higher proportion of the total and the filling of a skilled vacancy obviously requires greater care and consideration than one for an unskilled man. The shake-out which followed the economic measures of 1966 has resulted in a higher proportion of older people on the registers and older people are harder to place.

'It may also be that employers, having weeded out the least useful members of their labour force, are being more careful to maintain high standards. The effect of the selective employment tax has been to make some employers in sectors of industry, particularly service sectors, think carefully about taking on extra men.

'It looks as if it is not only workers who have become more choosy, but employers, too. And the result is likely to be a permanently higher level of transitional unemployment.'

be, in its combination with other Government economic policies bearing upon the position of the low-paid worker, the balance that results from the last three years is an adverse one for the low-paid.'

In other words, 'social justice' has become a casualty of the economic stringency in which the Government has found itself. When the unions were originally coaxed into cooperation with the Government in its economic policies, there *was* good reason for them to look out means for securing an overall, social attack on all the linked problems of deprivation which we have been discussing. As Mr Ron Smith, then General Secretary of the Union of Post Office Workers, put it:

> We have heard a lot about free-for-alls and how in free-for-alls the unions are part of the all. ... My people are not part of the all, and the majority of the people that you represent here are not part of the all in a free-for-all society. Why the hell do we want to get rid of a free-for-all, I'm-all-right-Jack society if we really believe our people can make progress in it? Of course they cannot, and you know as well as I know that even within our society the vast majority of the people we represent here are not within these fantastic brackets of wages and of recognition that so many people pretend we are getting in a full employment society.
>
> I believe that within a policy such as has been adumbrated by the N.E.D.C. and has been adumbrated by the General Council there has got to be a recognition of the distorted wage structure that we have. And there has got to be a recognition of the problems of the service industry, of the unskilled workers, of the lower-paid people – nearly 2 millions of them adult men still earning only £10 and less a week in this country. We have got to do something in their interest as well as in those of the other sections of the community.
>
> The alternative I believe is a planned society ...

Indeed, that is the alternative: but implied within Mr Smith's view were a series of assumptions about *for whom* such plans should be made. Four years after Mr Smith had helped to carry the unions into support for 'planning', his successor, Mr Tom Jackson, was finding it necessary to speak about 'putting the Government to the test' by submitting a claim for Civil Service Unions which would compel it to meet the issue of the hosts of low-paid workers toiling in its own backyard. There is, it need hardly be said, no real sign that the Government is even going to attempt to pass any such test. The fact is all too plain: the rhetoric about 'the language of priorities' which accompanied the rise to office of Mr Wilson's administration can now be judged in relation to its *actual* priorities, made manifest through several years.

In this context, the question before the unions is not simply 'what policies do you wish to have implemented?' Already this has been amply answered. There is no need for elaborate research to buttress the claim for a minimum-wage guarantee which will ensure that family standards at least meet the standards of social-security entitlements, or to underpin the demand for meaningful further increases in Family Allowances.

It is true that more detailed information about the extent and causes of low pay would be helpful to the Government in rationalizing its policies, if it had any serious intention of attacking these problems. But the appeal for more information, made by the N.U.G.M.W. and endorsed by the T.U.C., should not in any way be construed as an alibi for the lack of such action. The beginning of wisdom in this matter is the appreciation that nothing will be done if the demand for amelioration is not backed by real social power. Had the Prices and Incomes Board been remotely concerned with 'social justice', it would, upon its constitution, have set its ample staff to work immediately to analyse such problems. Of course it did no such thing, and for good reason. In reality, Government 'planning' today is concerned above all to avoid the resolution of the problem of low pay, the elementary solution to which it has always known, but has come to regard as at best inflationary, and at worst rankly communist. In either event, to mention it seriously is, for the Treasury, akin to dalliance with the Devil himself. In such circumstances the question the unions must answer is not so much how they should formulate their demands, but far more urgently, how they should mobilize to secure their implementation. If you are concerned to rally forces for action, you need simple rallying-cries: detailed blue-prints for the reform of social security are neither necessary nor helpful. While the complexities of draft legislation may well reinforce the popular view that social priorities are fixed by extremely clever specialists, and require mastery of infinite mysteries, everyone can perfectly easily understand the social justice involved in a £15 minimum wage. It is even arguable that everyone can understand that if the economy as it is now constituted cannot afford such a meagre concession to adult full-time workers, this is so much the worse for the present con-stitution of the economy. For sure, it will be generally agreed that if a General Strike were to impose such a demand to-morrow, there would be convulsions in the economic order. It should be as generally understood that this event would only serve to establish what planning is *about*. If social justice is a priority, then society, including the economy, must be so arranged as to enforce it. It is sheer mythology to argue that the necessary rearrangements are impossible: they are entirely simple, provided that you are prepared to attack the authority of wealth and property. But if you regard yourself as subject to this authority, it becomes transparently plain that social justice is not only not a priority, but that it weighs nowhere in the scales. For it to become important, the unions will need above all to put force behind their arguments. Talk alone will not only be insufficient, but will actually worsen the position, because its guaranteed lack of effect will serve to extend still further the active process of demoralization which has already afflicted the Labour Movement since the apostasy of its Gov-ernment. Talk will only deepen the already profound apathy which is engulfing the working population. But a series of mobilizing actions would have the opposite effect.

Of course the fundamental difficulty in which the unions are caught is that Mr Ron Smith's strategy for social reform, which was until recently the orthodoxy of every union, and almost the whole Left, has now proved totally inoperable. All present-day studies of the problem of poverty draw added poignancy from the fact that the traditional agencies for reform have proved themselves irremediably bankrupt. Given the choice between helping the poor and maintaining the existing social order, the Labour Party in office has chosen, at every turn of policy, those measures which uphold the received *status quo*. It is very pretty to talk about 'putting the economy right, and then paying ourselves a dividend'. But even in the unlikely event that the economy can be righted by Mr Jenkins' efforts after a whole series of Conservative chancellors applying nearly identical formulae have abysmally failed, the reward for such a rectification will probably be defeat at the polls at the hands of all those whose modest claims have been set aside in order to ensure it. In the course of this evolution, the claims of 'planning' had already been reduced to cover purely the 'rationalization' of the existing condition of things, and have long since ceased to connote any kind of encroachment by the needs of social welfare into the domain of market sovereignty. Everywhere, indeed, welfare contracts to admit more of the market, in which power becomes more and more concentrated in fewer, and more untrammelled, hands.

Today there is an increasingly apparent crisis in the political structure of this country, necessarily occasioned by the defection of the Labour Government to the camp of conventional wisdom. In the middle-term, provided always that democracy itself is not, in the interim, extinguished in a 'strong state', the answer to this will be the regeneration of the socialist movement, embracing the important trade unions and most of the supporters of what is left of the present Labour Party. This process will require an active onslaught on all the circumstances of poverty and deprivation, in a thorough-going agitation which will bring to the slums and housing estates an awareness of the vast social power which sleeps within them. But in the short run, the unions will have to act for themselves, because it is unfortunately clear that the socialist forces are so divided and disoriented as to be quite incapable of constituting, quickly, any overall political alternative to the moribund hulk which Mr Wilson has left of the Labour Party's principles and organization. Indeed, until open war breaks out within that organization, on the issue of its failure to honour any of its fundamental pledges and its total present lack of optimistic perspective, it will be very difficult for socialism to reassert itself, since the basic questions for socialism, both as an ideal and as a movement, are all posed by the collapse of the moral credibility of the Labour Government. The movement to clean up house within the Labour Party cannot be indefinitely deferred, but it is to be feared that it may be held off until after the catastrophe of the next election. If anything could accelerate it, and thus avert the worst disasters for the Labour Movement, it would be the speedy development of an aggressive initiative by the trade unions on this very question.

What, then, could the unions do? One immediate action which they might undertake would be a campaign to organize the poor. Such a move would not be unprecedented. In the United States, last August, the Teamsters' and United Automobile Workers' Unions met in Chicago and agreed upon an Alliance for Labour Action. They adopted a fifteen-point programme, the basic purpose of which was to organize the unorganized. They agreed to set up a network of Neighbourhood Unions for the unemployed and the poor, and to develop a series of actions 'to achieve equal opportunity and equal rights' for social minorities. Significantly, they also agreed to work, in the course of this campaign, to 'repair the alienation of the liberal-intellectual community and the youth of our nation in order to build and strengthen a new alliance of progressive forces'. As a beginning, they gave a million dollars for the organization of refrigeration workers, and discussed means of addressing the problem of organizing agricultural workers. Of course, both of these two organizations have been excluded from the A.E.L.-C.I.O.: and they operate in a political context in which an American Labour Party is still, largely, undreamt of.

In Britain, by contrast, there exists a significant number of unions already individually committed to the £15 minimum claim, and these have at least secured the moral commitment of the T.U.C. to the same goal. In the local Trades Councils there already exists a whole network of organizations which could promote and carry through a recruitment drive – at any rate among the poorer areas and industries of their own towns. They could also act as a clearing house for membership, allocating newly joined members to their appropriate organizations. But, of course, no recruiting campaign would meet with any significant success unless it were centred around plausible activities. The low-paid have been promised so much, so often and have received so little, so generally, as to have become somewhat immune to verbal blandishments. A national one-day stoppage, in which all trade unionists were asked to spend their time recruiting among the poorer housing areas, or visiting and picketing non-union areas of business, might be far more credible than the most carefully researched briefs, as far as the poor are concerned. If necessary, such a device could be repeated several times until it was taken seriously. Within such a strategy, increasing attention could be given to the servicing of inter-union field stations among poor housing areas, the provision of competent advice and representation before such bodies as rent tribunals, and the block-by-block attack on inferior working conditions in shops, offices and sweated workshops. There is ample organizing capacity available within the local organizations of the trade-union movement for such a labour. To begin it would not only be to start to dispel the almost universal cynicism about the political process which now exists throughout the country, but also to provide a powerful corrosive solvent to the generalized sentiment, so carefully inculcated in the newspapers, that trade unions are unconcerned with general welfare and entirely preoccupied by the search for their own sectional advantages. This notion has always been a libel on the trade-union movement, as has been amply demonstrated for all who care to see, by its overlong acceptance of the ill-considered Incomes Policy. The forged credentials of this policy were all, as we have shown, testimonies to the need for re-distribution of income and the protection of the poor, while its real charter was the continued control of wages in order to guarantee the continued dominance of profit-mongers and bond-forgers over the economy and society. If the victims of the present policy were originally persuaded to accept it for good reasons, in a spirit of concern for greater equality, there can, today, be no good reason for their spurning the search for other, more effective, means to the same end. As we write, all Italy has just stopped work in order to secure an adequate level of old-age pensions. There can be little doubt that any genuine reforming tendencies which may linger in either the Italian or the British Governmental structures would be powerfully reinforced by such a demonstration. The forces prepared to seek a real social transformation would gather cohesion and strength within it. If anything could halt the political slide to the obscurantist Right, it would be this. And if there is anything else that would compel the uncomfortable administrators who hold sway over all of us to see the stark face of deprivation and accumulated social neglect which is veiled in all our major cities by their neon promises of so-called affluence, we do not know what it is.

11 Wanted—A New Radical Attack

I

Much of the (admittedly dilatory) public discussion about poverty, and most of the measures prescribed for dealing with it, have been concerned with what has been seen simply as a welfare problem, requiring more or less major alterations in our social-security system. But in a community like St Ann's (and such communities will be found in every major town and city) poverty is seen to be infinitely more complex than this. To begin with, poverty is a great deal more than an impartially calculated shortage of money. It is also a profound and permanent sense of insecurity which afflicts those who hover around a poverty line as much as, and maybe more than, those living permanently below such a line. Poverty is often aggravated by poor housing, in a way that is readily apparent in St Ann's, and although these two problems of housing and material hardship can be bureaucratically distinguished, in real life they are often interlocked with one another so intimately as to become in practice inseparable. More: they feed off one another, because shortage of money can make substandard housing virtually uninhabitable, while the continued inconvenience of bad housing highlights and continuously emphasizes impoverishment. Again, as we have already argued at length, areas like St Ann's suffer from generations of public and social neglect, a neglect which meshes in with the 'private' distress caused by housing and money worries, and reinforces the sense of despair as a way of life, of hopelessness as the normal condition, which one so frequently encounters. Now the problems of poverty, of housing, and of environment are all recognized by authority, but are usually recognized separately. Thus any official social policy is liable to be at best, fragmentary and partial, and in certain instances can do as much harm as good. For example, a perfectly laudable desire to improve housing standards will, if it involves (as it usually does) substantial increases in the level of chargeable rents on the new properties, put yet another pressure upon family budgets already stretched to their limits; the poor family's living standards will then have to be further reduced to meet the new rent, or the demoralizing search for cheaper (and probably overcrowded as well as substandard) accommodation will start again. Similarly, expenditure on primary school improvements in the aftermath of the *Plowden Report*, although desirable in itself, poignantly highlights the shocking inadequacies of the overcrowded homes for whose children the improved schools are to cater.

Clearly what is required is a systematic, simultaneous and integrated assault upon all these areas of deprivation. All the social policies mentioned have an essential role, not as alternatives to one another, but as essential complements to one another; and for any one policy to succeed there must be a parallel success in all the others. Piece-meal reforms by bureaucratically separate agencies can contribute little; the commitment that is required is a whole-hearted and comprehensive one involving traditional social-welfare measures, a properly conceived and heavily redistributive incomes-policy, a housing programme, and, equally crucial but only recently acknowledged, the active encouragement of community-action programmes which reactivate grass-roots democratic and collective participation in decision-making at all levels.

II

To consider, first of all, the part that social-welfare policies have to play in the fight against poverty, we can fairly distinguish between social security, that is to say policies of income maintenance on the one hand; and social work, or the specialist social-work services currently carried out in the local-authority children's and welfare departments, on the other.

Appropriate nationally sponsored schemes of income maintenance through social security should not be considered separately from wages policies. As we have already seen, the largest number of poor people live in households with no social-security entitlement, dependent wholly upon the bread-winner's earned income. One could conceive of a social-security system based upon the Speenhamland principle, that is as a set of payments designed to supplement wages where these are thought inadequate; the principle of the wage-stop, however, demonstrates that the present social-security programme is based upon the very opposite principle, on that of the reduction of entitlement to below the wage-level, no matter how inadequate that may be. Not only is social security as a supplement to low wages an unlikely development, it is also an undesirable one. The wages question in itself involves a consideration of human rights.

Is it altogether too naïve to argue that we should aim to achieve a social order within which all men at work could expect to command a wage adequate to support themselves and their families? Is it altogether too radical to argue that this aim can best be achieved through the establishment of a statutory national minimum wage which would protect the weak, the ill-informed and the isolated from further exploitation? The only substantial argument we have seen against this viewpoint was put by *The Times*, when it commented on the preliminary report of our survey. 'The trouble with a minimum wage,' it said, 'is that it might make it uneconomic to employ a number of people now in work – and it lacks flexibility for bringing help to those most in need.' Of course, this is likely to be true. But the alternative canvassed by *The Times* is not, properly speaking, an alternative at all, but a parallel attack upon the same problem: 'positive discrimination', such as is advocated in the *Plowden Report* on primary schools (making an attempt to compensate children for their unsatisfactory home environment by giving them above-average schools). Even if this is extended throughout the field of present welfare services it is not likely to be available either on the scale or in the form necessary to meet the major problem, which is to restore self-respect, and with it both individual and collective initiative, to the poor.

If it is true that a living minimum wage would squeeze out some areas of employment, there are two points which should be made. Either the uneconomic jobs are socially necessary, or they are not. If they are, and are genuinely incapable of providing a proper livelihood for those employed in them, then they must enter the province of public-welfare control and support. If we want coalminers or corporation gardeners we must pay them. If, on the other hand, these jobs are *not* socially necessary, why should they continue to be done? If the expensive bar which employs an adult barman at a wage which would insult a school-leaver really cannot afford to pay him more, ought it not to release him for other work? Such a 'shake-out' might be rather more productive and rather more humane than the one we have experienced recently: would not a minimum wage redistribute labour with greater efficiency and greater kindliness than an induced recession? It seems to be a somewhat defeatist argument which can see no prospect of the maintenance of full employment other than by the tolerance of wage levels which compare unfavourably with the standards of public relief. If the present social order is incapable of a more optimistic assessment of human rights than is implied in such an assumption, it is high time it made way for another.

Having said this, however, there still remains one difficulty. There is as yet no system of payment of wages which is sensitive to the earners' specific responsibilities; thus an unmarried man with only himself to support will usually earn the same wage (for the same job) as a married man with wife and children to support. True, the income-taxation system attempts some limited redistribution, but this is least effective among the lower-paid who pay little or no income tax anyway. The Family Allowance, however, is an administratively simple benefit, which is immediately and directly sensitive to the most vital of changes in family responsibilities, namely the arrival of dependent children. The Family Allowance, then, is a benefit of particular significance; and the Child Poverty Action Group has lobbied most persistently for the development of a more generous system of Family Allowances. The first and most obvious development should be the payment of an allowance for the first child. In many cases the first child imposes the most severe strain on a family budget; if the wife has been at work before the birth, the loss of her income requires a substantial adjustment in expenditure, while the capital outlay on a first child is considerably higher than on subsequent children who can use many of the articles bought for the eldest. Secondly, the allowances themselves, although they have been substantially improved in the last four years, are still parsimonious when compared with the allowances paid in many other advanced countries. A substantial increase would be possible and the net additional burden on the Exchequer would be very slight if such an increase were linked with the abolition of the tax allowances on children. These tax allowances already cost the Exchequer considerably more than the Family Allowances, and they are difficult to justify on any count. They benefit most those with higher incomes (and hence a higher taxable income) whose needs are presumably more easily satisfied out of earnings, and it is hard to see why the 'running costs' of a child in a high-income household should be significantly different from those of a child in a low-income household. Yet, as the C.P.A.G. has been able to demonstrate most clearly, the value to the recipient of the combined family and tax allowance rises steadily with income. This can be justified neither as an efficient use of resources nor as an exercise in social justice.

The poor in dependency situations (that is, the old, the sick, unsupported families and similar people) will, while the existing order of things survives, continue to rely on Supplementary Benefits. The short-run target here must be to ensure that the levels of benefit paid are adequate to support personal and family life at a tolerable level. Here again we must not divorce the rates of benefit from overall wages policy. On the day when a meaningful statutory minimum wage is fixed, it would appear to be sensible to establish rates of Supplementary Benefit in some proportion to this minimum wage. Equally important is some device for adjusting rates of benefit to take account of changes in the cost of living and the value of money. The target should be to avoid the situation we have known since the war, where the real value of benefits (low to start with) has been systematically eroded by inflation. The proposed social-security reform does in fact promise to maintain the value of benefits by regular biennial alterations in rates to match changes in living costs, and if this promise is fulfilled then it will be a significant and overdue improvement in social policy.

Changes in social-security provisions are made at national level; the bulk of traditional social work, however, goes on very much at local level, through the various departments of the local authorities. Until fairly recently, as has already been observed, most social workers, although familiar with the continuing problems of poverty and deprivation through their own first-hand professional experience, were nonetheless confident that, given time, the development of social services and social work would finally eradicate all but the most recalcitrant problems. In other words, most social workers felt that the genesis of social problems was now more in the personalities of their clients than in the structure of society, and that such structural flaws as remained were a passing hangover from the pre-Welfare State. In recent years this piously optimistic assessment has been substantially modified, and it is fair to say that social work today is in a state of profound and, one may hope, creative ferment. Part of this ferment can be attributed to the inability of the public sector of the economy to hold its own, and the constant succession of cuts and retrenchments which have affected social-work departments no less than such services as education. Social workers today are not the least alienated of employees, and are increasingly prone to view the arrangements they are supposed to administer in a critical light.

In so far as it is a reaction to the problems of their clients, this mood among social workers has developed for two principal reasons; the first is the growing realization among social workers that the Beveridge Revolution has not in fact revolutionized society and that there remain obvious and, at present, insurmountable flaws in the structure of society which change the practice of social work from a progressive and ameliorative process into a rearguard, even regressive activity. To quote a vivid but simple example, where ten years ago it might have seemed reasonable to teach old-age pensioners how to eke out their stipend by shrewd budgeting, it now seems more reasonable, indeed, imperative, to agitate for an increase in the pension. In essence what is happening is that social workers are increasingly recognizing that their clients, far from being a social inconvenience or worse, a menace, are, all too often, victims of a social order which appears as far from just. This recognition is forcing a radical reassessment of social work's role and contribution to society.

At the same time, there is an imminent organizational revolution, which, hopefully, offers the possibility of establishing new social-work agencies of a scale and character hitherto only dreamed of. Ultimate judgements on this must await the implementation of the *Report of the Royal Commission on Local Government*, which will radically reform the system of local administration, by the creation of a smallish number of city-regional authorities. With these significant changes in the air, the *Seebohm Committee Report on Local Authority and Allied Personal Social Services* has recommended a most far-reaching and imaginative reorganization of the local-authority services. In a nutshell, the Seebohm Committee would amalgamate into one 'new local-authority department, providing a community-based and family-oriented service, which will be available to all', all the social-welfare work that is at present the responsibility of several different local-authority departments. This recommendation goes far beyond a mere organizational change; it also involves a new orientation for the practice of social work. No longer will social workers be divided into narrow specialisms, each engaged with a specific and defined set of problems; instead they will be encouraged to identify with a family in its communal setting, helping to deal with all the problems that may arise for that family, and acknowledging all the direct and indirect pressures which may be precipitating family or community difficulties. This has enormous significance for social work as a profession, as it marks a decisive step towards the notion of the general social worker. But it will point up, in a most direct way, a problem of which many social workers already know, the problem of their relationship with the authorities which employ them. Although by no means inevitable, it is highly likely that the more successfully a social worker identifies with the community he serves, and the more he in turn is appreciated by the community, the more he will find himself in conflict with his employing body. This difficulty exists already under the present system of administration, as we discovered most poignantly in the aftermath of the first St Ann's Report. As we have already mentioned, certain of our findings were denounced in the most forthright terms by some of the city's leading politicians and administrators; yet in the following weeks and months, on the many occasions when we encountered social workers in the council's employ, we were given emphatic, even at times enthusiastic, support. Yet none of those social workers felt able to express this support publicly, in some cases because their employers specifically forbade their staff to make any public statement which affected the department, in others out of a fear of the possible consequences which might fall upon them should they be seen to disagree with their masters. This tension, which is by no means surprising, could well be considerably aggravated if social workers should be encouraged to develop a communal rather than a departmental loyalty. One of the most fascinating aspects of the 'Seebohm Revolution' will be to see how this question is handled.

The lessons of the American poverty programme, where there are many examples of a growing alliance between social workers and their clients in opposition to the local authorities, are revealing, but do not encourage the hope that reform of the social-service agencies will be without convulsive conflicts. For, let it be clearly understood that while progress through cooperation is always pleasant to contemplate, there are all too many situations where progress is manifestly only likely to be achieved through conflict. Local authorities, as institutions, greatly favour consensus, and have little taste for conflict, particularly if they are centrally involved in it. Very frequently, then, local authorities attempt to muzzle their more restive employees.

In brief, social work is about to embark upon a series of changes which could substantially remodel its contribution to society. Social workers are, however, situated within the political fabric of the community, and their professional freedom of action is liable to be substantially curtailed to suit the convenience of their political and administrative chiefs. The way out of this dilemma has already been repeatedly hinted at; alone, the social worker can do little, but in alliance with real forces in the community a great deal can be achieved. Given suitable income and social-security policies, given a reformed local social service, the third and essential ingredient, without which no war on poverty can succeed, is a reawakening of the demand for genuine participation in their own affairs by the people, or, as it is sometimes called, community action. But there is little evidence that either adequate income or security policies are remotely likely in the present economic and political climate. This means that an integrated social-work service will either be irrelevant, or become increasingly hostile to the social order. In either event, community action will be no platonic endeavour, but, from the beginning, a resolute and intractable struggle.

III

'Ours is a society in which, in every field, one group of people makes decisions, exercises control, limits choices, while the great majority have to accept these decisions, submit to this control and act within the limits of these externally imposed choices. It happens in work and leisure, politics, and education, and nowhere is it more evident than in the field of housing.' [1]

1. Colin Ward, 'Tenants Take Over', *Anarchy*, No. 83, January 1968.

The relevance of this comment in communities like St Ann's should by now be obvious, and the rapidly growing interest in experiments in forms of community action is a direct response to the nation-wide need for some form of direct and meaningful grass-roots participation in and control over the affairs of the community.

Although it is true that tenants' associations have existed for many years as one form of community association, and although after the Second World War there was a widespread (though short-lived) revival of interest in the community-centre movement, the great impetus to the community-action programmes of today has been the far more urgent, dramatic (and successful) confrontations with authority by the homeless families in a number of local-authority hostels.

As early as 1962 Mrs Sheila Jones, of the tenants' association at an L.C.C. halfway house, was writing:

> To some of us it is beginning to be clear that if we want anything done we will have to do it ourselves. The L.C.C. tries to keep these places as terrible as possible to prevent others taking advantage of the 'facilities' provided. An imaginative and selective breaking of the artificial L.C.C. rules might be an effective method of protest. What would happen for instance if a group of families got together and decided to bring in their own furniture to replace the L.C.C. stuff? Would the L.C.C. wardens call the police in … against tenants whose only crime was that they had tried, at their own expense, to make living conditions more bearable for themselves and their children? [2]

The following year saw precisely such a confrontation at Islington's notorious Newington Lodge, and in 1966 there were further persistent disturbances at the Kent County Council's King Hill hostel. Here the point at issue was the right of husbands to remain with their wives and children, rather than being limited to specific visiting hours laid down by the authority. Both these campaigns resulted in some welcome improvements in the administration of the hostels, and strikingly demonstrated that persistent and concerted action, even by the

2. See the pamphlet 'Homelessness', Solidarity, 1962.

(initially) most demoralized and apparently powerless groups, even against the most authoritarian and insensitive of administrators, could be highly successful.

More recently, community groups have established themselves in towns and cities all over the country, and it has become quite modish to talk of citizen participation; indeed some see the creation of viable community groups as the definitive answer to our urban problems. The most widely-known experiment is the Notting Hill Community Workshop, and the ambitious hopes of such groups are well expressed in an open letter from the Chairman of the Notting Hill People's Association.

A FORUM FOR NEW THINKING AND COMMUNITY ACTION
From the Chairman of the Notting Hill People's Association,
33 Colville Square, London, W.11

Dear Friend,

Are you concerned about the helplessness and frustration of people everywhere within the present political and social situation? We ask the question directly because we would like you to give serious consideration to the case and suggestions which follow.

The Notting Hill People's Association was formed a year ago and, throughout last summer, was engaged in a project involving hundreds of people, many living here in the houses and streets of North Kensington and many from towns and cities elsewhere with similar problems. Their concern was the effect bureaucratic indifference and political irresponsibility were having upon people's lives, particularly here where the reports and surveys revealed a condition near to social breakdown.

An Environmental Slum. What we discovered was far worse than expected – a paradise for racketeering landlords, where the cheaply furnished single room was a standard tenancy at £5 per week and upwards, where whole families lived in these single rooms, where basic and essential repairs went undone because, it seems to us, the local Council, now legendary for its lame excuses, is more concerned with its policy of protection for private landlordism than it is for the people it is supposed to serve: where the highest population of children in London literally have nowhere to play – not even a bomb-site – and where the death and accident rates are the highest in the Metropolitan area, where streets are permanently dirty, where minimal services are provided to people paying the highest rates in the country, and where thousands of families are left to live out their lives in what is virtually an environmental slum. Of course, this does not apply to the tree-lined terraces and avenues of South Kensington. The amenities and services provided there are paid for at the expense and neglect of the North. We also found that the schools were grossly overcrowded and understaffed and nurseries for working mothers non-existent, except for those run commercially and making extortionate charges. So, caught somewhere between the facelessness of officials, the cynicism of so-called political representatives and the unrestricted profiteering of commercial and retail interests, PEOPLE ARE TREATED AS MERE VICTIMS, TO BE PUSHED AROUND AND MILKED.

Something Bigger than an Ombudsman is called for. Another voice is needed — a people's voice, independent of the Party machines, strong enough to remind officials and politicians alike that they are public servants and accountable to the people who pay their salaries, a voice also to remind people that their voting every few years is really non-involvement in affairs which govern their lives and which, if left to bureaucrats and politicians, must and do resolve into party power and gimmickry.

It is clear, too, that the party system has ceased to be a safeguard of democracy. The legislation of both Tory and Labour Governments has become consistently alike and repressive, under which, despite advancing technology and accelerating production, the quality of life for most people shrinks and deteriorates. WE FEEL BOUND, THEREFORE, to recommend the formation of a third and independent way, which would begin to discipline and make demands from both Government and opposition, particularly local. We feel that out of such an attempt can grow a new and honest system of representation — at street level, perhaps — containing within it direct accountability and referendum to people's opinions and desires.

A Discussion to Create a Forum for New Thinking and Action. It is not our aim to form a new political party, rather to avoid this, but simply to explore the possibility of action for organizations and people concerned about the misuse of power and authority, and who feel they have no means of expressing criticism and ideas as things are. A forum for ideas and demands to create maximum pressure and embarrassment to those who do not represent the people of Notting Hill, and yet occupy positions of power at the

Town Hall. We are aware that people will come to such a meeting with conflicting ideas and allegiances. This would be natural. Some have already remarked that it would be naïve to expect common sympathy and issue. WE DO NOT ACCEPT THIS. We believe that people everywhere are tired of the old lies, are seeking new forms of collective expression and that an attempt should be made. We invite you to take part in this first discussion at the People's Centre, Clydesdale Road, off Talbot Road, on Monday, 13 May at 7.30 p.m.

BILL RICHARDSON

25 April 1968

The issues in St Ann's have been different in a number of ways from those raised in Notting Hill. The basic dissimilarity has been the fact that the whole area of St Ann's has been scheduled for clearance by the corporation, so that, while extortionate rents are paid by some people, and while the general deterioration of the area is universally resented, the fact remains that everybody in the district has a special set of problems in his relations with the local council.

The birth of the St Ann's Tenants' and Residents' Association (S.A.T.R.A.) came after the announcement of the intended demolition. The inhabitants had already learned, often through a grapevine in which unfounded rumour filtered as freely as fact, that the area was about to be flattened. Almost everyone in St Ann's is torn between two suppositions: that their house will be knocked down next year, or sooner, a belief which is encouraged every time an official-looking stranger walks down the road; and that they will rot on another twenty years without being rehoused, an assumption which floats up to the top whenever the public authorities make any statement about the progress which is imminently to be expected. Hope is somehow less rational than cynicism in St Ann's. And until the public clamour reached deafening pitch, communications between St Ann's residents and officialdom were perhaps as intimate as they might be expected to be between, say, Chairman Mao Tse Tung and Generallissimo Chiang Kai Shek. Each side has, for a long time, known of the other's existence, and, in a more or less calculated way, tried to predict the other's movements. But aside from an occasional long-range broadside, or a hasty spy flight, neither has sought or found any contact with his opponent closer than that of occupying adjacent columns in a distant neutral newspaper. When the original phasing of the whole area into separate demolition zones was undertaken, hardly anyone in St Ann's understood it, and virtually nothing was done by the corporation itself to ensure that it be understood. The result was that, when Ray Gosling called a public meeting on this issue, over five hundred people turned up, primarily in order to try to find out what they might expect to happen to their house or street. If the corporation were so tardy in communicating their decisions to the people, it need hardly be said that the amount of positive prior consultation about what sort of decisions ought to be made was minimal.

There was clearly a place for S.A.T.R.A. in this context. But at the same time, the demand for better communications with, and prior consultation by, the corporation, is not the only demand which needs to be made in the districts. Absentee landlords *do* exist there. Rack-renting *does* go on. Repairs *are* neglected. And most people are tenants, not owner-occupiers. But S.A.T.R.A. preoccupied itself with the demand for improvement grants for houses, so that its natural appeal was first of all to owner-occupiers. While, of course, there is every reason to press for improvement grants to be made available, and over a very much shorter run than the fifteen years which is the general rule, it remains true that an owner-occupier can still much more easily avail himself of such a facility than can a tenant. So that if a campaign is to be mounted on such an issue, it must be accompanied by a whole series of other campaigns aimed at assisting tenants, if the community association is not to become unbalanced in its composition and unrepresentative of the population at large.

We think this has happened in S.A.T.R.A., in spite of the fact that a lot of valuable work has been put in by Ray Gosling and his colleagues. An initial recruitment based on the main demand for improvement grants resulted in the local membership being formed from a narrow sector of the St Ann's community, and this in turn resulted in the new Association taking up more and more of its time with problems of less and less general concern, such as the difficulties of small shopkeepers faced by redevelopment which would remove their locale. These are important problems, but need to be construed in a total context, which can only be provided by a community association which represents a genuine cross-section of the local people, and can voice all their most pressing needs.

The way in which S.A.T.R.A. found itself campaigning increasingly on behalf of minority interests draws attention to a danger that faces all community groups of this sort. A few days after we had contributed to a correspondence in *New Society* on this very question, we received a letter from a reader who described a very similar situation in the Rye Hill area of Newcastle. He wrote:

It is a much smaller area [than St Ann's] of 16 streets of (mostly) large, once upper-middle-class houses. Smaller houses of a similar age have been demolished to the south and will be demolished to the north. But for the Rye Hill oblong our former Planning Officer, Wilfred Burns (now Chief Planner at the Ministry of Housing) decided that 'revitalization' was the answer.

He seems to have decided on intuition, with not even a survey of the condition of the houses having been made until much later. It was to be another instance of Newcastle ('Venice of the North') giving the whole country a pioneering lead. When the Council got round to doing a few pilot modernizations last year the cost was £3,300 for a five-room house.

The people of the area who are predominantly tenants in multi-occupation were first 'represented' by a body called the Rye Hill Residents' Association. Like S.A.T.R.A. it was dominated by owner-occupiers and long-established 'respectable' tenants (it also included one big landlord) who held the other 'slum' tenants to be largely responsible for the decay of the district.

The Residents' Association was against the Council's revitalization policy, it is true, but because it was being applied with a rigidity that meant that owners would lose their houses if they could not afford to bring them up to the Council's very high standards. They did not mind revitalization if they were left out. They were largely concerned with getting themselves excluded.

The bulk of tenants, on the other hand, had no confidence in revitalization, since earlier Council modernizations in the area had produced very damp and defective results. Anyway most wanted to be out of the area. So a group of us formed the West End *Tenants'* Association to fight along these lines. We argued that most of the houses had deteriorated so far that either revitalization would be no cheaper than new housing and would produce high rents; or if the Council tried to economize on revitalization the people would not have homes fit to live in.

Eighteen months later we have more or less won (aided of course by the Minister's refusal to confirm the compulsory purchase order). The Council now says it will demolish most of the streets. The Residents' Association curled up and died after the compulsory purchase order was refused. We are still going pretty strong. Maybe St Ann's needs a tenants' association?

In groups of this description it would seem to be the case that the relatively more articulate people and those whose felt interests are most immediately threatened, easily become dominating influences. To the extent that community-action groups do not remain open to the whole population of their area, creation of a multiplicity of sub-groups may be called for. Indeed it would be naïve to suppose, even in a small community (let alone a district as large as St Ann's) that there is ever a perfect harmony of interests, exactly balanced and reflected in a community group. There is more likely to be a conflict, or partial conflict, of interests which will disrupt and fragment any local group which claims to defend the interests of all. The resolution of local and area tensions of this kind is impossible without the establishment of overall policy objectives capable of unifying all slum-dwellers in the recognition of a common interest, an interest which can only be determined in relation to the overall social obstacles to its realization. Of course, tenants, owner-occupiers, and even small landlords, taken in abstraction from their immediate environment, could easily be seen to have a great deal of common ground, if against their interests were weighed the alternative concerns of, say, merchant bankers, or captains of industry. But the last two groups of men do not commonly walk in St Ann's, and the vicissitudes of the interest rates which determine so much of local-authority housing policy are seen, not as the actions of a human agency, but almost as natural phenomena, like earthquakes, or rainstorms on Cup Final Day. To develop the sense that poor people share a common interest is not simply to urge them to act together in order to resolve immediate problems, although this is always the beginning of wisdom. It is also to begin to bring to life among them a real picture of the actual state of society as a whole, by reference to which they can overcome the bondage of the partial view, and judge their condition by standards which are, as nearly as possible, 'objective' ones. Needless to say, the development of this view is a profoundly *political* labour. But the balance sheet for this kind of work cannot be drawn up on three cases: the move to agitate and organize in poor neighbourhoods has only just begun, and will develop very seriously as more and more young people devote their attention to it. For this reason generalizations about community action cannot be made with great assurance: action programmes have a spontaneity and a commitment to specific local anxieties so that they differ markedly one from another. Nonetheless, there are some general points which we would stress, mainly because we fear that they have been ignored or underrated by the community associations themselves.

The first point to emphasize is that community action at the local, face-to-face level is a more appropriate response to some problems than to others. The open letter which we quoted stressed the presence of rent-racketeering landlords and indifferent councillors, two elements in a community which vigorous local activity could expose and might, conceivably, ultimately eliminate. In fact, most aspects of activity at present covered by local authorities are suitable for effective lobbying by community groups.

There are some problems, however, which, no matter how heavily they may weigh upon a community, are yet not *of* the community in a way which makes a local solution possible. Poverty in most of its manifestations, is one such problem. That the poorer people can be found in greater concentration in some districts rather than others, does not mean that the causes of their poverty lie in the districts themselves. To talk in terms of local solutions in this situation is both misleading and misguided; indeed to encourage a search for local solutions could be positively harmful. That there is widespread material hardship in St Ann's cannot be denied, but there is no St Ann's solution to it and to suggest that there is may prevent the poor of, say, St Ann's from developing a sense of community with the poor of other districts, and other towns.

This leads us to a second general point about community action. Among many of the people most deeply and successfully involved in community work, there is a considerable and profound mistrust of other forms of association. Not only is the local council execrated, but so are the radical or one-time radical political parties, the trade unions, and other associations of a functional, rather than local, type. Very often the distaste for such associations arises out of many years' frustrating personal experience of their ways, and many people will feel a considerable sense of sympathy for this reaction. To ignore such organizations is, however, not a fruitful strategy; whether one likes it or not, they not only exist, but are really the only ones that can deal with those problems at national and structural levels, rather than in purely local terms. That the established organizations fail, and fail miserably, is all too plain. But unless that failure is the subject of insistent public reproach, both from outside and from within them, the danger is that the overall policies that are necessary will never emerge as practical options. Direct action on the many grievances of the deprived members of the population is a crucial lever to the development of their self-respect and social understanding: but it is not a sufficient remedy for their problems, which demand overall solutions such as can only be canvassed by nationally structured political and social organizations. Unless a serious effort is made at this level, it is unlikely that any basic change will take place. To assume that such bodies can be by-passed is blithely optimistic; to assume that they would remain impregnable to insistent campaigning on these issues seems crudely pessimistc.

Very often the feelings expressed by community workers reflect a fear of being absorbed or taken over by national bodies, and hence losing both their sensitivity to local conditions, and their flexibility of response. There is in consequence a resistance to alliances between the community-action groups and the trade unions and relevant political bodies. It seems to us that whether to encourage such alliances on the formal level or not is very much a local decision, but that participation in the affairs of the larger associations by no means necessarily assumes such formal alignments. If a community group succeeds in arousing into meaningful social action people who have hitherto confined themselves to seeking private solutions to their public problems, then many of those people, aware of shared interests which cut across local and geographical boundaries, might well express themselves through political organizations and trade unions as well. Indeed, in this way, the more moribund constituency parties and union branches might be not merely revitalized themselves, but transformed into bases for the re-education and regeneration of their parent bodies.

Of course, historically, the vehicle which could have linked the separate efforts of community groups, trade unions, local councillors, and other bodies to provide both local servicing and communications, and a framework for the elaboration of national policy and demands, has been the Labour Party. The present crisis for the poor is aggravated in the extreme by the fact that it is no longer able to play any of its major traditional roles. Possibly it can never be recaptured for its own original purposes. It remains true, however, to put the matter at its worst, that before such a vast organization can disappear from the scene, to make way for something more effective, all the issues it is now avoiding must be seriously faced within it.

Sooner or later this is bound to begin to happen, and then will be the time to judge whether the attempt must fail. In the meantime, while agitation must be renewed on all other possible fronts, it must also be brought to bear on this one.

Afterword

In the last play he wrote, Aristophanes posed a series of questions which mankind has yet to answer. His conundrum runs like this: Ploutos, the God of Wealth, blinded and wandering the Earth in rags, befriends the peasant Chremylos, who offers to cure his blindness if he will stay close by him. Ploutos hesitates, fearing the jealousy of Zeus: blind Wealth and social misfortune go hand in hand; yet the social order, no less in heaven than on earth, depends upon Wealth. Could this same Wealth only see, he could then direct his powers, deliberately, for good. This understood, at last Ploutos agrees to be taught again to see. Other peasants hasten to assist Chremylos, and to join in his prosperity. But now the goddess Penia, Poverty, appears, claiming herself to be the authentic source of all that is good. A debate ensues, which Penia wins, by showing that a society which she did not rule could provide no compulsion to labour. Her logic appears invincible. Everyone must concede that the argument is hers. Yet in spite of her reasoning, the peasants remain unsatisfied: they drive her out, enthrone the seeing Ploutos, and inaugurate an era so joyous that the gods themselves return to Earth, since people no longer need them in their old capacity.

The story of Ploutos has been the democratic dream for at least as long as men have written plays about it: but the interesting thing about it is that Poverty has to be exorcized by force, not logic, which means that the establishment of the rule of planned Wealth is, inevitably, a leap in the dark. Civilization has always up to now been predicated on the assumption that since wealth equals idleness, work must be done under the scourge of controlled deprivation. But Aristotle saw a way in which this dilemma might be overcome: 'If every tool, when summoned, or even of its own accord, could do the work that befits it, just as the creations of Daedalus moved of themselves, or the tripods of Hephaestus went of their own accord to their sacred work, if the weaver's shuttles were to weave of themselves, then there would be no need of apprentices for the master workers, or slaves for the lords.'

Today, in the light of modern technology the tripods of Hephaestus seem a little lame: and we can call on numerous technical-school pupils who could give Daedalus advice for which he might be thankful. It is perfectly thinkable that the weavers' shuttles should weave of themselves, and likely, before the turn of the next century, that they may be doing so on the moon.

But as men's powers have expanded, so their dreams have shrunk. While the ancient Greeks could envisage a polity in which all men could share in what any man had it in himself to be, modern British politicians seem unable to hope even for a world in which every boy knows some Algebra and French, or in which every woman has a hot-water supply in her house, or in which every workman can afford to come home after eight hours' work without precipitating his family into want. We can fly faster than sound, but in our cities there are thousands of lovers who cannot make love without being overheard in the next house. We can create new materials whose lightness and strength dazzle the senses, but we cannot keep the damp out of hundreds of thousands of our dwellings. We may synthesize life wholesale before we have finished with the diseases of poverty and malnutrition.

It is clear that there is no rational impediment to prevent us from ordering our affairs differently. There are, it is true, vast official rigmaroles about banking, and balances of payments, and returns on investments, which apparently preclude a humane polity as far as our rulers are concerned. But we have the resources, and we have the techniques, to begin to live like people. It is time we found the imagination and courage to match them.

Index

INDEX

MORE ABOUT PENGUINS
AND PELICANS

Penguinews, which appears every month, contains details of all the new books issued by Penguins as they are published. From time to time it is supplemented by *Penguins in Print*, which is a complete list of all titles available. (There are some five thousand of these.)

A specimen copy of *Penguinews* will be sent to you free on request. For a year's issues (including the complete lists) please send 50p if you live in the British Isles, or 75p if you live elsewhere. Just write to Dept EP, Penguin Books Ltd, Harmondsworth, Middlesex, enclosing a cheque or postal order, and your name will be added to the mailing list.

In the U.S.A.: For a complete list of books available from Penguin in the United States write to Dept CS, Penguin Books Inc., 7110 Ambassador Road, Baltimore, Maryland 21207.

In Canada: For a complete list of books available from Penguin in Canada write to Penguin Books Canada Ltd, 41 Steelcase Road West, Markham, Ontario

POVERTY AND EQUALITY IN BRITAIN

J. C. Kincaid

If you are complacently satisfied that the British system of
social security is the finest in the world, this important book
by Dr Kincaid may shake you.

Quoting estimates that suggest that 2,000,000 people in Britain
are living in acute poverty, he argues that their poverty is a
direct consequence of inadequate social security schemes,
that the Welfare State does nothing effective to iron out
inequality and the services offered are far less egalitarian
and more punitive than generally believed.

In the belief that poverty and inequality are integral
components of a competitive social order, the author urges
that we re-think our ideas about the poor. Working-class
militancy, in his view, lacks political expression: if the unions
were prepared to take action over the sores that fester in our
society 'neither a Labour nor a Conservative Government
would dare treat the old, the sick and the unemployed
as they do at present'.